Israeli Nuclear Deterrence
A Strategy for the 1980s

ISRAELI NUCLEAR DETERRENCE

A Strategy for the 1980s

Shai Feldman

Columbia University Press
New York   1982

Shai Feldman is a research associate at the Center for Strategic Studies, Tel Aviv University. The views expressed in this book are his own, and do not necessarily reflect the views of the Center, its trustees, officers, or other staff members or the organizations and individuals that support its research.

Library of Congress Cataloging in Publication Data

Feldman, Shai, 1950–
    Israeli nuclear deterrence.

    Bibliography: p.
    Includes index.
    1. Israel—Military policy.   2.Deterrence (Strategy)
3. Atomic warfare.   4. Near East—Strategic aspects.
I. Title.
UA853.I8F44   1982   355'.0217'095694   82–9679
ISBN 0-231-05546-3
ISBN 0-231-05547-1 (pbk)

Columbia University Press
New York   Guildford, Surrey
Copyright © 1982 Columbia University Press
All rights reserved
Printed in the United States of America

Clothbound editions of Columbia University Press books are Smyth-sewn and printed on permanent and durable acid-free paper.

Contents

Preface and Acknowledgments

Strategy must evolve from a clear conception of political purpose, since it is but an operational grand design for achieving one's aims. Strategy without purpose is an exercise in futility; once political aims are lost sight of, the entire enterprise is doomed to failure. Potentially, political goals may bias strategic analysis, but awareness of this danger may best permit its containment. Such bias should always be guarded against, but not at the expense of abandoning political purpose.

This book, written by a fifth-generation Israeli, evolves from an intense concern for Israel's security and a strong determination that Israel is in the Middle East to stay. Yet, it is also the result of a very strong belief that Israel cannot remain oblivious to the domestic effects of her national security policy. Israel's strategy must provide not only for the defense of the state, but for the defense of a state endowed with a particular character and purpose. Our founding fathers wished it not only as a Jewish state, but also as one based on the principles of social democratic justice. An Israeli national strategy that compromises Israel's values of democratic government and social justice negates the very purpose of the exercise. This strong conviction has guided me during the many months of writing this book.

In this enterprise, I was fortunate to receive much help from many generous people. My excellent teachers at the Hebrew University of Jerusalem, where I took my undergraduate studies, provided me with an initial insight into history, politics, and strategy. Among them were Shlomo

Avineri, Yehezkel Dror, Galia Golan, Ehud Sprinzak, and Nissan Oren.

My friendship with Uri Maimon, to whose memory this book is dedicated, flourished during my years in Jerusalem. The years 1969–1973 now seem like one continuous dialogue with Uri. Invariably, the discussions revolved around Israel's politics and national security. Though very different in style, he and I shared a common vision of Israel's future as a Jewish state. It was after Uri's death on the Egyptian front at the twilight of the Yom Kippur War that I determined to attempt to contribute to the improvement of Israel's foreign and defense policies.

I also owe an enormous debt to my teachers at the University of California, Berkeley, where I went in 1973 to pursue my doctoral studies in political science. I am particularly grateful to two individuals, Nelson W. Polsby and Kenneth N. Waltz. Nelson has done much more than teach me most of what I know about American politics; at critical junctures he provided appropriate measures of encouragement and discouragement. Ken Waltz is not only a master at teaching how to think about international politics, but also provided invaluable instruction on how to express these thoughts in writing. He has guided this enterprise from its first stage as a two-page proposal to the final copy-editing stage, with enormous patience and endless goodwill. This book would not be what it is without his limitless help.

During my years in the United States, no single person has taught me more or has provided so much assistance as my friend and colleague Stephen Van Evera. Steve is a truly extraordinary scholar; he has more original ideas in a normal week than most scholars have in a year. Most of my own conceptions about international affairs were forged during endless conversations with him over the past eight years. No one could ask for a better friend and colleague.

My trip to the United States was supported by a Fulbright Travel Grant. Daniel M. Krauskopf, Executive Secretary of the United States–Israel Education Foundation, deserves a special thanks in this connection. At Berkeley I was supported by numerous research and teaching assistantships. I am particularly indebted to Sanford Elberg, former Dean of the Graduate Division, for having supported my scholarship application, awarded in 1976. Finally, a special thanks to Robert Lieber, then Chairman of the Department of Political Science at the University of California, Davis, where I enjoyed my first teaching job as lecturer, in the spring of 1976.

I returned to Israel in the summer of 1977, and soon joined the Center for Strategic Studies at Tel Aviv University. I will forever be grateful to Major General (Res.) Aharon Yariv, Head of CSS, for his support. We, at the Center, are very fortunate to be led by a person who is not only a brilliant strategist, but also extremely open-minded, always willing to consider and examine new ideas.

An earlier version of this book served as my doctoral dissertation, and a grant for that purpose from the Edward C. Congdon Memorial Trust of Duluth, Minnesota, was indispensable. I am indebted in this connection to Mr. and Mrs. William P. Van Evera of the Congdon Trust. Without their belief in the worthiness of the project, I could not have undertaken the task.

In early 1979 I spent six weeks in Washington, D.C., interviewing pertinent people in and out of the government. I am grateful to those people for having allotted me some of their precious time. During my sojourn in Washington I enjoyed a comfortable office at the American Enterprise Institute. I wish to express my thanks to Austin Ranney and Robert J. Pranger of the A.E.I. for their thoughtfulness and consideration.

In 1981 I received a postdoctoral fellowship from Stanford University's Arms Control and Disarmament Program. I am extremely indebted to the Program's director, John Lewis, to its associate director, Coit (Chip) Blacker, and to its assistant director, Condoleezza Rice, for structuring such a conducive environment allowing me to turn my dissertation into a book. My deepest gratitude goes to Barbara Johnson, the

Program's secretary. Her remarkable humor, efficiency, and goodwill provided continuous support during the final months of bringing this book to the press.

Many people were generous in providing helpful comments on the various drafts of this work. I am particularly grateful to my doctoral dissertation committee: Kenneth N. Waltz (chairman), Paul Seabury, Walter A. McDougall, and Sidney Drell (Stanford University); to the senior staff of the Center for Strategic Studies at Tel Aviv University, and particularly to Yair Evron, Mark A. Heller, Nimrod Novik, Aryeh Shalev, and Aharon Yariv; and to others of goodwill: Gloria Duffy, Philip Farley, Shalhevet Frier, Richard L. Garwin, Shlomo Gazit, Galia Golan, Robert Lieber, Baruch Raz, Ya'akov Ro'i, Haim Shenhav, Ehud Sprinzak, Stephen Van Evera, and David Vital.

I am also grateful to Moshe Grundman, Faith Erickson, and the staff of the C.S.S. documentation center and to Rose Toeg, Library Director at the American Cultural Center in Tel-Aviv, for enormous help in gathering the data for this study. Phyllis Maceoghan, Ruth Reginiano, Zeva Baron, Florence C. Myer, and Pauline B. Tooker typed the various drafts of this work, and Anita Safran edited an earlier draft of the manuscript.

The senior management of Columbia University Press deserve much gratitude for their efficiency, patience and goodwill. I am particularly indebted to Bernard Gronert, Executive Editor, and to Joan McQuary, Managing Editor, for their invaluable help.

This book would never have come about without the endless support I received from my close and extended family. My wife, Yochy, with whom I have exercised interdependence for over a decade, has endured admirably my preoccupation with international politics. Yochy is also my severest critic, and the only reason this book is not better is that I have a terrible habit of sometimes rejecting her advice. My son, Amos, who had to accept a father whose interest in strategy overshadows his enthusiasm for Lego bricks and Tinker Toys. My wife's parents, Sophia and Yeshayahu Jerud, who graciously parted with their daughter during our various long trips to the United States. And above all, to my parents, Lea and Michael Feldman, I owe everything. They have always provided me with endless encouragement and unlimited assistance.

Finally, a very special thanks to our lovely friends and neighbors, Hanna and Giora Pinhasi. By extending enormous help over a three-year period, they enabled us to keep our sanity.

Stanford, California
March 1982

Abbreviations

Military Terms*

AWACS   Airborne Warning and Control System. A converted Boeing 747 Transport aircraft equipped with long-range surveillance, and tracking radars, including "downward-looking" tracking radar that can identify intruders flying at very low altitudes. The aircraft is also intended as a decision-making control system for orchestrating air operations.

CEP   Circular Error Probability. A measure of the delivery accuracy of a weapon system used as a factor in determining probable damage to targets. The radius of a circle around the target within which the warhead has a .5 probability of falling.

EURATOM   European Atomic Energy Community. The organization provides the framework for cooperation among Western European states in the field of atomic energy. It provides for the sharing of scientific and technical information, joint research, cooperation in the construction of research facilities, and the control of nuclear material.

ICBM   Intercontinental Ballistic Missiles. A land-based rocket-propelled vehicle capable of delivering a warhead within intercontinental ranges (in excess of about 3,000 nautical miles).

---

* Definitions of military terms are based on Wolfram F. Hanrieder and Larry V. Buel, *Words and Arms: A Dictionary of Security and Defense Terms*; and Edward Luttwak, *A Dictionary of Modern War*.

IDF   Israel Defense Force. Official designation of Israel's armed forces, encompassing all land, air, and sea branches of the Israeli army.

INFCE   International Fuel Cycle Evaluation. A two-year study undertaken in the October 1977 meeting of 66 states and organizations to examine the extent to which alternative routes to nuclear power production involve the danger of nuclear weapons proliferation.

MIRV   Multiple Independently-targeted Re-entry Vehicle. A nuclear delivery system based on providing each booster with several warheads, each of which is separately guided to its target.

NATO   North Atlantic Treaty Organization. Formed to implement the treaty signed in 1949, its members are Belgium, Britain, Canada, Denmark, West Germany, Greece, Iceland, Italy, Luxemburg, the Netherlands, Norway, Portugal, Turkey, and the United States. France signed the treaty and remains strongly associated with NATO, but officially is no longer a member.

NPT   Non-Proliferation Treaty. Signed on July 1, 1968, this U.S.-USSR inspired treaty is aimed at preventing the spread of nuclear weapons.

PGM   Precision Guided Munitions. PGM refers to bombs, missiles, and artillery projectiles with single-shot kill probabilities from ten to one-hundred times greater than unguided munitions. This increase in accuracy is made possible by new guidance technologies that reduce the CEP of delivery vehicles to twenty meters of less.

p.s.i.   Pounds per square inch. A measure of the blast effect from detonations, including nuclear ones. It is expressed in terms of overpressure, namely by the extent to which the transient pressures created by the blast exceeds the normal atmospheric pressure.

SACEUR   Supreme Allied Commander Europe. Responsible, under the general direction of NATO's Military Committee, for the defense of the Allied countries in Europe. In time of war, SACEUR would control all land, sea, and air operations in the area.

SAM — Surface-to-Air Missile. A surface-launched missile employed to counter airborne threats.

SLBM — Submarine Launched Ballistic Missile. A ballistic missile carried in and launched from a submarine.

STOL — Short Take-Off and Landing. Aircraft capable of clearing a 50-foot obstacle within 1,500 feet of commencing take-off; or in landing, of stopping within 1,500 feet after passing over a 50-foot obstacle.

TNW — Tactical Nuclear Weapons. Nuclear weapons employed against enemy targets in the area of military operations.

Triad — The term used in referring to the basic structure of the U.S. strategic deterrent force. It is comprised of land-based ICBMs, the strategic bomber force, and the submarine fleet (SLBMs).

VTOL — Vertical Take-Off and Landing. Aircraft capable of taking off and landing vertically and of transferring to or from forward motion at heights required to clear surrounding obstacles.

Sources

AFP — Agence France Presse. (French News Agency).

AP — Associated Press.

BBC — Service of the British Broadcasting Company monitoring radio stations in various regions, and translating the monitoring broadcasts to the English language.

FBIS — Foreign Broadcast Information Service. A service monitoring radio broadcasts in various regions and translating them to the English language. FBIS is provided by U.S. Department of Commerce's National Technical Information Service, 5285 Port Royal Road, Springfield, Virginia.

INA — Iraqi News Agency. The official news agency of Iraq.

JPRS   Joint Publications Research Service. Provides trans-
            lation to the English language of written press reports
            from various regions. JPRS is provided by National
            Technical Information Service, 1000 North Glebe
            Road, Arlington, Virginia.

MENA   Middle East News Agency. Egypt's official news
            agency.

SNA   Saudi News Agency. The official news agency of
            Saudi Arabia.

UPI   United Press International.

Israeli Nuclear Deterrence
A Strategy for the 1980s

Introduction

This work examines the risks and benefits that may be involved in a possible shift of emphasis in Israel's political–military strategy: from one dominated by principles of conventional defense–offense to one of overt nuclear deterrence. An overt nuclear deterrent posture must include capability and doctrine. In the Mideast context, the capability component might comprise an arsenal of 30 to 40 deliverable nuclear weapons in the 20 to 60 kiloton range. The contemplated doctrine is countervalue—that is, threatening the destruction of cities and resources. It would consist of a simple but intentionally vague declaration that any attempt to cross Israel's borders by a significant military force would be countered by extremely high levels of punishment. The strategy's purpose would be to deter the Arab states from pursuing most forms of violence against Israel by letting them know that she possesses the means for devastating punishment.

The risks and benefits that may be involved in instituting the proposed changes in Israel's strategy will be examined from an admittedly partisan viewpoint—Israel's. The implications of this shift for regional and global stability will also be examined because of their direct effect on Israel's security and well-being. The study revolves around three central questions.

First: Will the adoption of a nuclear-deterrence posture deter the Arab states from posing strategic challenges to Israel's survival? Would such a posture ensure Israel's *security*?

Second: To what extent would a nuclear posture deter or reduce lower levels of warfare such as limited conventional war, a war of attrition, or guerrilla warfare? To what extent would such a posture offer Israel *peace*?

Third: What type of nuclear-deterrence posture must Israel adopt in order to maximize the odds of peace and security? In particular, to what extent must the posture be overt and explicit in order to be effective?

The first chapter addresses the third question, concluding that a nuclear-deterrence posture must be explicit in order to increase the odds favoring peace and security. It then provides the underlying theoretical rationale for a deterrence-dominant national security policy.

The first two central questions will be discussed in the second and third chapters, which will investigate the advantages of the contemplated strategic change. Chapter 2 will provide an assessment of the extent to which a nuclear-deterrence posture might enhance Israel's security by deterring the Arab states from posing strategic challenges to Israel's survival. Chapter 3 will debate whether nuclear deterrence might also offer peace to Israel by preventing or reducing Arab willingness to engage in lower levels of violence against her.

The risks involved in adopting a posture of overt nuclear deterrence will be discussed in chapters 4 and 5, the fourth chapter addressing the various risks inherent in the Middle East structure itself. Risks originating outside the region will be addressed in the fifth chapter, which will examine in particular the likely reactions of the United States and the USSR to Israel's adoption of overt nuclear deterrence.

The study does not assume that nuclear weapons are already at Israel's disposal. Due to his ignorance on this matter, the author cannot make such an assumption. Therefore, if such weapons are now in Israel's "basement," the questions addressed here concern the implications of announcing their existence. If Israel does not already possess nuclear weapons, however, these questions concern the implications of developing and producing such weapons, and announcing their introduction subsequently.

Many of the arguments advanced here have far-reaching implications that stretch far beyond the confines of the Middle East. These could be formulated as generalized propositions applicable to other small states and regions. However, it is left for the reader to distill the more generalized applications of this study and to draw the appropriate conclusions. People living in the Middle East are somewhat prejudiced against general propositions on the grounds that the region's peculiarities preclude attempts to draw conclusions about it from generalizations about "small states" or "regional subsystems." Conventional common wisdom maintains that analogies cannot be drawn to the Middle East. I decided to meet these critics on their own ground, rather than make a futile attempt to dissuade them. Even though the Middle East will be addressed directly, however, general propositions will also be generated and formulated.

A few words may also be appropriate in regard to the empirical evidence presented herein. A criticism often leveled at strategic analysis centering on deterrence is that even if the analysis is perfectly logical, a potential adversary may see things differently and may not be deterred. In anticipation of this common criticism, I try to present evidence of Arab perceptions with respect to the issue of Israeli nuclear weapons. The reader may judge the extent to which the evidence supports the propositions advanced here. The evidence consists of statements made by Arab statesmen and commentators alike. Some words of caution may be appropriate. First, it is necessary to emphasize that there is no single and internally consistent Arab philosophy with respect to nuclear weapons. Rather, what I have attempted to do is to organize, and make some sense of, a multitude of verbal and written statements on this subject. The reader must continuously bear in mind that the organization is artificially superimposed upon all this material. At times it is risky not to do justice to the available data. In this case, I should like to warn that it is also risky to do too much justice to the data.

In addition, I am assuming that these statements represent real perceptions: namely, that they say what the particular source really thinks, rather than what he would like others, possibly Israelis, to think he thinks. This assumption is open to criticism, but cannot be avoided. One can speculate endlessly on the possible motives that lead to each of these statements, but such speculation is not likely to be useful. Moreover, since the scope for imagination is very wide and various alternative explanations are likely to be equally plausible, such speculations may simply cancel each other out.

There is also a technical limitation. Some of the data presented in the various chapters and sections appeared in their original form in Arabic. I translated some of the quotations into English from a Hebrew translation. Thus, some of them were twice translated. As with organization, we must also be aware of both hazards when a translation is involved: not doing enough justice and doing too much justice to the data in their original form.

In the course of the study, the reader will be led to five central conclusions: First, a nuclear posture must be overt and explicit in order to provide the benefits of security and peace. Second, accurate perceptions of the cost involved in suffering nuclear retaliation will deter massive Arab attacks intended to challenge Israel's survival. Third, an Israeli withdrawal to lines approximating those held prior to 1967 will limit Arab willingness to suffer enormous punishment in order to obtain further territorial gains. The fear that exercising limited challenges might escalate to costly nuclear war is likely to deter Arab states from attempting lower levels of violence against Israel after she withdraws to such lines. Fourth, although the risks entailed in nuclearization of Israel and perhaps additional countries in the Middle East cannot be dismissed lightly, they are actually less significant than most analysts believe. Finally, although the superpowers would not applaud the contemplated change in Israel's strategy, competing interests will moderate their negative response if the change is made wisely and with great care.

Despite a clear preference for deterrent strategies, I stop short of recommending that Israel adopt a nuclear-deterrent posture. The approach is policy oriented, but *not* policy prescriptive. My aim is to analyze a wide range of policy considerations pertinent to the possible shift from conventional defense to nuclear deterrence. Yet I do not claim to have exhausted the spectrum of possible considerations. I do stress that *if* Israel wants to maximize her deterrent capacity, she must adopt a doctrine of explicit strategic nuclear deterrence. This rests on the assessment made of the benefits and risks of overt nuclear deterrence. However, a recommendation to alter Israel's strategy from conventional defense to nuclear deterrence can be made only after these costs and benefits are compared with the advantages and inherent risks involved in the continuation of Israel's present defense strategy. Such a comparison remains beyond the scope of this essay. Thus, Israel's economic ability to sustain her enormous conventional force is not analyzed. Neither have I addressed Israel's ability to match the planned and likely growth of Arab conventional forces in the 1980s. To have covered these important issues responsibly would have required an effort far beyond the time allotted to this present project.

A number of limited recommendations can nevertheless be distilled from this study. First, in order to avert the political costs involved in being a test case for the superpowers' antiproliferation efforts, Israel should attempt to postpone the adoption of overt nuclear deterrence until a few more states have developed a nuclear capability. It would be still more desirable for Israeli disclosure to follow the acquisition of a nuclear capability by at least one Arab or Muslim state. A deterioration of the conventional balance, however, might make it unwise to await such a development. Second, both to avert enormous political costs and to enhance the credibility of her deterrence, Israel should not "go nuclear" unless she concomitantly adopts a flexible political posture with respect to the territories she has held since the 1967 war. The adoption of a nuclear-deterrent posture that seems to be aimed at maintaining Israel's present hold over the West Bank, the Gaza Strip, and the Golan Heights would result in prohibitive political costs. If nuclear deterrence is not coupled with political flexibility, not only would the Soviet, American, and Western European reactions be extremely negative, but a dramatic deterioration of relations between Egypt and Israel might also be expected. To avoid such costs, disclosure should accompany dramatic steps that increase the prospect of a regional political settlement. Finally, once Israel does go nuclear, she should refrain from developing a doctrine and capability for counter-Soviet nuclear deterrence. In order to avoid extreme Soviet responses resulting from unnecessary anxieties about Israel's nuclear capability, Israel should try to convince Moscow that her nuclear-deterrent posture does not constitute a threat to Soviet security.

No one should underestimate the difficulties of weighing the advantages involved in the adoption of an overt nuclear deterrent against its inherent risks. The costs and benefits do not yield to common measurement. All we can do is to air the full range of considerations pertinent to each of the issues involved, and weigh them in our own minds, even if imprecisely. Thus, the goals I set for this study are limited to two: to lead to a debate in Israel on the possible role of nuclear weapons in Israel's strategy—a debate that might clarify and refine the arguments advanced here; and beyond Israel, especially in the capitals of the free world, to help persuade influential opinion-makers to adopt a more balanced attitude toward the prospect of a nuclear Middle East.

CHAPTER 1

The Logic of Going Nuclear

What might be the strategic rationale for going nuclear? And if a nuclear posture were adopted, why should Israel prefer an overt posture? The first section of this chapter addresses the second of these questions. Assuming that reliance on nuclear deterrence is advantageous, it asks what type of nuclear posture should be adopted. The following four sections provide the conceptual and theoretical basis for Israel's possible adoption of a nuclear posture by analyzing the general effects and implications of nuclear deterrence.

A Proposed Posture: Overt Nuclear Deterrence

Three kinds of nuclear postures are often discussed in the Israeli context. The first is the "nuclear-option" posture. The second is a "bomb-in-the-basement" posture. The third is "disclosed" or "overt" deterrence. A nuclear-option posture implies that operational nuclear weapons have not yet been assembled but that the capability exists to do so within a relatively short time. A bomb-in-the-basement posture implies that nuclear weapons have been assembled but that this fact has not been disclosed. Finally, overt deterrence implies that the acquisition of nuclear weapons is disclosed and becomes part of the public domain.

Most of what has been written so far about Israeli nuclear strategy attempts to guess whether Israel's present posture is the first or second of these alternatives. Among those who believe that Israel merely has a nuclear option, guesses with respect to the length of time Israel would require to convert the option to actual weaponry range from a few weeks to a few years. Among those who believe that Israel has weapons in the basement, estimates of the number of weapons range from a few to more than two dozen. The wide spectrum of guesses demonstrates the futility of the guessing game.

A comparison between the nuclear-option and the bomb-in-the-basement postures reveals that their deterrent effect is similar. In both cases the exact status of the weapons program is kept secret. Unless intelligence reveals Israel's exact status, Arab perceptions of her nuclear status remain equally clouded, regardless of Israel's true posture. Consequently their deterrent effect is the same. The two postures differ, however, in their sensitivity to three important factors: first, to incorrect intelligence estimates of the opponents' conventional forces; second, to failures of deterrence; third, to the opponents' ability to verify the exact status of the weapons program.

Clearly, the length of time Israel would regard as acceptable for turning its nuclear option into actual weaponry depends on her estimate of the length of time it might take for the Arabs to acquire the conventional capability that might threaten her survival. In addition, the length of this lead time would depend on Israel's confidence in her intelligence estimates. While the bomb-in-the-basement posture allows the immediate utilization of nuclear weapons for deterrent purposes, the option posture does not. Hence the nuclear-option posture is much more sensitive to failures of intelligence estimates. If the adversaries' strength is underestimated, the lead time taken for the option may turn out to be longer than the period of time it takes the enemy to achieve superiority, and conversion of the option to actual weapons will occur too late to be of any use. From Israel's perspective, one wishful assumption after the surprise of the Yom Kippur war is that confidence in intelligence estimates has somewhat diminished. Consequently, if Israel's present posture is that of an option, the lead time taken should be very short. But once the lead time becomes very short, the nuclear-option and bomb-in-the-basement postures become essentially indistinguishable.

Once Israel's adversaries are in a position either to inflict military defeat or to do enormous damage to Israel's major cities, the two postures will manifest different sensitivities to failures of deterrence. The option posture is useless if deterrence fails and the Arab states attack under the conditions stipulated; a bomb-in-the-basement posture promises some probability of restoring deterrence. Israel would be able to explode a device in an unpopulated region of the Arab world so as to communicate to the Arabs that they would incur great costs if they continued their advance or the bombing of Israel's cities. Thus, the second posture permits "carrying deterrence into war."[1] Needless to say, the nuclear option offers no such alternative.

Finally, the two postures manifest different sensitivities to the possibility that the exact status of the Israeli nuclear program becomes known to the Arabs. In the case of the option posture, this would significantly reduce whatever deterrent effect its ambiguous status might provide. If the lead time is discovered to be very long, the result might be a renewed Arab attempt to launch a massive preventive war. In the case of a bomb-in-the-basement posture, discovery would simply have the effect of turning Israel's posture into one of disclosed deterrence. The overriding conclusion is that although the deterrent effect of nuclear option and bomb-in-the-basement are similar, the former is much more sensitive to a number of important factors. Because it provides a margin of safety, the second posture is much more appealing.

A comparison between the bomb-in-the-basement posture and that of disclosed deterrence shows that the latter has four major advantages: First, a disclosed deterrent lends greater credibility to Israel's deterrent threats. Second, an overt posture facilitates the elaboration of a doctrine for the use of nuclear weapons, thus reducing the likelihood of their misuse. Third, disclosure permits the development of a strategic dialogue between the parties, which would lead to mutually shared definitions of what might result in nuclear retaliation; this, in turn, would minimize the probability that war might occur through misunderstanding. Fourth, a disclosed deterrent permits the socialization of the Mideast elites to the realities of life in a nuclearized region.

Possibly the most important of these advantages is that it would give Israel's nuclear deterrence far greater credibility. Israel's present policy of ambiguity creates too much uncertainty; as a result, at critical moments Arabs may disregard Israel's implicit threats. Israel's present policy of ambiguity is said to produce "deterrence through uncertainty." The premise is that Arabs are not sure that Israel *does not* have nuclear weapons, which deters them from taking undesirable action because of their uncertainty that such action would *not* elicit an Israeli nuclear response.

Strategists have been aware that since nuclear retaliation elicits threats of extremely costly counterretaliation, states may be self-deterred from executing their deterrent threats. Consequently, a measure of uncertainty is associated with any nuclear-deterrent threat; one can never be sure that the threatener will in fact carry out the promised punishment. Deterrence, however, can survive such uncertainty because one is never sure that the threatener will *not* carry out his threat. This has traditionally been the meaning of the concept of deterrence through uncertainty. Israel's present policy of ambiguity stretches the limits of this concept, however, because of too much uncertainty. In Israel's case, the uncertainty with respect to the will to carry out a nuclear threat is compounded by the additional uncertainty as to whether Israel has the ability to execute such threats. Together they may reach a degree of uncertainty high enough to render Israel's nuclear threats ineffective. A survey of Arab pronouncements since the October 1973 war reveals an enormous amount of confusion as to whether Israel does or does not have nuclear weapons. Part of the survey indicates belief that Israel has nuclear weapons, part concludes that Israel does not have such weapons, and some evidence suggests that the Arabs are simply not sure. Egypt's President Anwar

Sadat was very explicit in an interview he gave to *Der Spiegel* in March 1976 in stating that he did not believe that Israel has nuclear weapons: "I believe they are capable of manufacturing such bombs anytime, but I do not believe they already have them."[2] Sadat specifically referred to the reports that appeared in the American press to the effect that Israel has 10 to 20 nuclear bombs, by saying that to his best knowledge "the report is not true and Israel does not have such weapons. However, Israel does have the know-how and capability to assemble such bombs."[3] A month later, in an interview with a Danish newspaper, Sadat said: "I believe that the Israelis can manufacture atomic bombs, but I do not believe that they have a nuclear weapon."[4] At other times Sadat referred to the introduction of these weapons into the area by Israel as a possibility of the future, i.e., as something that has not yet occurred. He used such expressions as "if Israel introduces nuclear weapons to the area";[5] "Israel would be the loser if it did";[6] or "it must be made clear that we cannot possibly stand idly by if Israel introduces atomic weapons into the area."[7] Egypt's then Foreign Minister, Ismayil Fahmy, repeated in 1976 Sadat's assessment that Israel does not have nuclear weapons: "Scientifically, Israel has reached the capability to produce nuclear weapons. What is left to do is make the political decision to produce these weapons."[8] The *ifs* that characterize Sadat's statements are shared by Fahmy.[9] At one point Fahmy demanded that Israel commit herself not to produce or acquire nuclear weapons, which implies a belief that Israel had not already done so.[10]

Late in 1976 Egypt's Minister of War, Abd-al-Ranny Gamassy, said that "Egypt has clear information to the effect that Israel can manufacture nuclear weapons but does not have available bombs because it does not have means to test such weapons."[11] Gamassy talked about the introduction of nuclear weapons by Israel in the future tense.[12] Later, in mid 1977, Gamassy was only willing to say, "After the October war Israel increased its interest in the military aspects of the nuclear field."[13] A year later, Gamassy repeated his 1976 statement: "Israel . . . produces enough plutonium to make nuclear weapons. However, there is no proof that Israel has conducted a nuclear test."[14] In 1980, Gamassy's successor, General Ahmad Badawi, still referred to the Middle East as a nonnuclear arena: "The transformation of the Middle East from a conventional to a nuclear arena harbours enormous dangers. We hope that such transformation will never occur."[15] Later that year, in a speech to the People's Assembly, Egypt's Minister of Foreign Affairs Kamal Hasan Ali explained: "Since the 1960s, Israel has the capability to produce nuclear weapons in the Dimona reactor. However, there is no evidence that Israel has actually produced such weapons or that it has conducted a nuclear test."[16] In 1981 Ali said, "We have no information confirming that Israel has nuclear weapons because there is no evidence that it has detonated a nuclear device." Ali referred to Israel as having a peaceful nuclear program.[17]

Syria's President Hafez Asad also indicated a perception that Israel does not yet have nuclear weapons. In 1976 he was willing to say only that "it seems that Israel is indeed on its way to the acquisition of nuclear weapons."[18] In April 1977, he said he could not exclude the possibility that Israel has nuclear weapons, but still talked about it in terms of the future: "If Israel does get nuclear weapons, we shall get them as well,"[19] or "We in Syria have a counterplan, in the event that Israel gets nuclear weapons."[20] Saudi Arabia's King Faisal, when confronted by a leading Egyptian journalist, also indicated a belief that Israel had not produced nuclear weapons. Asked Faisal: "Do you imagine that in Israel they are producing the bomb? This is an adventure fraught with danger and I do not think they will embark on it."[21]

A second set of evidence suggests that at least Sadat, if not many others, was simply not sure whether Israel does or does not have nuclear weapons. President Sadat said that the reports of Egyptian intelligence have "confirmed to a certain extent the report [that appeared in the press] that Israel has tactical nuclear weapons."[22] In Rome in 1976, Sadat said that he "could not know whether Israel has nuclear weapons at present,"[23] and at the Riyadh conference he said "it is pos-

Arab elite – think IS has Nukes

sible that Israel has nuclear weapons."[24] Jordan's King Hussein was slightly more reserved. In an interview he gave in 1978 to the Lebanese *Al-Nahar*, Hussein said: "We don't even have guarantees that Israel does not possess nuclear weapons ready for us if the need arises."[25] One of Egypt's foremost journalists, Muhammad Hasanayn Haykal, explained the nature of the confusion: "No one doubts Israel's capability to produce an atomic bomb, but the question is whether a political decision to produce an atomic bomb has been made, or whether such a decision has been postponed."[26]

In addition to statements that show Arabs' disbelief in the existence of operational Israeli nuclear weapons, and those that show uncertainty about it one way or another, other evidence of no lesser weight can be brought to show that Arabs do believe that Israel already has nuclear weapons.[27] This does not diminish the impact of the other statements; indeed, it lends strong support to the proposition that an ambiguous Israeli posture elicits an ambiguous Arab perception of Israel's capabilities. Nevertheless, it could be argued that the third set of evidence, indicating Arab belief that Israel already has operational nuclear weapons, reflects the true thinking of the Arab elites. The negative and doubting statements can be explained away by arguing that the Arab leaders could not be expected to admit officially that Israel already has nuclear weapons. Such an admission would expose them to enormous domestic pressures to produce an adequate response. Presently unable to come up with such a response, these leaders have no choice but to pretend that the problem does not exist. This proposition has compelling logic, but it remains unsupported by evidence. It is irrefutable in the way it is formulated; no set of evidence can be brought to show it false. We can only repeat that the evidence at our disposal does not indicate that in any of the Arab states—with the possible exception of Iraq—a "national estimate" exists to the effect that Israel has operational nuclear weapons.

Moreover, the fact that Arab state leaders have not reached a conclusive assessment about whether Israel has operational nuclear weapons is not surprising at all. Having looked at the question in some detail, some careful scholars have reached the conclusions either that Israel does not have nuclear weapons or that the evidence available is much too shaky to enable one to draw definitive conclusions to the contrary. A group of experts, nominated by United Nations Secretary General Kurt Waldheim to prepare "a study on the Israeli nuclear armament," submitted their report on September 18, 1981. It said: "On the basis of the available authoritative information, the Group of Experts is unable to conclude definitively whether or not Israel is at present in the possession of nuclear weapons."[28] In another study, India's P. R. Chari, director of the Institute for Defense Studies and Analyses in New Delhi, articulated more definitely the view that Israel does not possess nuclear weapons: "It must be pointed out that to extract the plutonium produced in a nuclear reactor a plutonium separation plant would be necessary. There is no evidence of such a facility having been set up by Israel, even at the pilot plant level. It is not possible to conclude, therefore, on the basis of objective scientific considerations, that Israel has already manufactured nuclear weapons." Chari further bases his evaluation on the lack of evidence of Israeli nuclear tests. He doubts that Israel "would proceed towards building up a nuclear arsenal with untested devices. It is difficult to believe that it would find it possible to place its faith, indeed complete trust, in the efficiency of nuclear devices without having tested them."[29]

A study prepared for the United States government has reached a similar conclusion.[30] Michael Mandelbaum also holds this view, holding that "a state may not actually fabricate a weapon despite a demonstrated or widely accepted capacity to do so, as in the present case of Israel."[31] Alan Dowty best expresses the view that the proposition that Israel has nuclear weapons has never been adequately supported:

Insofar as it deals with the actual presence of nuclear weapons in Israel's arsenal, what is striking about [the] body of weighty testimony is the almost total absence of concrete evidence to support it. Given the deliberately created fog that envelopes the subject, it is hardly surprising that experts must speculate, but the inventiveness of the speculations is sometimes astounding. Problems of evidence are solved by citing other expert opinions, which in turn are based on other unconfirmed reports, creating a "preponderance" of opinion. "Israel apparently has been actually building nuclear weapons" says one typical recent study that was widely publicized as a scholarly finding. On closer examination the "evidence" is the same body of speculative literature (to which this study will no doubt be added, and cited by others). Technical hurdles to Israeli nuclear weapons production are either ignored or their solution is assumed in unexplained fashion. Thus, the International Institute of Strategic Studies (Strategic Survey, 1974, pp. 35–36) assumes, without explaining the shape, size or form of the "plant" or adducing an iota of evidence, that Israel has a "plutonium separation plant," which Israel denies having and which would by any account be extremely difficult to conceal.[32]

These quotations demonstrate that, given the present ambiguity surrounding Israel's nuclear program, it is not unreasonable for scholars to conclude that Israel does not have a nuclear arsenal. Likewise, it is not unreasonable for Arab leaders to be uncertain as to whether Israel does or does not have nuclear weapons. The significance this has for Israel's deterrence is that the usual uncertainty associated with the will to carry out a nuclear threat is compounded by a high degree of uncertainty about Israel's capabilities. The impact of such compounded uncertainty may be a reduction of the credibility of Israel's deterrent threats to an unacceptably low level.

The policy of undisclosed deterrence stipulates that Israel would announce its capability only if she faced an Arab attack that appeared overwhelming. The danger is that such an announcement at the last moment would tempt the Arabs to assume that Israel is simply trying to bluff her way out of a crisis. Under such circumstances nothing short of a demonstrative explosion would be likely to convince the Arabs of Israel's capabilities. The nuclear threshold would then have been crossed. Intentional ambiguity may easily lead to misperceptions and then to nuclear war. As Jeremy Stone put it with regard to the United States, "uncertainty is itself undesirable . . . we should have our deterrent capacity unequi-vocal."[33] General Pierre Gallois also reflects the view that disclosure of capabilities is a prerequisite to effective de-terrence. Gallois argues that "it is necessary that each side be perfectly informed of the other's potentialities."[34] Typi-cally, Bernard Brodie best articulates this view. In 1959 Bro-die wrote that "if we consider the problem strictly from the point of view of achieving the maximum deterrent effect from our retaliatory force before hostilities, the answer is appar-ently simple. We assign the hard-core elements in our retal-iatory force to the enemy's major cities, provide for the max-imum automaticity as well as certainty of response, and lose no opportunity to let the enemy know that we have done these things."[35] Almost twenty years later, a similar view was articulated in a Congressional study. The study notes that "being able to carry out a retaliatory strike is not the only requirement for nuclear forces. Strategic forces are designed for appearance as well as for possible use. It does no good to possess a powerful deterrent force if at some critical mo-ment it is not perceived as such."[36]

Lawrence Freedman applies the same conclusion to Israel: "The announced existence of the deterrent must precede those events which it is intended to deter. Israel could not allow herself the benefits of ambiguity. She would not be able to keep her weapons hidden until such time as the Arab armies were almost upon her; sudden claims about 'bombs in the basement' would not necessarily have the credibility required to avoid disaster. Thus, Israel could not shift to a nuclear strategy surreptitiously."[37]

Nowhere is this more vividly put than in Leonard Harris' novel, *The Massada Plan*.[38] His scenario includes a total Arab attack that Israel believes she is unable to stop; absence of disclosure by Israel of her nuclear capability prior to the attack; the issuing of an Israeli threat to detonate nuclear devices in Cairo, London, Paris, Berlin, Moscow, New York, and Los Angeles. The threat is designed to induce the two superpowers to force the Arabs to stop the invasion. After appropriate doses of sex, politics, and action, the book produces a happy ending in the best tradition of Hollywood. The threat finally becomes credible, the interests of the two superpowers converge, and Washington acts to stop the Arabs.

The Massada Plan's happy ending fails to convince us of the merits of undisclosed deterrence. Instead, everything that happens before this ending is reached convinces us of the opposite. The sequence of events that take place to make the threat finally credible is entirely dependent on individuals, timing, and chance. No one could stake his nation's survival on the expectation that they, or similar events, will occur. Harris bases the credibility of the threat on three components. First, an official message is sent by the Israeli government to the United Nations, the United States, and the USSR. It asks for an immediate cease-fire and states that the Arab invasion affects the world, and would trigger a world war. Second, the Israeli government makes it clear, unofficially but authoritatively, that they have nuclear weapons and when a nation's life is at stake, it reserves the right to use *any* weapons in *any* way it sees fit, with *no* limitations in its response. Third, the nuclear threat is conveyed "precisely and specifically, but irregularly, . . . in such a way that it does not appear to be coming from our mouths." The plan calls for leaking the threat so that "there'll be no question of its authenticity" (p. 21). An American woman television reporter is set up in circumstances that enable her to photograph the secret documents related to the Massada plan at the Israeli Embassy to the United Nations in New York. These photos are eventually shown to the President and the Secretary of State and convince them that the threat is real. Thus this third step is the key element to making the threat credible. Yet it rests on a number of events that, even if more or less likely in themselves, are extremely unlikely to occur in the real world in just the right combination, in exactly the right sequence, and at exactly the right pace. Thus *The Massada Plan* only strengthens the conviction that disclosure at a time of grave crisis may raise suspicions of a bluff. Israel could not risk such misperceptions.

The second big advantage of disclosing the nuclear deterrent is that it facilitates the elaboration of a sound doctrine, which reduces the likelihood that nuclear weapons would be misused. The doctrine has better chances of being sound if the process of its elaboration involves the participation of a large number of people. In the case of nuclear weapons, this should include soldiers, statesmen, physicists, civilian strategists, and the like. The ability to draw a wide variety of opinions must come at the expense of secrecy. Hence, the development of sound doctrine necessarily involves disclosure.

Lacking a sound doctrine developed through an overt process, nuclear weapons may be misconceptualized. For example, decision makers may come to regard them as simply another "war-fighting" weapon with a bigger bang. This would increase the danger that nuclear weapons would actually be used, while wasting their deterrent effect.

The risks and dangers involved in the absence of doctrine become most apparent at times of grave crisis. It is then that decision makers, acting under enormous pressure and extremely severe time constraints, cannot pause to reflect afresh and tend to rely on standard operating procedures (SOPs). If the SOPs have been elaborated wisely within a doctrine, disaster may be averted. If absence of disclosure prevents the development of sound doctrine, and SOPs are developed in an incomplete manner, the worst may indeed occur. Situations that have not previously been envisaged may elicit either paralysis or overrections. The result could be costly for all the parties involved.

The "bureaucratic-politics" and "organizational-process" perspectives on decision making both point to the importance of elaborating a doctrine. Both were developed by Graham Allison and related directly to deterrence by Patrick Morgan.[39] From the bureaucratic-politics perspective Morgan argues that in time of severe crisis, the "interaction of internal games" may "indeed yield nuclear war as an outcome."[40] From this perspective it may be desirable that the internal fight be conducted prior to an actual crisis. If the internal

Organization process

struggle yields dangerous results, inputs by extrabureaucratic communities would still have an opportunity to check such results. This, in turn, would increase the chances of avoiding the kinds of dangerous outcomes that Morgan describes.

The organizational-process perspective stresses "the impact of agency routines in shaping a state's perceptions, its selections and definition of problems, and its 'realistic' alternatives for dealing with them." The impact is greatest at times of grave crisis when "most of the behavior is determined by previously established procedures" (*ibid.*). In military-strategic terms such procedures are precisely what is meant by "doctrine." Since these "previously established procedures" have such a compelling effect at times of crisis, it would be wise to avoid creating procedures that may have detrimental consequences at such times.

A major advantage of nuclear weapons for deterrence, to be elaborated later on, is that they allow a state to communicate threats more clearly. Disclosure is, of course, a prerequisite to this. It is impossible to communicate threats if the ability to carry them out remains undisclosed. This points to the third big advantage of disclosure: namely, that it facilitates the development of a strategic dialogue between conflicting parties. Such a dialogue is likely to lead to mutually shared definitions of what is likely to result in nuclear retaliation. This, in turn, will significantly reduce the danger that war may occur through misunderstanding. If war is initiated, mutually shared concepts and definitions will facilitate the maintenance of thresholds and will thereby reduce the threat of uncontrolled escalation. Furthermore, once disclosure facilitates the development of sound doctrines along the lines previously portrayed, a dialogue between doctrines can take place, a process in which the conflicting parties communicate to each other their respective doctrines. The parties can then modify their postures and doctrines so that these may constitute an effective response to all aspects of their counterparts. Such a doctrinal dialogue then facilitates both the prevention of war and the efforts to keep war controlled once initiated.

clear threats

Disclosure

dialogue

communications code for shared conduct

The importance of communicating doctrines has been emphasized in a number of prescriptions for U.S. national security. Bernard Brodie recommends communicating to the Soviets not only the nature of the capabilities at the disposal of the United States, but also her intentions about using them. By communicating the doctrine, the United States would also enhance the deterrent effect of her capabilities. In Brodie's words, "Such an arrangement must surely maximize the deterrent effect of our retaliating force. We assure the enemy by assuring ourselves, that we will not reconsider the matter in the event he attacks us."[41] Michael Brenner points out that the very creation of "nuclear doctrines and plans [is] guided by a desire to project certain conceptions, attitudes, ideas about objectives, capabilities, and tolerances—and expectations."[42] Richard Garwin shares this view: "An important part of any nuclear defense posture is that which is announced about it—within a nation, to other nuclear powers, and to non-nuclear powers. Like the physical force posture, the declaratory posture influences the actions of adversaries, allies, the neutrals in building their own nuclear and non-nuclear forces as well as their willingness to use these forces. Both postures should be chosen with this in mind."[43] Donald Brennan, Manfred Warner, and Colin Gray have stressed the importance of the "declaratory policy" in enhancing the deterrent effect of various elements of NATO's posture.[44]

The communication of intentions, price lists, and thresholds is the key to the formation of a mutually shared code for nuclear conduct. Such a code facilitates not only the prevention and control of war, but also the ability to check other destabilizing processes. A strategic dialogue provides an opportunity for one state to persuade its rival that it should avoid certain steps for the benefit of both. An excellent example is the lecture that United States Secretary of Defense Robert S. McNamara gave to Soviet Prime Minister Alexei Kosygin at Glassboro on the destabilizing nature of antiballistic missiles.[45] Needless to say, an educational process of this type cannot take place before the very existence of capabilities is disclosed.

Viewed from this perspective, an important dimension of

SALT, beyond any specific agreements reached, is the process itself. The strategic dialogue—the *T* of SALT—is central to the avoidance of undesired and unintended consequences. The enormous importance of the fact that the conflicting superpowers are continuously exchanging views on strategic matters had led David Gompert to ask that all efforts be made to continue this dialogue: "No matter what stresses and strains weaken that dialogue in the coming decade, it is essential that the channel be kept open. Soviet–American negotiations have engendered a common theoretical base for arms control over the past decade, and each side has taught the other quite a bit about its own strategic fears and needs. The ability of the two countries to manage their nuclear affairs in less stable days than ours will depend heavily on the availability of bilateral consultative machinery."[46]

In the Middle East, with the possible exception of the Israeli–Egyptian exchanges following the 1979 peace treaty, bilateral consultative machineries are not yet realistic. However, other channels for conducting the dialogues exist: through announcements broadcast by the mass media, through declassified publications of various kinds, through third-party intermediaries, and through direct communications in covert ways. The establishment of such a dialogue is as important in the Middle East case as in the Soviet–American context.

It is possible to argue that the importance of a "code for nuclear conduct" has been overplayed, that price lists are less important in the nuclear era because nuclear weapons make the prices clear without them, and that escalation would be controlled even without the communication of thresholds, because when nuclear weapons are involved everyone becomes very cautious. As will be argued in a later chapter, it is doubtful that nuclear war could be all that controllable. But even if it were, and the fear radiated by the specter of holocaust can make prices clear without price lists, it would be highly irresponsible to ignore mechanisms that could further diminish the likelihood of war and the likelihood of uncontrolled war.[47] The dialogue resulting in a code for nuclear conduct is precisely such a mechanism.

To sum up: disclosure facilitates the development of a

"strategic dialogue." The strategic dialogue enhances deterrence and the limiting of warfare in case deterrence fails. Deterrence is improved by the communication of price lists, by the reduced likelihood of misperceptions, and by the greater automation of deterrence. The limiting of warfare is enhanced by the conceptualization of thresholds and their integration within standard operating procedures. None of these advantages can be obtained without prior disclosure of the existence of a nuclear force.

The fourth advantage of disclosing the deterrent is that it allows the entire debate on strategic matters in the Middle East to surface. The discussion of the implications of nuclear weapons for the regional system will then be in the public domain. Newspapers will write about it, universities will research and then teach it, politicians will address it, and the people will discuss it wherever they gather on warm Friday nights. Above all, television, the most ubiquitous of all media, will bring the realities of life in a nuclearized region to most homes. Thus a process of socialization to the facts of nuclear life will take place in the Middle East. Both elites and mass will be the objects of this socialization.

Such socialization is likely to have three interrelated effects. First, it is likely to reduce the general level of misunderstanding among the governments possessing these weapons. Given disclosure, Gallois' opinion on this effect is instructive: "The knowledge of the laws of atomic strategy accompanies or at least follows the proliferation of this armament where it is being created and tested. So that among the major governments—that is, those which possess nuclear weapons—there exists an increasing similarity of outlook."[48]

The second effect of this socialization is that it would minimize the pressure of some segments of the Middle East elites on their respective governments. Aware of the constraints imposed by nuclear weapons, such as the constant possibility of massive nuclear retaliation, large numbers among these elites would cease demanding that governments follow unreasonably aggressive policies. In the Arab world the effect of this would be to reduce pressures to pursue policies aimed at Israel's destruction. Belligerent elements within the Arab

[handwritten annotation: "Is future in clouded ambiguity"]

body politic would be likely to lose ground. In Israel the effect would be similar. Disclosure would reduce pressures to take frequent preventive action. In addition, it would enhance the government's ability to persuade both elite and mass that it is possible to withdraw to borders not very far from the pre-1967 lines without jeopardizing Israel's survival. In general, a disclosed deterrent would decrease domestic opposition to moderate policies. Appreciation of the security provided by nuclear deterrence would reduce the sense of paranoia with which the Middle East publics are so afflicted.

The third major effect of socialization would be in the realm of strategic stability. Among the elites undergoing socialization to the realities of nuclear weapons, the military elite will probably be the most important. Disclosure would mean that nuclear weapons would be addressed at every level of military training, from officer staff colleges to schools and academies of high command. Since the participation in coups d'etat in the Arab world comes primarily from within the armed forces, socialization of these forces to the realities of nuclear weapons would minimize the likelihood that a new set of leaders would be ignorant of the constraints imposed by nuclear weapons and follow reckless policies. The likelihood of strategic instability resulting from changes of leadership would be reduced by widespread socialization.

In summary, the exact state of Israel's progress in the nuclear field remains clouded in ambiguity, and we do not know whether Israel does or does not already possess nuclear weapons. Looking toward the future, an undisclosed bomb-in-the-basement capability seems preferable to a nuclear-option posture, while a disclosed deterrent seems preferable to an undisclosed one. A disclosed nuclear capability would lend greater credibility to Israel's deterrent threats; it would reduce the likelihood that nuclear weapons would be misused; it would facilitate the development of a strategic dialogue; it would lead to commonly perceived price lists and to shared definitions of thresholds; and it would allow the socialization of elites of the Middle East to realities of life in a nuclear region.

After this elaboration of the rationale for preferring an overt nuclear-deterrence posture to an undisclosed posture, we are left with the more fundamental question: Why should Israel adopt any nuclear-deterrence posture? The following sections will provide the conceptual and theoretical rationale for Israel's possible adoption of a nuclear posture by analyzing the general effects and implications of nuclear deterrence.

The Nature of Deterrence

Understanding the implications of altering Israel's strategy from conventional defense to nuclear deterrence requires that the concepts of defense, offense, deterrence, and compellence are distinguished carefully:

—Offense is a strategy of using force to defeat the opponent or to conquer his territory.
—Defense is a strategy of using force to deny the objectives of the adversary.
—Deterrence is a strategy of using threat to dissuade an opponent from attempting to achieve his objective.
—Compellence is a strategy of using threat to persuade the opponent to perform some desired action.

Central to the strategies of defense and offense are the state's war-fighting capabilities. Central to the strategies of deterrence and compellence is the concept of punishment; deterrence is achieved by a threat that the opponent's attempt will result in very high costs. The cost must be higher than the maximum worth attached to the attainment of the objective by the prospective attacker.[49] Similarly, compellence is achieved by a threat that the opponent's refusal to carry out the desired action will result in very high costs. These costs must be higher than the maximum price that the opponent is willing to pay for his refusal.

Defense and offense, subsumed under what Thomas Schelling calls "brute force," and deterrence/compellence, subsumed under "coercion," must be kept distinct.

[T]here is a difference between taking what you want and making someone give it to you, between fending off assault and making some-

Deter, Compellence, Defense, Offense

one afraid to assault you, between holding what people are trying to take and making them afraid to take it, between losing what someone can forcibly take and giving it up to avoid risk or damage. It is the difference between defense and deterrence, between brute force and intimidation, between conquest and blackmail, between action and threats. It is the difference between the unilateral, "undiplomatic" recourse to strength, and coercive diplomacy based on the power to hurt.[50]

In the hope of clarifying and sharpening the distinctions between the four strategies, we may look at them from various angles. For example, offense and compellence may be said to be positive in the sense that a change in the status quo is intended. The effort is to achieve an objective or to induce an opponent to perform some desired action. Defense and deterrence would, by contrast, be negative in the sense that the goal is to prevent a change in the status quo. The effort is directed at denying the opponent his objectives or dissuading him from even attempting to achieve them.

Military strategies may have an active or a passive orientation.[51] Thus, defense and offense require active fighting. One must use force to defeat an opponent or to deny him his objectives. Deterrence and compellence are passive in that they use the threat, implicit or explicit, to inflict damage should the opponent attempt to achieve his objectives or refuse to perform the desired action.

Another distinction may be drawn with regard to the target of the strategies. The emphasis in defense and offense is on the opponent's forces. Defense is an effort to stop the opponent's forces and to deny them their objectives. Offense usually requires that enemy forces be defeated in battle. With deterrence and compellence the emphasis is on value: the threat is to inflict punishment on the adversary by destroying what he values most—life and the means of livelihood.[52] In order to spare what he values most, the opponent will have to refrain from undesired activity (deterrence) or to perform some desired action (compellence).

Finally, whereas defense and offense work on the opponent's forces and thus imply that the adversaries' interests are absolutely opposed (i.e., a zero-sum situation), deterrence and compellence work on the opponent's interests and thus imply a kind of bargaining situation. In Schelling's words, "[c]oercion [deterrence and compellence] requires finding a bargain, arranging for [the opponent] to be better off doing what we want—worse off not doing what we want—when he takes the threatened penalty into account."[53]

Although both deterrence and compellence have a passive character, they may involve various forms of activity designed to make the threats appear more credible. Such activity usually falls short of the actual employment of violence. However, both deterrence and compellence may have active and quite violent variants.

Active deterrence is a strategy of inflicting punishment on the opponent in order to dissuade him from continuing some undesired action.[54] The opponent is then expected to cease his activity so as to avoid further punishment. Likewise, active compellence is a strategy designed to inflict punishment on the opponent in order to persuade him to conduct some desired action.[55] The opponent is expected to conduct this desired action in order to avoid further punishment. In both cases "it is not pain itself but its influence on somebody's behavior that matters. It is the expectation of more violence that gets the wanted behavior, if the power to hurt can get it at all."[56]

We have so far reviewed four pure types of strategies and two variants. Some examples may be in order. Deterrence is best exemplified by present American–Soviet strategic nuclear relations. American nuclear deterrence is designed to dissuade the Soviet Union from attacking Europe and North America by threatening the Soviets with unacceptable punishment. This strategy is sometimes called "the doctrine of finite deterrence."[57]

An example of compellence is the Arab—and particularly the Saudi—putative use of the oil weapon. This putative use is designed to compel the United States to adopt a distinct line of policy vis-à-vis Israel. Another example is Israel's reaction to the Syrian invasion of Jordan in September 1970. Israeli mobilization of forces, their movement to the north with the explicit threat to intervene, coupled with a successful Jordanian defense, compelled the Syrians to withdraw from Jordan.[58]

The events leading to Jordan's attack on the PLO in September 1970 demonstrate the dynamics of active compellence. Israel's constant raids into and against Jordan, in retaliation for PLO activity originating from Jordanian territory, were designed to compel the kingdom of Jordan to put an end of this type of activity. Some more recent Israeli activities in Lebanon have had a similar objective.

In the case of wars of attrition or guerrilla warfare, the distinction between active deterrence and active compellence becomes less sharp. Wars of attrition correspond more closely to our conception of active compellence. For example, Egypt's strategy during the 1969–70 war of attrition was designed to inflict costs on Israel, coupled with the promise of worse to come, with the purpose of compelling Israel to relinquish her hold over the Sinai. Egypt's strategy was to make the punishment sufficiently severe that Israel's refusal to withdraw from the Sinai would not be worth her while.[59] But this example may be used to support a different interpretation. One can state the Egyptian goal as having been to dissuade Israel from continuing to hold onto the Sinai. Such a formulation does not focus on Egypt's attempt to change the post-1967 status quo, but rather on her attempt to restore the pre-1967 status quo. Israel then appears as the party that altered the status quo and Egypt as attempting to deter Israel from turning her change of the status quo into a fait accompli. This formulation makes Egypt's strategy look much more like active deterrence. In fact, the Egyptian leadership itself defined the initiation of the war of attrition as the beginning of "the stage of active deterrence."[60] A similar lack of clarity surrounds guerrilla warfare. It comes closer to fulfilling the ingredients of active compellence but sometimes looks more like active deterrence. Guerrilla warfare usually develops when a group or movement lacks the power to meet the opponent in open battle. Such a group, like the Vietcong, uses punishment to signal to the opponent that more punishment

Mixture
NATO deter *by denial*

is to come if he does not stop the ongoing activity. The strategy is designed to compel the opponent to stop or to deter him from continuing by promising to increase, and by actually increasing, the amount of punishment to more than the maximum level of costs that the ongoing activity is worth to the opponent.[61] For instance, since the continued occupation of Palestine was not worth more than a limited price to the British, the Jewish underground movements adopted a strategy aimed at raising the actual price above this threshold. As Thomas Schelling put it, "the Jews in Palestine could not expel the British in the late 1940's, but they could cause pain and fear and frustration through terrorism, and eventually influence somebody's decision."[62]

The strategies mentioned so far represent "pure types." Actual strategies are mixtures of the above. For example, NATO's so-called forward strategy combines deterrence, defense, and offense. U.S. strategic nuclear forces are expected to deter the Soviets from launching an attack on Western Europe; NATO's conventional and later tactical and theater nuclear weapons are meant to halt the attack should it nevertheless occur; and, in conjunction with reinforcements from North America, conventional and tactical nuclear forces are to carry the war into the adversary's territory.[63] Another mixed strategy, one that deserves particular attention because in the main it has been part of Israel's past and present posture, is the strategy of "deterrence by denial."[64] This concept is basically a mixture of defense and deterrence.[65] Promises of failure and denial are expected to induce the opponent to refrain from attempting to achieve his objectives. As Dennis Ross has put it, "by 'deterrence through denial' we mean actor A deters actor B by convincing B that he cannot carry a successful attack. . . . B can be so convinced by A's visible capacity to disarm B (at least partially) and limit damage to himself. A deterrence through denial strategic posture, therefore, clearly requires some combination of the ability to destroy the other side's military force and at the same time provide additional measures for one's own defense."[66] Thus, in deterrence by denial—as distinct from pure deterrence—

general & specific deter

the threat is not to inflict punishment at a level higher than the maximum level of costs that the prospective attacker is willing to pay for a certain objective. Rather, the threat is to inflict the losses that are associated with his failure to achieve the envisaged objective. These costs may involve the complete destruction of the attacking forces.[67]

Having seen how the six strategies differ, we may make a further distinction between general deterrence and specific deterrence.[68] Whereas the former implies deterrence of ultimate threats to the survival of the national entity, specific deterrence implies heading off specific lower-level adversary action. General deterrence involves deterring massive conventional or nuclear attacks; specific deterrence assumes lesser challenges. The target of a lower-level adversary action may be one of the state's allies or some other object or value abroad to which the state is committed. In addition, lower-magnitude actions may be directed at the nation itself by presenting it with challenges that are of a more limited character. Achieving successful specific deterrence may be difficult because limited challenges often do not merit the execution of massive deterrent threats at the risk of possible counterretaliation. Thus, whereas the United States is so far successful in deterring a direct attack on the North American continent, she has not been as successful in deterring attacks on her allies such as South Vietnam, or on other third parties such as Afghanistan. Likewise, the events leading to the June 1967 Mideast war demonstrate that it is one thing to deter a total Egyptian assault on Israel and quite another to be able to deter Egypt from closing the Straits of Tiran and from later proceeding to remilitarize Sinai.

The Nature of Deterrent Power

The winners of wars conducted in the realm of defensive and offensive strategies are determined by the distribution of power. This distribution encompasses a wide variety of factors: the quality and quantity of arms and men, the com-

power

implict costs for absorp punishment

mander's skills in management and combat, the morale of the forces, the relative geographical advantages, and the general stock of resources determining the state's staying power.[69]

In determining winners in the realm of deterrence/compellence, two factors appear to be crucial. The first is the relative capability to inflict costs. The higher the level of punishment the state can promise to deliver, the greater its deterrent power. The capacity to inflict costs depends on each country's weapons and delivery systems and on the extent to which its adversary's "values" are vulnerable. A second factor determining deterrent power is *the relative willingness to absorb punishment*.[70] This component is of the utmost importance because in most confrontations both parties are equipped with some capacity to inflict punishment. In most cases, when states are threatened with punishment they can threaten to counterpunish. Counterpunishment may trigger further retaliation, and so on. Consequently, each state must consider whether the issue at stake justifies taking a path that may result in the absorption of high levels of punishment. The willingness to absorb punishment may be as important as, if not more so than, the comparative ability to inflict punishment in determining the outcome of deterrent/ compellent confrontations.

Indeed, a nation blessed with superior will may win a deterrent confrontation despite its inferior ability to inflict punishment. However, if the weaker state is to win a deterrent confrontation, it must be able to inflict more costs than the opponent is willing to absorb in order to win the dispute. For instance, in a conflict of mutual active deterrence, North Vietnam was able to produce an American withdrawal from South Vietnam not through a superior ability to punish but through superior willingness to absorb punishment. Of course the latter had to be coupled with the capability to inflict a higher level of punishment than the United States was willing to absorb over the issue of its continued presence in Southeast Asia. A nation's capacity for specific deterrence varies with the nature of the issue in dispute. The relative significance of the issue determines the level of willingness to absorb

Vietnam

punishment and the effort made to avert the challenge.[71] Thus, for example, America's capacity for successful deterrence against Vietcong-type raids would be different if these were to originate in Canada against upstate New York rather than from North into South Vietnam. The issue would then be different, its salience would be different, and hence the will to absorb punishment would be different.

The concept of specific deterrence is best exemplified by superpower nuclear relations. Where both sides can inflict unacceptable punishment, the capability factor in each half of the deterrence equation may be considered identical and hence may be canceled out. The winner in any dispute between such parties is determined by only one factor: relative will.[72] Will is determined by the subjective significance of the issue at dispute. This explains why the Kennedy administration "won" the Cuban Missile Crisis of October 1962[73] and why the Johnson administration could not intervene to prevent the Soviet invasion of Czechoslovakia in 1968. The first issue was more important to the United States; the second, to the Soviets.[74]

This leads us to the next proposition: When each party can inflict unacceptable punishment on the other, the party defending its own sovereignty and survival will win any confrontation between the two. The assumption on which this proposition is based is simple: the willingness to defend one's state will be greater than the willingness to conquer another state.[75] The attacked state's territory and population are worth more to it than they are to the attacker. When sovereignty and survival are challenged, leaders of states will manifest little hesitation and much will. As Henry Kissinger put it, "the most agonizing decision a statesman can face is whether or not to unleash all-out war; all pressures make for hesitation short of a direct attack threatening the national existence."[76]

The defender will manifest a level of will higher than the offender. A state whose survival is threatened may feel that it has nothing to lose and may therefore be willing to absorb enormous punishment. The offender will then face an op-

threatened have greater will

ponent who has fewer incentives to refrain from activating his deterrent threats. As Pierre Gallois puts it, "faced with an alternative of servitude or invasion, a nation could gamble on the policy of dissuasion [deterrence] to save its independence."[77] The offender, by contrast, has more reason to hesitate. He knows that conquest will be to no avail if he is nearly destroyed and no longer able to enjoy the fruits of victory. He will show less willingness to place the defender in a position of unleashing his deterrent weapons. Hence, the more the defender feels that conquest is likely to result in his physical extermination, the greater the extent to which the balance of deterrence will tilt against the attacker. The probability of a holocaust lends great credibility to Samson-like deterrent threats.[78]

To sum up, a major change from the concept of defense to that of deterrence is that the determination of the winners of conflicts shifts in favor of those with greater will; the greater the importance of will the greater the advantage of being a state whose survival and sovereignty are threatened. We can therefore conclude that the greater the degree to which states move from defense to deterrence the greater the advantage for the state whose survival and sovereignty are threatened. In the realm of pure deterrence the absolute winner will be the party whose survival is absolutely threatened.

From Conventional to Nuclear Deterrence

The advent of nuclear weapons carried by aircraft and missiles has dramatically increased the likelihood of successful deterrence. This may be seen by considering the prerequisites to stable and effective deterrence.

In order to conduct successful deterrence, a state must meet the following conditions: First, it must have the capability to inflict high levels of punishment on its adversaries. Second, the level of punishment involved must be clearly perceived by the opponent. Third, the opponent must be sen-

Successful deterrence conditions

sitive to costs. The threat of costs will not dissuade a completely insensitive opponent.[79] Fourth, threats must be delivered in the clearest form so as to reduce the likelihood of misperceptions.[80] The aim of the threat must be clearly stated. Fifth and last, to ensure that deterrence is reliable and stable, the means of inflicting punishment must be immune to a preemptive or preventive strike by the opponent.

The ability to meet these prerequisites has been dramatically affected by the advent of the aircraft and missiles and by the military application of nuclear energy. The advent of air power made it possible for the first time to inflict punishment on another state prior to the attainment of victory.[81] Nuclear energy has increased the levels of punishment that can be delivered to the extent that punishment can now come not only prior to victory, but also in its stead.[82] Nuclear weapons represent a phenomenal miniaturization of explosive power. The blast–weight ratio of nuclear devices is on the order of magnitude of a million times greater than the same ratio for dynamite.[83] The absolute level of destruction achieved by nuclear weapons is equally impressive. Raymond Aron estimates that "the explosive power of a single thermonuclear bomb is greater than the total explosive power of all ammunition used in all the wars of the past, including the first two World Wars of this century."[84] As a consequence, unacceptably high levels of punishment can be delivered and the first prerequisite to effective deterrence is easily met.

The second prerequisite—that the level of punishment be clearly perceived—is largely met through the examples of Hiroshima and Nagasaki.[85] In view of the fate of these two cities no doubt can exist of the costs entailed in nuclear retaliation. As Patrick Morgan put it, with nuclear weapons "the sheer simplicity of the calculation is compelling—one side simply threatens destruction so grave in a retaliation that no rational opponent will ever find any objective of an attack worth it."[86] The advent of air power has also contributed to increasing the clarity of perceptions of punishment.[87] Because before aircraft the delivery of punishment was largely dependent on first attaining victory, anticipation of punishment that might result from ignoring deterrent threats depended on the uncertain estimate of who was likely to attain victory. In a delightful book, Geoffrey Blainey has demonstrated how easy it had been throughout history to misperceive the distribution of power and to exaggerate the likelihood of victory.[88] The threat of punishment, the delivery of which was dependent on the opposite outcome, could hardly deter.

That the level of punishment could not be assessed correctly in the prenuclear era was not accidental but systemic. Correct perception of costs depends on precise assessments of capabilities. But in a system in which punishment depended on victory, and in which victory might be a function of the ability to surprise, capabilities could not be advertised. The greater the secrecy, the greater the probability of victory. But the greater the secrecy, the easier it was to misperceive capabilities and to assess costs incorrectly and the smaller the likelihood that successful deterrence would result.

In the realm of conventional arms there is always a trade-off between defense/offense and deterrence. The former require maximum secrecy; the latter requires maximum disclosure. Since victory was a prerequisite to punishment, defense/offense had the upper hand; secrecy was enforced and the likelihood for successful deterrence was undermined. This has changed with the appearance of aircraft, missiles, and nuclear weapons. The dichotomy that evolved between deterrent weapons, on the one hand, and weapons for defense in case deterrence fails, on the other, permits the adoption of a two-tier policy of maximum disclosure for the former coupled with a degree of secrecy surrounding the latter. This has made for an increase in the accuracy of perceptions of the costs of policies that risk activating an adversary's deterrent force. Hence the second prerequisite for successful deterrence can be met.

One final remark about the increased accuracy with which punishment is perceived in the nuclear era: it has at times been questioned whether nuclear weapons are more effective deterrents than conventional weapons. The argument

Nuclear wa Comment.

has been made that the destruction and death inflicted by the bombings of some German and Japanese cities during the Second World War was greater than the damage done to Hiroshima and Nagasaki. There are two important reasons that this comparison is misleading. The first is that the destructive capability of presently deployed strategic nuclear weapons is very much greater than that of the weapons used at Hiroshima and Nagasaki. As Alain Enthoven pointed out, "Hiroshima was destroyed by a 20 Kiloton bomb. [The U.S.] now [has] weapons a thousand times that size. Roughly 2.5 million tons of TNT were dropped on Germany in World War II. One B-52 can now deliver many times that destructive power, and [the U.S. has] the ability to deliver the equivalent of thousands of millions of tons intercontinentally."[89] The second, and possibly the more compelling, reason is that as far as the impact on perceptions is concerned, it makes a great deal of difference whether the punishment is inflicted incrementally or by a "single shot."[90] Incremental bombings allow decision makers to postpone difficult decisions. They will tend to avoid considering the cumulative effect of the bombings and will primarily consider their incremental effect. Nuclear weapons do not permit such psychological defense mechanisms. The enormity and swiftness of the punishment requires that decisions not be postponed. The punishment must be considered in its entirety because only in such a form will it appear. The chance that decision makers will be deterred prior to the initiation of hostilities is therefore far greater.[91]

The advent of nuclear weapons has also facilitated meeting the fourth prerequisite—that threats be accurately communicated. Communication is essential for effective deterrence; in the absence of precise messages it may not be clear what one is to refrain from doing in order to avoid punishment.[92] In general, precise and open communications are a prerequisite to the avoidance of war through misunderstanding.[93] Increasing clarity of communication between the parties is an additional bonus of the overall decreased level of secrecy in the realm of nuclear weapons. As the need to conceal

" Second strike "

intentions has diminished with the declining role of surprise, states can afford to convey intentions in the clearest form. In contrast to the prenuclear era, it is now both necessary and possible to spell out in advance and with a degree of precision what one's strategy and intentions are in a developing dispute. This is exemplified by President Kennedy's televised address on the eve of the Cuban Missile Crisis. The message he delivered to the Soviets was perfectly clear.

The fifth and final condition for stable and reliable deterrence is that the ability to inflict punishment be immune to an adversary's preemptive or preventive strike. This is usually referred to as the acquisition of "second-strike capability," the purpose of which is to assure the ability to inflict high levels of punishment regardless of what the adversary does. This "independence" of deterrence is what gives it stability and reliability. Raymond Aron has gone so far as to state that "a deterrent force does not exist until such time as it is capable of inflicting reprisals, and therefore of surviving an attack by an enemy whom one tried to deter."[94] Pierre Gallois concurs by looking at the problem from the perspective of the potential attacker:

> If the potential aggressor were convinced that by attacking his victim's vital targets he would not paralyze his victim's reaction; that, even in the chaos of surprise and destruction, the nation thus attacked would nevertheless launch its reprisal forces; that, in short, by pressing the attack button the aggressor would also pull the reprisal trigger; then the recourse of force must be abandoned and the strategy of dissuasion would have achieved its purpose.[95]

Nuclear weapons are particularly well suited to the creation of such stability. The increased stability of deterrence based on nuclear weapons results from their high cost-exchange ratio against answering or neutralizing weapons. They are relatively cheap and easy to make, protect, and deliver. This means that an attempt to prevent nuclear weapons from doing their damage must cost far more than the use of the weapons themselves, under present technologies. As Stephen Van Evera points out, neutralizing nuclear delivery systems "can be done, but only at a very poor cost-exchange ratio. The tremendous blast-size and blast-cost nuclear ratios mean that a system to deliver nuclear weapons need operate only at very low efficiency, while a system to prevent nuclear delivery must operate at near-perfect efficiency before it is useful. Small improvements in delivery must be met with great improvements in defense."[96]

Another argument for stability lies in the nonreductivity of nuclear weapons. While counterforce weapons are mutually reductive in the sense that one state's counterforce weapons can subtract from the counterforce capability of another state, this is not the case with deterrent nuclear weapons. Nuclear weapons are given countervalue roles: their purpose is to inflict punishment by destroying what the enemy values most. As Robert Jervis has put it, "[d]eterrence comes from having enough weapons to destroy the other's cities; this capability is an absolute, not a relative, one."[97] An addition to the countervalue capability of one state does not subtract from the countervalue capability of its opponents. The outcome of this is increased stability because the countervalue deterrent capability of each state remains highly independent of anything a potential adversary does. Each state can act with confidence that its nuclear retaliatory capability cannot be endangered by developments in its adversary's force structure. If the enormous destructive capability of nuclear weapons is often said to have made them "the great equalizers," it is their cost-exchange ratio that has made them "the great stabilizers."

Recent developments in weapons technology have shaken the confidence of some analysts in the nonreductive character of nuclear weapons. In the realm of American–Soviet strategic relations the advent of weapons precision as well as MIRVing is feared to have eroded the stabilizing cost-exchange ratio of nuclear systems. Increased accuracy implies a reduction in the number of warheads a state must deliver in order to make sure it knocks out each of its adversary's missiles. The introduction of MIRVs has had an equal if not greater destabilizing effect: the fact that each missile can now be fitted with, say, ten warheads means that a single incoming missile carries the capability to destroy a number of silo-based missiles. The implication of this is that the traditional attacker–target ratio of nuclear weapons has been overset. As a recent Congressional Budget Office study put it, this means that "if the U.S. and Soviet ICBM forces were constrained to be of roughly equal size, either by arms control agreements or by cost considerations, . . . an attacker using MIRVed missiles might be able to destroy a large part of the other side's ICBMs while expending only a fraction of his own force."[98] Thus an advantage of the defense is said to have been transformed into an advantage for the offense. Nuclear preemption, once considered a futile proposition, now seems a distinct possibility to some. Mutual fear of preemption is now said to be turning into reality.

This trend is said to be particularly detrimental to the safety of the American nuclear delivery systems since the MIRVing and increased accuracy of Soviet ICBMs are added to a Soviet advantage in throw-weight that has existed for some years.[99] The MIRVing and accuracy bestowed on a force already superior in throw-weight are expected, within five to ten years, to provide the USSR with the ability to destroy U.S. land-based missiles.[100] Yet Soviet vulnerability would probably be even greater than that of U.S. forces because a greater proportion of the Soviet nuclear force consists of the most vulnerable land-based missiles.[101]

Soviet advantage in throw-weight probably could not offset this disadvantage, because once MIRVing is coupled with high accuracy, differences in throw-weight matter little when it comes to knocking out the adversary's hardened missiles. MIRVing and increased accuracy of nuclear forces on both sides propels the superpowers toward the use of these forces in mutually reductive roles. This is true for the United States no less than for the Soviet Union. As another Congressional study recently noted, "it is simply the latest manifestation of an old tendency of the Defense Department to build Strategic forces to fight Soviet Strategic forces."[102]

To summarize, MIRVing and increased accuracy of the superpowers' strategic nuclear forces are said to threaten the stability provided by what had previously been a very favorable cost-exchange ratio. The transformation of this ratio in turn causes states to ascribe mutually reductive roles to nuclear weapons. This may endanger the second-strike capability (i.e., the immunity to preemption) that both nuclear forces have long enjoyed. The fifth prerequisite to effective deterrence will therefore be undermined.

There are, however, three important factors offsetting these potentially destabilizing trends. Because of them the ability to inflict punishment remains immune to an adversary's preemptive or preventive strike and the potential use of nuclear weapons in preemptive counterforce roles in the U.S.–Soviet context is extremely unlikely.

First, in examining the vulnerability of U.S. strategic-nuclear forces, it is clear that only one of the three elements of the American triad—the land-based Minuteman force—is likely to become significantly vulnerable by the mid to late 1980s. Indeed, it is the smallest of the three; only a quarter of U.S. strategic delivery systems are land-based.[103] Furthermore, its share of the total system will become even smaller once a large number of cruise missiles are deployed aboard B-52s and would shrink even more if some of the new MX ICBMs were to be deployed aboard wide-bodied transport planes.

The other two components of the American triad, the SLBMs and the bombers, would remain as safe as they are now. In addition, that part of the U.S. ICBM force that does survive the Soviet first strike could easily penetrate the Soviet homeland. Developments in antisubmarine warfare (ASW) are not likely to threaten the invulnerability of the SLBM, at least not before the 1990s. The nuclear submarine will continue to enjoy a favorable cost-exchange ratio. As Michael Mandelbaum has pointed out, "for one of the superpowers to pose a serious threat to the entire submarine fleet of the other, it would need an enormously sophisticated, highly reliable, and closely coordinated system that would be of substantial cost in national resources." In addition, it would be far cheaper for the defenders to work on decreasing whatever vulnerabilities the submarine may develop. "They can reduce the noise their submarines make to complicate the task of finding them. They can give them the means to fire their missiles at longer ranges, move faster and stay submerged longer than is now possible."[104]

A similarly favorable cost-exchange ratio will continue to be enjoyed by the bombers of the Strategic Air Command (SAC). As Richard L. Garwin has noted, "despite one's instinctive preference for defense over offense, despite the historical Soviet emphasis on defensive systems, and despite the large resources spent by Moscow over the years, no one suggests that even the expensive Soviet air-defense network can prevent a majority of the B-52s from completing their mission."[105] This situation will be further improved once the B-52s are fitted with cruise missiles. The cost-exchange ratio involved in any Soviet attempt to defend the USSR from incoming U.S. cruise missiles is likely to be prohibitive and its effectiveness questionable. The primary future threat to the U.S. cruise missile is likely to be the Soviet SA-X-10 surface-to-air missile system. However, it is estimated at present that the Soviets are unable to field the five to ten thousand missiles needed to form an effective anti-cruise missile defense. According to William J. Perry, U.S. Defense Undersecretary during the Carter administration, "there is a tremendous advantage to the offense over the defense in this game, not only in the relative economic advantage but in the speed with which we can respond because we have much easier things to do. I believe we will be able to sustain the penetrating power of cruise missiles for the indefinite future under any set of defense responses I'm able to conceive of."[106]

Apart from concluding that both SLBMs and bombers are likely to remain relatively invulnerable, there are also good reasons to doubt that U.S. land-based missiles are becoming as vulnerable as some claim. There is room to question whether the worst-case scenario of a successful Soviet disarming strike against the Minuteman force is a realistic one.

First, it assumes that the Soviets are able to achieve near-perfect surprise when executing their disarming strike.[107] Needless to say, if surprise is not achieved the United States could launch its strategic nuclear forces against the Soviet Union before those forces were hit. Yet the Soviets would find it extremely difficult to achieve such a perfect surprise, because it requires that their strike against all three components of the U.S. strategic nuclear force would follow near-perfect attack sequencing. As a 1977 study points out,

Under current and feasible future conditions, a coordinated Soviet strike at the land-based portions of [U.S.] forces—the ICBMs and the bombers—would require the use of Soviet ICBMs against U.S. ICBMs and Soviet SLBMs against U.S. bombers. Only ICBMs currently have sufficient speed, accuracy and yield for a surprise attack against hardened targets such as other ICBMs. Only SLBMs launched on low trajectories from areas near U.S. shores have short-enough flight times to destroy bombers before they can escape from their bases.

The need to use two strategic systems to destroy U.S. land-based strategic forces creates an attack timing problem for the Soviet Union. If the Soviets wished to strike U.S. ICBMs and bombers simultaneously, they would have to launch their ICBMs first because their flight time is longer than that of the SLBMs. That entails a risk. U.S. detection of the ICBM launch would warn of the attack, and the alert portion of the bomber force could take off before their bases were destroyed. On the other hand, if the Soviets launched their ICBMs and SLBMs simultaneously, the SLBM warheads would detonate over U.S. bomber bases before the Soviet ICBMs arrived on their targets. In this case, the Soviets would confront the risk that the United States might launch all or part of its ICBM force before it could be destroyed.[108]

In addition to near-perfect surprise and near-perfect attack sequencing, launching a preemptive counterforce strike requires that the attacking forces possess near-perfect operational reliability. Yet this, again, is extremely difficult to achieve. Great uncertainty surrounds the actual accuracy of any given guidance technology. Gaining sufficiently high confidence in estimates of a missile's CEP requires a large number of tests for each missile and for each change in its guidance system. Such testing is constrained by the enormous costs involved. In addition, "actual operational performance can be degraded by variable atmosphere conditions and small perturbations in the earth's gravitational field. As a result, actual CEPs can only be estimated within a fairly large range of uncertainty." Furthermore, according to the cited Congressional study, "similar uncertainty surrounds estimates of warhead yield, missile and warhead reliability and silo hardness."[109]

Another obstacle to a wholly successful disarming strike is the so-called "fratricide effect"—the distinct possibility that one incoming warhead's nuclear detonation might itself destroy or disable other incoming warheads. Because of this, enormous uncertainty surrounds missile performance in an actual large-scale attack.[110] Moreover, uncertainties about fratricide will probably never be settled because "the prohibition on atmospheric testing prevents real world evaluation of a nuclear warhead's ability to withstand the various effects of a nuclear explosion."[111]

The third important factor arguing against a Soviet counterforce strike is that MIRVing not only improves the likelihood of a successful counterforce strike but also increases the retaliatory capability of the forces that do survive such a strike. As David Gompert points out, "the effects of [MIRV] technology—which both superpowers have mastered—is not unambiguously destabilizing, for while it is true that an increase in the number of warheads usable in a first strike would worsen the odds that a given retaliatory weapon could survive an attack, each missile that did survive would, with its own multiple warheads, be that much more potent as an instrument of retaliation. Thus it might be argued that despite increases in warhead numbers, yield and accuracy, the greater lethality of each surviving retaliatory weapon will ensure that the price for launching a nuclear attack can be kept unacceptably high."[112]

The overall effects of the destabilizing trend mitigated by factors offsetting it can be seen in a 1978 Congressional study postulating a worst-case Soviet counterforce strike against U.S. strategic nuclear forces by the mid to late 1980s. By that time, assuming that the Soviets deploy ICBMs accurate to about six hundred feet and that the size of the U.S. submarine force shrinks as a result of the block retirement of the Poseidon fleet, a Soviet attack against U.S. strategic nuclear forces is expected to destroy 90 percent of the Minuteman 3 force, 70 percent of the B-52 force, and 34 percent of the Trident force (namely the portion not at sea). Yet this worst-case scenario would still allow the United States to answer the Soviet counterforce attack with over 4,500 warheads and 1,400 equivalent megatons.[113] In other words, a Soviet attempt at nuclear preemption, even when the worst possible situation is postulated, would still allow the United States to visit retaliation upon the Soviet Union with thirty-five thousand times the destructive power visited upon Hiroshima and Nagasaki together.[114] To suggest that the Soviets would willingly initiate a counterforce strike that would result in retaliation of such magnitude does not seem to me to be altogether serious.

Such calculations have lead Bernard Brodie and others to argue that even in the realm of U.S.-Soviet strategic relations nuclear weapons continue to enjoy a favorable cost-exchange ratio. This lends stability and reliability to nuclear deterrence and makes it relatively insensitive to what a potential adversary might do. As Brodie put it, "it has become abundantly clear ... that the balance of terror is decidedly *not* delicate."[115] What is even more certain is that nuclear weapons' cost-exchange ratio will remain particularly high for new members of the nuclear club, as I shall argue in the next chapter.

Deterrence, Security, and Peace

The direct relation between nuclear deterrence and peace emerged clearly in the preceding discussion: there is less danger of war when the effectiveness of nuclear deterrence is high; fear of nuclear holocaust simply keeps potential adversaries from waging war. Yet, a further inquiry into the relations between nuclear weapons and peace is required, this time focusing on the extent to which nuclear deterrence reduces the likelihood of war by mitigating the various causes of war.

Kenneth Waltz, in a landmark inquiry, found war to be caused primarily, although not exclusively, by the anarchic nature of the international system.[116] He, Geoffrey Blainey, Robert Jervis, and Stephen Van Evera, among others, have examined the systemic incentives and constraints that propel or point states toward peace.[117]

The Permissive Aspect of International Anarchy

As Waltz pointed out, since the international system is composed of many sovereign states without a superior agent capable of enforcing laws among them, war is always possible. Because the condition of anarchy allows each state to judge its "grievances and ambitions" according to the dictates of its own objective and subjective interests, "conflict, sometimes leading to war, is bound to occur." In a state of anarchy, Waltz further points out, there is no automatic harmony. A state may use force to attain its goals "if, after assessing the prospects of success, it values these goals more than it values the pleasures of peace."[118] Since in anarchy each state is the final judge of its own cause, any state may at any time use force to implement its policies.

The permissive aspect of international anarchy may be summarized as follows: In the absence of a single agent equipped with a monopoly of force and capable of enforcing law, war is always possible. The nature of the system permits the occurrence of war and since conflict is bound to occur, it is inevitable that conflict will sometimes lead to war.[119]

The Insecurity-Breeding Aspect of Anarchy

The second consequence of international anarchy is that states are in a constant state of insecurity because they fear that war may at any time be waged against them. As Waltz points out, since in the anarchic realm any state may at any time use force, "all states must constantly be ready either to counter force with force or to pay the costs of weakness."[120] The linkage between anarchy and insecurity is thus established.

Nuclear deterrence increases the chances for peace primarily by increasing the overall level of security in the international system. Nuclear deterrence enhances the security of states primarily by strengthening their prospects for survival. When the state's security is most threatened it is likely to manifest greater will and its nuclear deterrent will be most credible. Nuclear weapons guarantee the survival of states by providing the ability to threaten unacceptable punishment in retaliation against threats to a state's survival. Thus the statement that in the realm of pure deterrence the absolute winner will be the party whose survival is absolutely threatened can be regarded as a guarantee of sorts. Contrary to other types of guarantees, this one is most effective when it is most needed. In this sense, then, nuclear deterrence "insures" states against the worst and thus enhances security. By insuring the survival of states nuclear weapons provide them with security and reduce their incentives to wage war in the quest for security.

Preemption, Prevention, and Offensive Advantage

In their constant state of fear, states cannot forego opportunities to enhance their security by launching preemptive and preventive wars. In the words of Jean Jacques Rousseau:

> It is quite true that it would be much better for all men to remain always at peace. But so long as there is no security for this, everyone, having no guarantee that he can avoid war, is anxious to begin it at the moment which suits his own interest and so forestall a neighbour, who would not fail to forestall the attack in his turn at any moment favourable to himself, so that many wars, even offensive wars, are rather in the nature of the unjust precautions for the protection of the assailant's own possessions than a device for seizing those of others.[121]

In the absence of a single authority with a monopoly of force, capable of providing and guaranteeing security, each state is moved to take self-help measures to enhance its security. The launching of preemptive and preventive wars is among such measures.

In turn, whether or not states will either fear preemption or decide to embark on such a strategy themselves is largely a function of the relative attractiveness of the offense over the defense. The greater the advantages of offense over defense, the more likely are states to feel insecure and to initiate offensive action. If geography and weapons technology are such that the offense has a greater advantage, then large investments must be made in defense in order to offset small investments in offensive capabilities. Under such circumstances states have strong incentives to adopt offensive postures, which causes all the other states to feel insecure. The inability to mount an effective defense means that some states are vulnerable and hence sensitive to developments in other states' offensive capability. The heightened sensitivity of states to their insecurity leads them to prefer to launch preemptive or preventive wars. Thus offensive advantage significantly affects the probability that states will launch preemptive and preventive wars.

When the defense has an advantage, the opposite is the case. If the defense has enough of an advantage, "not only will the security dilemma cease to inhibit status quo states from cooperating, but aggression will be next to impossible, thus rendering international anarchy relatively unimportant. If states cannot conquer each other, then the lack of sovereignty, although it presents problems of collective goods, no longer forces states to devote their primary attention to self-preservation."[122]

Since nuclear weapons enjoy a high cost-exchange ratio against answering or neutralizing weapons, the incentives for preemption have dramatically decreased. There is no sense in preemption if this does not reduce the opponent's retaliatory capability below the unacceptable level. By making preemption futile, nuclear weapons have decreased the like-

Nuclear neutralizing

lihood that any state will launch a preemptive war.[123] The consequence of this is a further increase in the security of all: each state recognizes that another state will not find it useful to preempt. In the words of Aron, "Peace will be maintained simply because any first strike, with either conventional or nuclear arms, will clearly be against the best interests of both sides."[124]

Finally, nuclear weapons also reduce the likelihood of preventive war. In the realm of nuclear deterrence, threats to one state's survival may result only from another's acquisition of first-strike capabilities: namely, the capacity to launch a nuclear strike so effective as to insure that the attacked state will be left without the minimum strength required in order to mount an effective retaliation. Only the prospect that an adversary might gain such capabilities can justify taking some form of preventive action. However, as has been pointed out, the attainment of a first-strike capability is exceedingly difficult. This reduces the incentives to launch a preventive war and another cause of war is thus mitigated.

In general, the high cost-exchange ratio of nuclear weapons has alleviated fears that prospective opponents might take the offensive by making an offensive attack highly unrewarding. It has reduced the incentives to adopt offensive postures, thus adding stability to the system. This is best exemplified by a statement of General Leslie Groves cited by Bernard Brodie: "If Russia knows we won't attack first, the Kremlin will be very much less apt to attack us. . . . Our reluctance to strike first is a military disadvantage to us; but it is also paradoxically a factor in preventing world conflict today."[125]

Exclusiveness of Security

Another cause of war has been the fact that in the conventional realm security is mutually exclusive. The capability of other states to project threats also serves to provide them with security. Hence, "many of the means by which a state tries to increase its security decrease the security of others. [Thus] . . . one state's gain in security often inadvertently threatens others."[126] This is what John Herz called a "security dilemma."[127] Since the dilemma exists for each state from its own perspective and since all states resist any effort to diminish their security, it is almost inevitable that the general quest for security often leads to war. Thus war becomes more likely to the extent that the security of both countries is mutually exclusive. As Henry Kissinger pointed out with respect to the nineteenth century, absolute security for one state implied absolute insecurity for its adversaries.[128] Aron's view is similar: "Security based on strength is a mirage; if one side feels safe from attack, the other will feel at the mercy of the enemy."[129]

Because defensive capability can often be converted to offensive capability, the general quest for security increases each particular state's "security dilemma." To the extent that what states do to increase their security is additive (e.g., two armored divisions provide twice as much security as one does) and to the extent that their achievements are convertible (e.g., tank divisions can have both an offensive and a defensive role), each state's quest for security presents its neighbors with grave threats. Since the latter are likely to resist such threats, the very quest for security may lead to war.

Indeed, when resources are additive and convertible, war often takes place not over security itself but rather over those resources that add to security. As Brodie has pointed out, states often interpret "their requirements for security expansively, and the objects sought in its name often become in themselves the causes of conflict."[130] For example, "in order to protect themselves, states often seek to control, or at least to neutralize, areas on their borders. But attempts to establish buffer zones can alarm others who have stakes there, who fear that undesirable precedents will be set, or who believe that their own vulnerability will be increased. When buffers are sought in areas empty of great powers, expansion tends to feed on itself in order to protect what is acquired, as was often noted by those who opposed colonial expansion."[131] Expanding one's buffer zones necessarily places one's forces in greater proximity to other states' centers, thus threatening them. Threatened states take preventive actions and this may lead to war.

Nuclear deterrence reduces the extent to which the security of states is mutually exclusive. As I pointed out in the previous section, deterrent weapons are countervalue rather than counterforce. Their purpose is to threaten to destroy what the adversary values most. While counterforce weapons are mutually reductive in the sense that one state's counterforce weapons can subtract from the counterforce capability of another state, this is not the case with deterrent weapons. An addition to the countervalue capability of one state does not subtract from the countervalue capability of its opponents. Consequently, large increases in the deterrent capability of a state—and therefore in its security—do not decrease the security of other states. The general level of security among the states is thereby enhanced.

Nuclear weapons also diminish the importance of various resources that states fought over in previous eras. We have mentioned the role of buffer zones in the realm of conventional defense/offense. Nuclear deterrence, by decreasing the importance of buffer zones, increases the likelihood of peace.

Buffer zones or simply greater area are not entirely unimportant in the realm of nuclear deterrence. A greater area provides more room to disperse one's nuclear forces, thus making them less vulnerable. However, as my discussion of the ability of a small state to have a credible second-strike force will show, dispersal is just one method of many for making one's nuclear force invulnerable. States are extremely unlikely to launch a war of expansion simply to provide themselves with better ability to disperse their nuclear forces; greater area, buffer zones, and "strategic depth" are vastly more important in the realm of conventional defense/offense. In the shift from conventional defense to nuclear deterrence, resources that constituted "a cause of war" under defense fortunately lose this urgency.

Optimistic Misperceptions

Within the realm of systemic pessimism caused by the anarchic nature of the international system, states are often driven to momentary optimistic misperceptions of the distribution of power. They may perceive what seems to be an opportunity to increase their security by expansion or defeat of the enemy and rush to exploit it before the distribution alters to their disadvantage. Thus many preemptive or preventive wars are the outcomes of momentary miscalculations of the distribution of power.

A temporary exaggeration of the odds in favor of quick victory, when coupled with long-standing pessimism with respect to the ability to attain security in the anarchic international system, often propels states to war. Geoffrey Blainey, in his book *The Causes of War*, examines various conditions that favor such optimistic misperceptions. The list is too long to be reproduced here. It is of interest, however, that both Blainey and Aron regard a rough balance of power as most likely to produce such miscalculations. Blainey found that a rough balance made leaders' calculations of the distribution of power more difficult to perform. The frequent misperceptions were often of the optimistic variety.[132] As Aron put it, "the more evenly balanced the opposing forces of states or coalitions appeared to be, the more easily an ambitious leader or an expansionist nation could come to cherish notions or delusions of superiority."[133] Optimistic misassessments of the distribution of power often lead to war; states will attempt to make the most of their advantage. Thus the balance of power, classical theory notwithstanding, caused not peace but war. World War I, the bloodiest in centuries, started from a state of equilibrium that both sides mistakenly thought they could overcome. The long years spent by the participating forces deadlocked in their miserable trenches are evidence of their undue optimism.

The adoption of nuclear deterrence postures strongly affects the trend toward peace by mitigating the effects of this cause of war. War becomes less likely because it will become more difficult to form misperceptions of the distribution of power. As pointed out earlier, in the realm of conventional weapons, the same weapons systems had a deterrent and offensive role. Because surprise was an important element of successful offense, states had to keep their capabilities secret. Systemic secrecy induced misperceptions and hence war. In the realm of nuclear-deterrent weapons, this would no longer be the case. Each state, wishing that its punishment-inflicting capabilities will be feared, would do its best to advertise these capabilities. As a consequence, the international press, the academic community, and the bureaucracies of the respective states will be saturated with information as to each state's capabilities. Under such conditions, it would be very difficult to form misperceptions of capabilities and harder still to launch a war based on an optimistic misperception.

Besides having freer access to more information, statesmen are bound to take greater pains to avoid misperceptions when nuclear weapons are present. This is because the penalties of misperception are far larger when such weapons are involved. In the prenuclear era, as Brodie has pointed out, "in most cases the penalty for a wrong prediction was sufferable without too great anguish. In the event of defeat, national humiliation counted far more than casualties. One critical reason for this was that casualties and other material losses were bound in any case to be relatively light, certainly by present-day standards. What nation could have been more decisively defeated than France in 1870–1871? Yet the price paid by the great majority of Frenchmen, especially those outside besieged Paris, was trivial."[134]

The character of nuclear punishment places the penalties for misperception in an entirely different league. The sheer horror of nuclear punishment wipes out any kind of optimism. When the explosive unit is so large and the punishment it can inflict is so grave, optimism can hardly develop. Even if the chance of nuclear retaliation is not thought to be very high, the recognition that this assessment may be mistaken is a heavy brake on optimism, given the enormous cost of a mistake.

So far the advantages of nuclear deterrence have been examined in some detail. Nuclear deterrence was shown to decrease the odds of war and increase the odds of peace by mitigating the effects of various causes of war. These advantages, however, must be weighed against the risks involved in adopting such a posture. These risks will be discussed in the next chapters, as the advantages and disadvantages of Israel's adopting a nuclear posture will be addressed.

CHAPTER 2

Israeli Security and Nuclear Weapons

To what extent would the adoption of a nuclear posture by Israel provide her with effective general deterrence? In other words, would the adoption of a nuclear posture deter the Arab states from posing strategic challenges to Israel's survival? This question will be addressed from two perspectives: first, under conditions of Israeli regional monopoly of an overt nuclear deterrent posture, of the kind outlined in the introduction and chapter 1. Second, the question will be examined under conditions of general nuclear proliferation in the Middle East. I shall investigate the extent to which an Israeli nuclear posture might continue to deter the Arab states from posing challenges to Israel's survival following Arab acquisition of nuclear weapons.

Deterrence with Israeli Nuclear Monopoly

The general proposition advanced in this section is that, having regional monopoly over nuclear weapons, Israel's adoption of an overt nuclear posture will deter Arab challenges to her survival. The following discussion will thus be limited to the interval of time between Israel's adoption of an overt nuclear posture and the adoption of such postures by one or more Arab states. I shall first argue that during such

Why IS should have overt posture [handwritten]

a period nuclear weapons are likely to provide Israel with effective general deterrence.

The general proposition is justified in terms of the five prerequisites to effective deterrence enumerated in chapter 1. First, nuclear weapons would provide Israel for the first time with the ability to threaten unacceptable punishment in retaliation to an Arab challenge to Israel's survival. Second, the sheer size of the punishment involved would make it nearly certain that the Arabs would correctly assess the damage they might suffer should they attempt to challenge Israel's survival. Third, the punishment involved in nuclear retaliation makes it very likely that the Arabs would recognize the extent to which this punishment removes any challenge to Israel's survival from the range of alternative actions open to them. Fourth, a nuclear deterrent posture would provide increased clarity of communications among the adversaries in the Middle East conflict. Fifth, the deterrent effect of Israel's nuclear force would be stable because Israel would be able to retain a retaliatory capability sufficiently immune to an opponent's first strike.

The ability to inflict massive damage would clearly provide Israel with effective deterrence for the first time. This ability results from the destructive capability of nuclear weapons, even if they are of the small Hiroshima type, and the vulnerability of the adversary states—a vulnerability that derives from the concentration of much value in a small number of targets and from the ease of penetrating those targets. Having already discussed the destructive capabilities of nuclear weapons in the previous chapter, I can now devote more attention to the specific vulnerabilities of the Middle East states. The most striking feature of these states is their very high concentration of value. In most of the region's states there are only three to five significant targets. The destruction of these targets with nuclear weapons would essentially destroy the societies as we now know them. From table 1 it can be seen that the complete destruction of three to four targets in each state might eliminate 21 to 30 percent of the population.[1] In U.S. terms this would translate to 46 to 66 million

Table 1
Mideast Target Populations as Percentage of Total Population

Country/Year	Target	Population (in millions)	Target Population as Percentage of Total
Israel			
1977		3.610	
1975		3.460	
1975	Tel Aviv	0.354	
	Haifa	0.360	 30
	Jerusalem	0.335	
Egypt			
1977		38.740	
1975		37.230	
1975	Cairo	5.921	
	Alexandria	2.320	
	Giza	0.893	 25
	Aswan	0.258	
Syria			
1977		7.840	
1977	Damascus	1.097	
	Aleppo	0.842	 28
	Homs	0.292	
Iran			
1975		11.910	
1968		8.860	
1965	Baghdad	1.491	
	Basra	0.311	 23
	Mosul	0.264	
Jordan			
1976		2.780	
1976	Amman	0.672	 38
	Zarka	0.251	
	Irbid	0.131	
Saudi Arabia			
1977		9.520	
1974		8.710	
1974	Riyadh	0.667	
	Jeddah	0.561	
	Mecca	0.367	 21
	Ta'if	0.205	
Libya			
1974/5		1.940	
1974/5	Tripoli	0.426	 41
	Bengazi	0.379	

casualties. While these numbers are terrifying in themselves, their implications for the future of the stricken societies go much further. For most of the states involved these three to five targets encompass all their hopes for a better future. Almost everything that enables them to participate in the twentieth-century marketplace is concentrated in those few targets: their entire business, technical, industrial, intellectual, military, and political elites reside there.

To the population concentrations illustrated in table 1 one must add a few more strategic targets in each state. In Saudi Arabia, Iraq, and Libya, the oilfields; in Syria and Iraq, the Euphrates Dam; in Egypt, the Aswan Dam. These additions clarify the dimensions of the possible nuclear punishment and exemplify what Richard Burt has pointed out: that "rapidly developing states may be more vulnerable to discriminate strategic attack than mature industrial societies. These states, like oil-producing countries, may possess only a single resource, which holds the key to their development plans, and, if attacked, would drastically affect their future."[2]

Certainly, if only three to five targets in each of the Arab countries were hit, the majority of the population would survive. However, Egypt for example would be destroyed as a nation if Cairo, Alexandria, Giza, and the Aswan were destroyed by nuclear weapons and if the waters of the Aswan Dam were contaminated by radioactive debris.[3] What would remain would be a rural population scattered in thousands of tiny villages, all carrying on a lifestyle more reminiscent of the Middle Ages, attempting to cope with the sudden disappearance of all the country's central organs. This would also be true for the other states.

The population centers listed in table 1 plus the oilfields and dams add up to some 25 to 35 salient targets. Their complete destruction, implying 100 percent casualties, might indeed require more than the upper limit postulated for the Israeli nuclear force—namely, 30 to 40 weapons in the 20 to 60 kiloton range. For the purpose of effective deterrence, however, such a force would be more than sufficient. No Arab state would be able to ignore the possibility that a disproportionate part of the Israeli nuclear force will be directed specifically at it. In addition, to cause unacceptable punishment does not require the full ability to destroy each and every resident of the target cities. The important business, technical, industrial, intellectual, military, and political elites are invariably located in certain sectors in each of the major cities. Such sectors house most of the important reference groups of the elite, not to speak of their families and friends. These quarters could easily be designated as prime targets for the nuclear deterrent forces. The ability to threaten their complete elimination would provide enough of a deterrent effect.

But vulnerability comprises not only the existence of a small number of high-value targets but also the ease of reaching and hitting these targets. The penetration capability of an Israeli nuclear force would obviously depend on the delivery systems employed. Robert Harkavy assumes a mix of specially configured F-4 Phantom or Kfir jet aircraft and indigenously developed Jericho SRBM missiles that are said to have a range of 280 miles. The Jericho can strike the major cities in most of the confrontation states, even from within the pre-1967 Israeli borders. Cairo, Alexandria, Helwan, Port Said, Damascus, Amman, Aleppo, Homs, and Latakia all fall within this range. Other targets, such as Riyadh, Mecca, Tripoli, Bengazi, Baghdad, and Basra, would have to be targeted by aircraft. While missiles are unlikely to encounter penetration problems, Harkavy warns that for jet aircraft this should not be taken for granted. Citing lessons of the 1973 war with respect to the vulnerability of aircraft to SAM interdiction, Harkavy warns that in last-resort situations Israel "might be left with a small force of aircraft challenging massive and alerted SAM and fighter-interceptor defense."[4]

Although Harkavy's caution is valid, there are three reasons for modifying it. First, the nuclear posture envisaged in this prescription is for the 1980s. By that time a different mix of delivery systems might be adopted possibly compensating for whatever vulnerabilities jet aircraft might meanwhile develop. Second, Harkavy is probably overstating the penetra-

tion problems of F-4s. Analogies from the 1973 war are of
somewhat limited relevance. Israel has since been equipped
with impressive defense suppression capabilities. More important, in 1973 the difficulties involved not only penetration
but actually hitting "point targets." These could indeed be
defended by thick SAM and ZSU-23 × 4 defenses. It is by
far easier to hit "area targets" such as cities. No air defense
system could be so potent as to convince Syrian decision
makers that none of Israel's aircraft would penetrate their
defenses. For the purpose of deterrence this is quite sufficient. Third, even Harkavy warns of penetration problems
only in a last-resort situation, when as a result of a successful
Arab attack Israel is left with only a small force of aircraft.
His point may well be a contribution to the argument for
Israeli nuclear deterrence. As part of its advance disclosure,
Israel might be wise to declare that she would retaliate *before*
being placed in a last-resort situation precisely because she
could not take for granted her ability to retaliate after that
situation is reached. Israel's presumed weakness would then
enhance deterrence rather than diminish it. Finally, since
Harkavy's concerns pertain only to aircraft, Israel could assign her nuclear-tipped missiles to targets that are likely to
present penetration problems.

The second prerequisite to effective deterrence is that the
opponent correctly perceive the amount of punishment he
is going to suffer should he attempt to ignore the deterrent
threat. With the introduction of nuclear weapons, whose effects are well known, the leaders of the Arab states would
clearly perceive the magnitude of the punishment they are
likely to suffer should they attempt to challenge Israel's survival. The Arab elites and the general public as well would
join in their perception.

In fact, some evidence suggests that leaders of the Arab
world, as well as other members of Arab elites, are already
acquiring a grim assessment of the costs of nuclear punishment. Typically, statesmen are more reserved than journalists
in expressing their perceptions of the enormity of the punishment. But among the statesmen, Egypt's Minister of War,

General Abd-al-Ranny Gamassy, called nuclear weapons "weapons of total destruction"[5] and elsewhere said that their introduction "will create a new and dangerous situation."[6] Egypt's Foreign Minister, Ismail Fahmy, called them "horrible weapons"[7] and said "the matter is very serious and will present us with the question of 'to be or not to be!'"[8] When President Sadat tried to emphasize Egypt's superior capability to absorb costs he also revealed a perception of the high costs of nuclear war. In interviews in 1976 and 1977 Sadat said the use of nuclear weapons by Israel against Egypt would result in a million or half a million dead, respectively.[9] In 1980, Egypt's Chief of Staff, Abdel Halim Abu-Ghazala, called nuclear weapons "the most dangerous of all weapons." He noted that Israel's possession of such weapons would "constitute a danger to the Arab world. . . . Its effectiveness and danger is focused on cities, concentration of population, and industry."[10] Jordan's King Hussein referred to a Middle East war involving the possible use of nuclear weapons as a "comprehensive and disastrous war."[11] In 1981, Iraq's Foreign Minister Sa'adun Hamadi referred to nuclear weapons as "Hiroshima-bombs," a clear indication that the first use of nuclear weapons has profoundly affected Arab perceptions of the costs of nuclear war.[12]

Arab journalists and commentators have been even more revealing in their pessimistic estimates. Muhammed Jabber al Nasr, a Lebanese commentator, stated that "it is expected that Israel will be able . . . to present a liquidizing blow on the Arab state [that becomes the object of an Israeli nuclear attack]."[13] Another commentator has suggested that "in the event of a nuclear attack, it is possible that millions of Arabs would die."[14] Lieutenant Colonel Hitam al-Ayubi (Retired), one of the more prominent military commentators in the Arab press, called nuclear weapons "weapons of total destruction," and reminded his readers that "the atomic destruction of the Aswan Dam will cause enormous floods which will flood the Nile Valley and destroy its cities and villages, and will pollute the land with radioactive dust carried by the flood waters."[15] The Egyptian newspaper *Al-Akhbār* pointed out that nuclear weapons mean "the mutual danger of complete destruction" (December 4, 1974). Hassan A'ah has argued that a nuclear war will be "a war of hopeless suicide," and added that nuclear weapons were "invented for the purpose of deterrence and the bombing of large cities and centers of innocent citizens. . . . The use of nuclear weapons against essential plants and projects or against the densely populated Arab cities will no doubt present the Arab states with enormous dangers."[16] The Jordanian daily *Al-Dustur* warned that nuclear weapons would provide Israel with the ability to present the Arabs with the specter of "a holocaust" (August 2, 1975). A commentary in the Algerian *Al-Sha'b* claimed that Israeli nuclear weapons "will present a serious danger to the existence and fate of the Arab nation."[17] In Syria, the biweekly *Al-Ard* has written that "if the possibility of threatening the entire Arab world by any weapon is being discussed, then nuclear weapons are the only such means. This weapon, with a sufficient quantity of bombs mounted on appropriate delivery systems, can cause serious damage to the cities and oil facilities. A large number of bombs may cause incalculable damage in all the Arab capitals and the destruction of the Aswan Dam."[18] These statements and more give testimony to an emerging perception in the Arab world of the costs of nuclear punishment.[19] Were nuclear weapons to be overtly introduced into the region such perceptions would be more widely shared. The second prerequisite to effective Israeli deterrence would thereby be met.

The third prerequisite is that Arab elites develop a sensitivity to nuclear punishment. By sensitivity I mean their realization that a possible nuclear punishment imposes constraints upon their freedom of action. The effectiveness of deterrence will be measured by the extent to which the Arabs will eliminate the option to challenge Israel's survival from the range of alternative actions open to them.

With the overt introduction of nuclear weapons this prerequisite could be met. Arab decision makers will judge that challenging Israel's survival is not worth risking punishment of the magnitude discussed above. Egypt is unlikely to at-

Iraq deter?

tempt to undermine Israel's survival through a massive conventional attack at the risk of losing a quarter of its population and of being set back some hundreds of years. Iraq is equally unlikely to threaten a conventional massive invasion of Israel at the risk of losing a similar proportion of her population, her entire elite, the Euphrates Dam, and a large proportion of her oilfields. Syria, for the same reasons, is not only unlikely to initiate a massive invasion of Israel, but will probably also resist any Iraqi effort to use her territory as a springboard. Saudi Arabia is even less likely to participate in a venture threatening Israel's survival at the risk of her own oilfields and four cities housing 21 percent of her population and some 80 to 90 percent of her skilled technical, business, military, and intellectual community. Libya, notwithstanding her verbal belligerence, is similarly unlikely to engage in actions aimed at challenging Israel's survival at the risk of her own oilfields and two cities containing some 41 percent of her population. Thus the sensitivity to the horrors of nuclear punishment likely to develop following the introduction of an overt Israeli nuclear posture will force the Arabs to eliminate Israel's destruction from the realm of possible goals.

Some evidence already exists that such sensitivity has begun to develop among Arab elites. President Sadat is reported to have stated at the 1976 Riyadh Conference that "in five or six years it is possible that Arab military power will be neutralized by the Israeli nuclear threat."[20] Another "senior Egyptian statesman" (possibly Sadat again), one said to be "well versed in the Arab–Israeli conflict," predicted that "there will come a day when the Arabs will have enough power to overcome Israel. Israel will then make use of [its] nuclear weapons in order to insure her survival."[21] Similar notions have been expressed by others in the Arab press. Egypt's *Al-Ahrām Al-Iqtisādī* wrote that the purpose of Israeli nuclear weapons is to "point out to the Arab world that her survival in the Middle East is an existing fact."[22] The Kuwaiti *Al-Qabas* considered that the purpose of these weapons will be to provide Israel with "a status which will . . .

ensure her survival" (May 11, 1976). Radio Damascus assessed that Israel is pursuing the acquisition of nuclear weapons "in order to put psychological pressure on the Arabs to
accept her policy of 'faits accomplis'" (February 7, 1976).
Jabbran Khuria, writing in the Syrian *Tashrīn*, predicted that
Israel would utilize this weapon "in order to dictate [her]
views to the Arabs and the entire community" (May 1, 1976).
A final example are the words of Tawfiq Hassan, a commentator on Damascus Home Radio. In reaction to revelations in
the April 6, 1976, issue of *Time* with respect to Israeli nuclear
weapons, Hassan commented that "it is obvious that the *Time*
report is merely an indirect Israeli attempt to intimidate the
Arabs and to make them believe that any new confrontation
with the Zionist entity involves the danger that a confrontation with conventional arms may develop into a confrontation in which Israel will use its nuclear weapons. In other
words, this means that if the Arabs insist on preventing Israel
from achieving expansionist gains and insist on the liberation
of every inch of their land, and achieving the Palestinian
people's rights, the Arabs will expose themselves to Israeli
nuclear strikes."

Thus there are some indications that the Arabs are already
developing a sensitivity to the costs involved in nuclear punishment, and that the introduction of nuclear weapons is
likely to induce them to drop the destruction of Israel as a
policy goal. In short, with the adoption of a nuclear deterrent
posture the third prerequisite to effective deterrence will be
met.

The fourth prerequisite is that threats be communicated in
the clearest form. In discussing the advantages of an overt
nuclear posture I essentially explained that this prerequisite
will be met with the adoption of such a posture. The argument
need not be repeated here. Having established that nuclear
weapons would provide Israel with impressive deterrent
power, we are left with the final proposition, namely that this
deterrence capability would be stable. Its stability would be
measured by the extent to which Israel's retaliatory capability
was immune to an opponent's first strike. In a situation of

Israeli monopoly such immunity would be relatively easy to accomplish and maintain.

As long as Israel enjoyed a regional monopoly over nuclear weapons, an Arab effort to preempt Israel's retaliatory capability would have to be based on commando raids, conventional surgical air strikes, or air-dropped chemical weapons. In the next decade conventional surgical air strikes would continue to mean the use of aircraft carrying conventional bombs. In the more distant future this could imply the use of conventionally tipped cruise missiles or other types of long-range Precision Guided Missiles. James Digby has argued that the introduction of such missiles into a region would enable the neighbors of small nuclear powers to "target the limited nuclear operations of those states with effective non-nuclear missiles."[23] Since the introduction of long-range PGM technology into the Middle East is not predicted for the next decade, however, it is safe to assume that by the time such weapons proliferate into the region, methods for decreasing the vulnerability of nuclear systems to a conventional first strike will proliferate as well. The following discussion would therefore be limited to the more foreseeable next decade.

A successful Arab preemption by conventional surgical air strikes is highly unlikely. Air strikes against dispersed point targets are extremely difficult to conduct because the prerequisites for success are very demanding. First, perfect intelligence is required. The attacking Arab forces must have precise information about the location of every Israeli nuclear weapon and they must *know* that their information is accurate and complete. The current guessing game as to whether Israel does or does not have nuclear weapons shows how difficult is it to meet this condition. The second prerequisite is perfect precision. All incoming conventional weapons must hit all nuclear weapons without exception. If the strike fails to destroy some Israeli delivery systems, this would leave Israel with a potent retaliatory force. Due to conventional bombing inaccuracies the Arabs are unlikely to meet this prerequisite.[24] Third, perfect attack timing and sequencing are necessary. All the components of the Israeli nuclear force would have to be hit at exactly the same time. Otherwise, Israeli delivery vehicles that were not hit by the first wave would be launched. The fourth requirement is perfect surprise, for in its absence Israel would be able to launch her own delivery vehicles first. Perfect surprise is highly unlikely. A conventional air strike against all Israeli delivery vehicles would have to be on a massive scale. To conceal such a massive attack almost until it began would be very difficult. Arab leaders are unlikely to attempt such a strike because a significant probability of revelation would always exist, and with it the danger that Israel would respond in time.

These considerations will be repeated and elaborated further when the possibility of an Arab first strike with nuclear weapons is considered. They are obviously more difficult to overcome when the strike contemplated is purely conventional. Some of these difficulties must have been raised when a conventional surgical strike against nuclear delivery vehicles was considered and rejected during the October 1962 Cuban Missile Crisis. A surgical conventional air strike was one of the options reviewed by the Executive Committee of the U.S. National Security Council. The option was rejected, however, after the Joint Chiefs of Staff stressed that an air strike of this sort would be militarily impractical. The Commander in Chief of the Tactical Air Command, General Walter C. Sweeney, told President Kennedy at the time that even a major surprise air attack would not be certain of destroying all the missile sites and nuclear weapons in Cuba.[25] There are reasons to believe that the Arabs would be even less confident in their ability to conduct such a strike. The distribution of power between the United States and Cuba was extremely asymmetric. The capabilities at the disposal of the U.S. air force were greater than anything the Arabs could ever hope for, especially in the realm of bombers. In addition, Israel's own ability to interfere with such an attack are and will continue to be greater than Cuba's rudimentary capability at the time.

A measured assessment of the likelihood that such an attack could be executed perfectly is likely to dissuade Arab leaders from adopting such a high-risk course. It is also worth mentioning that in contemplating a preemptive strike the Arab states would face a difficult trade-off between force-strength and surprise. A massive conventional aircraft and missile strike by a single Arab state is more likely to achieve surprise. However, its limited force-strength would hinder its effectiveness. A combined attack by a number of Arab states is more able to meet the requirements of minimum size. However, the difficulty of coordinating such an attack makes it less likely that the requisite surprise would be achieved.

Air-dropped chemical weapons and subconventional commando raids are unlikely to be adopted as tools of preemption. In addition to encountering the same problems facing conventional surgical air strikes, a chemical attack would be confronted by two additional problems. First, the party contemplating such an attack would have to enjoy perfect intelligence about the defensive measures taken by its opponents. The attacker would have to be certain he knows everything about the countermeasures taken by the crews manning Israel's nuclear force. This certainty is particularly important if the Arabs cannot rely on perfect surprise. The Arab states would have to consider the likelihood that countermeasures would allow the Israeli crews to withstand the attack and retaliate. The second problem involves operational reliability. The crews' defensive countermeasures notwithstanding, the attacker would have to be certain that the chemical agents used would operate so instantly and so perfectly that crews on constant alert would have no chance to launch some delivery vehicles before falling victim to the attack. Arab leaders are unlikely to risk their major cities on the assumption that their chemical attack would meet such perfect operational reliability.

The possibility of using "special forces" in an attempt to demobilize Israel's nuclear force should be mentioned if only to say that it would be exceedingly unlikely to succeed. With an excellent record against commando raids, Israel is surely able to meet such a challenge successfully. The high odds of failure to penetrate Israel, coupled with the insurmountable difficulties of coordinating a timely attack against all of Israel's nuclear delivery systems by commando forces, would dissuade Arab leaders from seriously contemplating such an attack.

Thus in an era of Israeli regional monopoly over nuclear weapons, a successful Arab first strike is unfeasible. The Israeli nuclear deterrent would be immune to preemption and the fifth prerequisite to successful deterrence would be met. Israel's "general deterrence" would be both effective and stable.

Toward a Multinuclear Middle East

In the preceding pages we saw how the adoption of an overt nuclear posture would enable Israel to meet all five prerequisities to effective general deterrence. The attractiveness of such a posture to Israel is apparent to the Arabs, and they have begun to ponder responses to it.

Yair Evron, in his article "The Arab Position in the Nuclear Field: A Study of Policies up to 1967," found that Arabs saw two possible responses. One was to call for the development of nuclear weapons of their own. Possibly as a result of censorship, however, only one reference to such a call, in an article by Hasanayn Haykal in 1965, could then be cited.[26] The second response was in effect to warn Israel that her development of nuclear weapons would elicit an Arab preventive war. Egypt's President Gamal Abdul Nasser stated in 1960[27] and again in 1966 that "if Israel produces the atomic bomb, then the only answer to such an action would be a preventive war [Arabic: harb wiqaiya]. The Arab states would have to take immediate action and liquidate everything that will enable Israel to produce the atom bomb."[28]

The possibility of preventive war was also raised by Haykal, who nevertheless argued that preventive action would be possible only after the fulfillment of certain preconditions such as the strengthening of Arab conventional military forces.[29] The call for a preventive war was also sounded by Ahmad Khalifa in a long article published by the Lebanese *Al-Huria*.[30] Much has changed in the Middle East since then. In recent years not a single reference can be found to preventive war as a feasible Arab option. My own survey of Arab attitudes since the October 1973 war indicates a grave Arab concern about the paralyzing effect of a possible Israeli nuclear posture. This concern is reflected indirectly in the sheer frequency with which Arabs address themselves to the issue, and directly in the extent to which they recognize the need to develop viable responses.

Since 1973, Arabs have made four types of response to the possibility that Israel might acquire nuclear weapons. The first has been to urge that Israel sign the Nuclear Nonproliferation Treaty and accept inspection by the International Atomic Energy Agency. The second has been an attempt to rely on superpower nuclear guarantees. The third calls for an effort to counter future Israeli nuclear threats by developing an Arab deterrent capability comprising chemical and biological weapons. The fourth response has been to threaten that this will lead the Arabs to do the same.

The demand that Israel sign the Nuclear Nonproliferation Treaty and accept inspection by the International Atomic Energy Agency was made by President Sadat in an interview given to the ABC television network on February 27, 1977. Prior to that, the demand was presented by Egypt's Foreign Minister, Ismail Fahmy, as an Egyptian precondition for a Middle East peace.[31] In an interview in 1976, Fahmy demanded that Israel "commit itself not to produce or acquire nuclear weapons; it must sign the Nuclear Nonproliferation Treaty and agree to international inspection of her activities in the nuclear field." He added: "Egypt is ready to accept similar conditions."[32] Two years later, in the framework of negotiating peace with Israel, Egypt proposed that both countries renounce nuclear weapons and also accept limits on conventional arms as part of their projected (1979) peace treaty.[33] Egypt's position, according to Secretary of State for

Foreign Affairs Butrus R'ally, was that "if Israel wishes to emphasize its pursuit of peace to Arab public opinion, it must sign the N.P.T."[34] Since 1974, both Egypt and Iraq have adopted a variant to this demand, calling for the establishment of a Nuclear-Free Zone in the Middle East. The demand was presented in the form of proposed resolutions, subsequently adopted by the United Nations General Assembly.[35] By 1981, Iraq's President, Sadam Hussein, also demanded that Israel "announce its readiness to destroy its nuclear weapons. . . . Israel must agree to open all her doors to an international investigative commission which will search for Israel's nuclear capability and nuclear weapons and will destroy them. After that, we—as Arabs—will be ready to provide the entire would with a written commitment that we will not produce nuclear weapons."[36]

A second Arab response has been an attempt to elicit a Soviet nuclear guarantee against possible Israeli use of nuclear weapons. Egypt attempted to elicit such a guarantee when Soviet–Egyptian relations were at their best, but the Soviets are reported to have refused. Egypt's former Minister of Foreign Affairs, Ismail Fahmy, recalls that "The Soviet Union refused to supply Egypt with nuclear weapons or to provide her with a guarantee against Israeli use of such weapons against Egypt."[37] This recollection was seconded by *Al-Ahrām* chief editor Ibrahim Nafi.[38] Over the years, Syria has shown a more active interest in as well as a greater willingness to rely on Soviet nuclear guarantees. Thus, in the summer of 1980, Syria's Minister of Defense, Mustafa Talas, warned Israel and the United States of the dangers involved in a possible Israeli nuclear attack on Syria: "Our friends, the Soviets, will not let us down should we face a war of destruction waged by American imperialism and Zionism."[39] Two months later, Talas told the Kuwaiti newspaper *Al-Qabas*: "The Soviet Union will defend Syria should we face an Israeli nuclear threat."[40] Thus, Syria gave the impression that she has in fact been awarded a superpower nuclear guarantee. Unconfirmed reports indicate that such a guarantee was provided as a secret clause to the Soviet–Syrian Treaty of Friendship signed in October 1980.[41] The odds that such a guarantee has indeed been granted, as well as its likely character, will be analyzed in a later chapter.

The third response to the deterrent effect of Israeli nuclear weapons has been an effort to counter it by developing an Arab deterrent capability consisting of chemical and biological weapons. Having conversed with the commanders of the Egyptian Armed Forces, William Beecher of *The Boston Globe* reported in 1976 that "Egypt has accumulated a substantial supply of nerve gas weapons, partially to deter Israel from using nuclear weapons first, in case of a major war."[42] Shortly after the October 1973 war, Egypt's Minister of War General Abd-al Ranny Gamassy told the Peoples' Assembly that nuclear weapons were not the only weapons of mass destruction, but that chemical and incendiary weapons could be equally effective.[43] In 1976 Gamassy warned that "weapons of mass extermination are not limited to nuclear weapons. Egypt has enough of the other types of weapons of mass extermination and it has the capability of retaliating to an Israeli nuclear blow by making use of these weapons."[44] Gamassy repeated the same warning on two other occasions,[45] as did President Sadat himself.[46]

Finally, the fourth and most frequent Arab response to the possibility that Israel will acquire nuclear weapons has been to threaten that this would lead the Arabs to do the same. In an interview in 1974, President Sadat promised that "if Israel intends to introduce nuclear weapons into this area, we too will find a way of acquiring such weapons."[47] Sadat repeated this statement in 1975 as well as on a number of other occasions.[48] Similar statements were issued by General Gamassy[49] as well as by Foreign Minister Fahmy, who warned the U.S. Senate Foreign Relations Committee that "it must be completely understood that should Israel produce nuclear weapons, Egypt will have the right to acquire this weapon in order to maintain her strategic integrity."[50] The Syrian leadership seems to be of the same mind. In an interview in 1976 Syria's President Hafez Assad declared: "It seems that Israel is on her way to the acquisition of nuclear weapons.

We are faced with two alternatives: to prevent Israel from such acquisition or to acquire or try to acquire such nuclear weapons ourselves. It seems that the second alternative is the more promising one for the Arabs."[51] In 1977 Assad repeated the warning: "If Israel possesses this weapon, then we will possess it [too]."[52] From Libya, similar intentions were voiced. One of the first hints that its leader, Muammar Qaddhafi, wanted a bomb came in a 1975 interview with the Sudanese newspaper *As-Sahafa*, which quoted him as saying he hoped to transform Libya into a nuclear power.[53] A delegation of the Federation of American Scientists was told in 1978 by Ah'mad al-Shahati, head of the Foreign Liaison Office of the Libyan People's General Congress, that "Libya is planning to acquire nuclear weapons as soon as possible."[54] Iraq expressed a similar response in 1978 and in 1981. Naim Hadad, a senior member of the ruling Revolutionary Command Council, stated that "if Israel owns the atom bomb, then the Arabs must get an atom bomb. The Arab countries must possess whatever is necessary to defend themselves."[55] In June 1981 this motivation was repeated in greater force. In a speech to his cabinet, President Sadam Hussein "called on 'all peace-loving nations of the world' to help the Arabs acquire the atomic bomb to balance Israel's nuclear capability."[56]

No one, however, has more persistently pleaded that the Arabs must acquire nuclear weapons than Egypt's Hasanayn Haykal. As editor of Egypt's influential *Al-Ahrām*, as well as later on the pages of the Lebanese *Al-Anwār* and the Jordanian *Al-Ra'y*, Haykal consistently called on the Arab leaders to watch what he perceived as Israel's growing nuclear capability. In 1973, still highly influential in Egypt, Haykal wrote that "the possibility that Israel has nuclear weapons is something [the Arabs] must be prepared for by meeting the challenge, not by running away from it. . . . The Arabs will act to develop their nuclear capabilities with tenacity and determination as long as international action is not taken to inspect [Israel's] reactor at Dimona."[57]

The process of matching words with deeds is already underway. Almost every major Arab state now conducts some activities in the nuclear field. Some have devoted their efforts to a slow buildup of a nuclear infrastructure; others have attempted a "quick fix" acquisition of nuclear weapons.

Egypt has had a nuclear program since the late 1950s. She founded her Atomic Energy Commission in 1955, and by 1956 had initiated research in radio isotopes in the fields of medicine, agriculture, and industry. In 1957 the Center for Nuclear Research at Inshass was opened.[58] By 1961 Egypt had acquired a small 2-megawatt Soviet-made nuclear research reactor, and began training a cadre of physicists.[59] In 1963 Egypt ordered a 130-megawatt reactor from Britain, but it was never delivered. Egypt next decided to try for a 150-megawatt reactor for desalinating seawater and generating electricity to be built at Borg al-Arab, on the Mediterranean coast near Alexandria. The project was shelved in May 1965.[60] Meanwhile, much effort was made to establish a scientific and technical infrastructure in the nuclear field; Egypt conducted surveys searching for uranium and thorium and by 1969 uranium-bearing "black sands" were discovered near Aswan, in the eastern desert, and in the Nile Valley.[61] In the early 1970s more explorations were conducted with Yugoslav aid, and Egypt has shown interest in the use of nuclear explosives for a variety of civilian projects, including the possible use of atomic blasts in digging the Al-Quatarah depression canal.[62]

During President Richard Nixon's 1974 visit to Cairo, he offered to provide Egypt with two 600-megawatt nuclear power reactors.[63] And, when President Sadat visited Washington a year later, an agreement was initialed allowing Egypt to purchase the two reactors at a cost of $1.2 billion.[64] Egypt pursued the project in the framework of a national program calling for the construction of up to eight nuclear power reactors by the year 2000. These were expected to produce 6,000 megawatts, representing 40 percent of the total amount of electricity to be produced in Egypt by that year.[65] Yet, actual purchase of the reactors was stalled by prolonged negotiations concerning safeguards. By mid 1976, when the successful conclusion of these negotiations finally seemed in sight,[66] nuclear proliferation had become a heated issue in the U.S. presidential election, and the sale was further postponed. President Carter's strict nonproliferation policy, combined with Egypt's refusal to ratify the 1968 Nuclear Nonproliferation Treaty, caused another four-year delay in implementation.

Meanwhile, uranium exploration continued, and in mid 1980 Egypt announced that deposits containing 5,000 tons of raw uranium have been discovered between Qina and Safajah in the Red Sea governorate. Egypt also announced that the largest factory in the Middle East for uranium production would be set up in this area, with cooperation from Canada.[67] Egypt was also reported to have signed an agreement with Zaire, allowing Egypt to develop the uranium deposits there in addition to establishing a joint Egyptian–Zaire company to market the extracted uranium.[68]

Egypt's nuclear program was dramatically accelerated in 1981. On December 24, 1980, Egypt announced its decision to ratify the 1968 Nuclear Nonproliferation Treaty.[69] Following that, an Egyptian–French agreement was signed, calling for the construction of two nuclear power reactors, at a total output of 2,000 megawatts.[70] Egypt's People's Assembly finally ratified the NPT on February 16, 1981.[71] By then, negotiations with Britain for the supply of two more power reactors were reported, and Egypt asked the United States to reopen negotiations for the supply of the two reactors promised since 1974.[72] An agreement for the supply of two 1,000-megawatt reactors was finally signed in Washington on June 30, 1981.[73] Two more agreements were signed with the Federal Republic of Germany, the first to establish a nuclear fuel processing plant in Egypt and to double the capacity of the research reactor at Inshass, and the second to provide the framework for the purchase of two 1,000-megawatt power reactors from West Germany.[74] Egyptian atomic scientists who emigrated during the 1960s and 1970s were asked to return home to participate in Egypt's new endeavors.[75]

Thus, already blessed with the Arab world's most advanced

infrastructure in the nuclear field, Egypt is currently launching a new and massive effort. Should it decide to enter the realm of the military application of nuclear energy, this infrastructure would prove invaluable. Egypt may also enjoy some important shortcuts. As an outcome of her agreement for nuclear cooperation with India, Egyptian scientists and engineers have been trained in Indian nuclear research facilities. Some of these scientists were trained at the Trombay facilities, where India's small chemical reprocessing facility for plutonium extraction is located. In addition, Egyptian scientists were present at the testing ground when India exploded her nuclear device.[76] According to Cairo Radio, on January 26, 1978, Egypt and India signed an agreement to further strengthen their cooperation in the field of "peaceful application of nuclear energy." Press reports give no indication of an Egyptian crash program for the acquisition of nuclear weapons; however, this does not prove that such an effort is not taking place. Fear of Israeli preemption may have led the Egyptians to surround their efforts with a thick cloud of secrecy.

Until Israel destroyed her nuclear research reactor on June 7, 1981, Iraq promised to become the first Arab state to obtain a military nuclear capability. Iraq's nuclear program began in the 1960s, when the Nuclear Physics Research Center in Tuwaitha, near Baghdad, was established. In 1968 Iraq received a 2-megawatt Soviet-made research reactor, its capacity later increased to 5 megawatts.[77] On October 29, 1969, Iraq signed the NPT. In recent years, Iraq's nuclear program has been dramatically accelerated; large-scale training of manpower and the purchase of appropriate facilities were conducted in order to establish a scientific and technical infrastructure in the nuclear field. In 1975, Iraq attempted to purchase a 500-megawatt uranium graphite reactor from France.[78] Since graphite gas reactors produce enormous quantities of plutonium, and since their production in France has long since been discontinued, the French balked at the proposed deal. Instead, they offered the 70-megawatt Osiris research reactor. Iraq agreed.

Thus, the French–Iraqi agreement of 1976 provided Iraq with a complete nuclear research center, to include the 70-megawatt Osiris reactor, called *Osiraq*, as well as a small 800-kilowatt Isis-type reactor. The French Atomic Energy Commission undertook to train the Iraqi personnel required for the running and maintenance of the reactors.[79] Both reactors were to be fueled by uranium enriched to over 92 percent. France was to supply Iraq with 70 kg of such weapons-grade material.[80]

Deferring somewhat to American nonproliferation pressures, France later attempted to amend her nuclear agreement with Iraq. An effort was made to persuade the latter to fuel the Osiraq reactor with the new "Caramel" fuel, enriched to only 10 percent—far lower than weapons-grade.[81] The new fuel was not yet in industrial production, and this provided an excuse for Iraq to dismiss the French request out of hand.

Iraq's nuclear program was thrice tampered with prior to the June 1981 raid. On April 7, 1979, on the eve of its shipment to Iraq, the core of Osiraq was sabotaged at a storage house in La Seyne sur Mer, near the French port of Toulon. The French police and security services said that the professional nature of the job betrayed the hand of explosives experts with an intimate knowledge of nuclear reactors.[82] Iraq demanded that the damaged reactor be repaired promptly and France promised to comply.[83] The damage caused by the April explosion turned out to be smaller than initially assessed, and the delay much shorter. By December 1979 the reactor had been repaired and shipped to Iraq. Renewed efforts to persuade Iraq to accept the less enriched Caramel fuel, as a substitute to the highly enriched uranium, failed again.[84]

Iraq's nuclear program was again impaired on June 13, 1980, when an Egyptian scientist, Yihya al-Meshad, was murdered in Paris. Al-Meshad, a metallurgist, was recruited by the Iraqis to head their nuclear program in 1975. Prior to that, he was Dean of the Faculty of Nuclear Sciences and Nuclear Reactors at Alexandria University.[85] A central figure in Iraq's nuclear program and in French–Iraqi nuclear dealings, al-Meshad's death was a significant blow to Iraq's efforts.

In September 1980 Iraq's nuclear program was stalled again; with the outbreak of the Iraq–Iran war, the French technicians and nuclear engineers were evacuated.[86] Later, on September 30, Iranian bombers, returning from another mission, dropped their remaining load on the nuclear research center. However, the Osiris reactor itself was hardly damaged; only infrastructure facilities were destroyed.[87] And by early 1981, many of the French technicians and engineers returned to their work at Osiraq.[88]

During the same period, further progress was made in Iraq's nuclear program. In June 1980 Iraq was reported to have purchased Iran's share in the French uranium consortium, Eurodif.[89] And, by July, a senior French official revealed that the small Isis reactor delivered to Iraq had become critical.[90] France also transferred to Iraq the first consignment of highly enriched uranium fuel.[91]

The new nuclear research center would have provided Iraq with options in both the uranium and plutonium routes to weapons-grade material. In the uranium route, Iraq could have diverted some of the weapons-grade uranium that the French were to supply under the agreement. France insisted that she take some precautionary measures against such a possibility. One was to make sure that at no time would Iraq have more than 24 kg of enriched uranium (12 kg of fuel for the Osiris reactor and a similar quantity for the Isis reactor). This quantity would have permitted the construction of no more than one nuclear bomb. Another measure was the preirradiation of the enriched uranium, to make its handling hazardous.[92] French experts themselves admitted, however, that these steps were not insuperable obstacles to the material's diversion. A more effective obstacle was that the construction of a nuclear bomb would have required the entire quantity of enriched uranium available to the Iraqis. There would have been no fuel for the reactor, the entire nuclear program would have suffered, and the diversion would almost certainly have been detected.

The plutonium route to fissile material would have been more promising. "Blankets" of natural uranium could have been irradiated at the Osiris reactor, thus producing large quantities of plutonium. Moreover, adjustments likely to have been made in the reactor's cooling system would have allowed the expansion of the reactor's capacity. This would have made plutonium production through blanket irradiation easier still. The Osiris reactor is particularly well suited to such a task. As a Material Testing Reactor (MTR), its principal function is to test the ability of various materials to withstand bombardment by a high flux of neutrons. Provisions for placing "targets" for such bombardments are therefore an integral part of the reactor's construction. Moreover, Iraq has purchased from Italy a Fuel Fabrication Laboratory (FFL) capable of producing such natural uranium "targets." Separating the plutonium produced in this process could have been conducted with Iraqi adjustments of the "hot cell" simulators that are also provided by Italy under agreement.[93] The purchase of large quantities of natural uranium from Brazil, Portugal, Niger, and West Germany[94] indicate Iraq's intention to conduct blanket irradiation and plutonium separation. Iraq's nuclear program has no other uses for such quantities of natural uranium.

Under the terms of the Iraqi–French deal, French engineers were to operate Osiraq until 1983.[95] Plutonium production and separation could have been initiated only after that date. Therefore, Iraq was unlikely to have had a primitive nuclear capability before 1984 or 1985, or a deliverable nuclear force before the late 1980s.

Then on June 7, 1981, Iraq's nuclear plans were at least temporarily shattered. Israeli warplanes flew 1,000 kilometers inside Arab territory and destroyed Osiraq completely. Consequently, a further three- to four-year delay in Iraq's nuclear program can be expected. Also, Osiraq's destruction provided France's new President François Mitterrand with an opportunity to restructure French–Iraqi nuclear relations. Contrary to Former President Valery Giscard d'Estaing, Mitterrand had long been both an ardent opponent of nuclear proliferation and an intimate friend of Israel. This increased the odds that Paris would reconsider its contribution to Iraq's nuclear buildup. One thing Mitterrand may do is insist that the new reactor be fueled with the less enriched Caramel fuel. Such an arrangement would not exclude plutonium production, but France could also insist on tighter safeguards, thus minimizing the risks of undetected blanket irradiation. Both President Mitterrand and his Foreign Minister, Claude Cheysson, have stated that tighter safeguards would be a prerequisite for supplying Iraq with a new Osiris reactor.[96] In light of her dependence on Iraqi oil, however, France's bargaining power is not very strong. President Sadam Hussein and Foreign Minister Sa'adun Hamadi have immediately proclaimed Iraq's determination to rebuild Osiraq, and Saudi Arabia's King Khalid promised to cover the expenses involved.[97] In August 1981 Iraq's Deputy Premier Tarik Aziz was sent to Paris to negotiate the reconstruction of the Osiris reactor. He later said that his talks were "crowned with success," that an "agreement in principle had been reached," and that "France will supply Iraq, as in the past, with the means of developing its nuclear technology for peaceful purposes."[98] France's Minister of State for Foreign Trade, Michel Jobert, said there was no doubt that France would reconstruct Iraq's nuclear reactor.[99]

In assessing the future of Iraq's nuclear program it should also be noted that the first consignment of 12 kg of highly enriched uranium remains in Iraqi hands, undamaged by the attack on Osiraq.[100] Also unharmed are the facilities supplied by Italy with a potential for plutonium separation.[101] In addition, Iraq is negotiating the purchase of a 500-megawatt power reactor from Italy, and a contract for expanding the capacity of her Soviet-made 5-megawatt reactor with Belgium.[102] Portugal has meanwhile announced that in 1981 it plans to sell 130 metric tons of natural uranium to Iraq, in addition to the 120 metric tons it exported to Iraq in 1980.[103] Also important are the nuclear cooperation agreements recently signed by Iraq with India and Brazil. The latter provides for the appraising and exploration of uranium reserves, the supply of natural and slightly enriched uranium, and the development of reactor safety systems.[104] Finally, Iraq is also reported to have taken steps to equip itself with an appropriate delivery system. A well-financed program designed to build a 3,000-km range surface-to-surface missile has been initiated.[105]

Syria's nuclear program is still in its embryonic stages. Only in 1976 was a Syrian atomic energy commission established.[106] In 1978 a number of firms in Western Europe were contracted to conduct feasibility studies of possible Syrian investments in the peaceful uses of nuclear energy.[107] In addition, President Hafez Asad asked France to supply Syria with nuclear technology. His request was apparently denied. But in the summer of 1978 progress was reported in French–Syrian negotiations over the transfer of nuclear technology as part of Syria's quest for nuclear arms acquisition.[108] More important, in April 1978 President Asad traveled to India in order to arrange a deal for obtaining nuclear technology. Rumors proliferated that Syria was again seeking shortcuts on the way to nuclear arms acquisition. Some reports have underplayed the results of the Syrian–Indian talks, while others have claimed that the Indians were more than forthcoming.[109] Given the Soviet Union's strong commitment to nuclear nonproliferation, Syria's consistent efforts to obtain nuclear weapons from her have failed.[110]

By 1979 the focus again turned to establishing a domestic nuclear infrastructure. Syria's Ministry of Energy asked for more studies of the feasibility of extracting uranium from Syria's phosphate reserves as well as of constructing a nuclear power reactor.[111] Discussions with Swiss and Belgian firms were held in 1980 and 1981, focusing on the possible construction of six 600-megawatt power reactors in Syria. On June 15, 1981, Syria's Minister of Electricity, Oman Yousef, promised that the first of these reactors will be completed by 1991.[112] Meanwhile, the establishment of a nuclear research center in Damascus was also initiated.[113] Thus, in both thought and action, Syria has made the first move toward entering the nuclear era.

Libya is the Arab state seeking a nuclear capability with the most fuss and clamor. Lacking a scientific infrastructure in the nuclear field, Libya focused her efforts on the importation of nuclear bombs.[114] These attempts began in 1970 with Premier Jalloud's trip to China. Jalloud attempted to purchase nuclear weapons, but China refused to sell. He tried again, in vain, in 1975 and 1978.[115]

In 1973 Libya formed an atomic energy commission under the direct supervision of leader Muammar Qaddhafi. Between 1973 and 1976 nuclear cooperation agreements were signed with France, West Germany, Argentina, and Sweden. In November 1974 a contract was signed with a West German firm for the construction of a heavy-water production plant.[116]

During the second half of the 1970s, Libya's nuclear efforts had four focuses. The first was France: in March 1976 the French agreed to supply Libya with a 600-megawatt nuclear power reactor. The agreement was concluded during a visit by France's Prime Minister Jacques Chirac to Tripoli. The French were reported to have made it clear, however, that they would not provide Libya with nuclear research facilities or the means to produce heavy water, which could be used to develop nuclear weapons.[117] Later, France is said to have had second thoughts about the deal and to have quietly backed out of it.[118]

Libya's second possible avenue to a nuclear capability is Pakistan. The latter's nuclear program has been in existence since the early 1960s. Since India's 1974 nuclear test, Pakistan's program has been dramatically accelerated. Insisting on covering all avenues, she has taken both the plutonium and the uranium routes to weapons-grade material, and two alternative paths are being simultaneously pursued along both routes. Thus, Pakistan now has four different projects aimed at the production of fissile material.

The two Pakistani projects aimed at plutonium separation are both planned to separate the plutonium from the spent fuel (perhaps as much as 200 kg) of the 135-megawatt Candu power reactor, in operation since 1972 in Karachi. The larger of the two is the French-built reprocessing plant at Chasma.

The latter's construction was delayed in mid 1978 when, under pressure of the Carter administration's nonproliferation policy, France suspended the full implementation of the deal and insisted that crucial components had not been delivered.[119] By that time, however, Pakistan had already acquired the plant's specifications, thus allowing her to complete its construction on her own.[120] The second separation project is smaller, but closer to yielding weapons-grade material. Some of its components having been acquired in the early 1970s from the Belgian firm Belgo-Nucléair, the project is adjacent to the Pakistan Institute for Science and Technology (PINSTECH) near Islamabad.[121] It consists of a hot-cells compound much larger than is ordinarily associated with research purposes, thus indicating large-scale separation. The project is expected to yield separated plutonium in the near future.[122] By late 1981 various "anomalies" and "irregularities" were detected at Karachi's Candu reactor. These included a high rate of failure of surveillance equipment and problems in accounting for used or spent fuel. Fears were raised that spent fuel was already being set aside for the purpose of plutonium separation.[123] Pakistan's announcement that it began indigenous production of nuclear fuel elements provided an additional source of concern. Such production increases Pakistan's ability to produce plutonium by irradiating fuel elements at the Karachi power reactor.[124]

Simultaneously, Pakistan is pursuing uranium enrichment. Two distinct projects can be identified. The first is the construction of a large-scale centrifuge enrichment plant in Kahuta, modeled on the Dutch enrichment plant at Almelo.[125] The project required the theft of the plant's specifications from the Netherlands and an impressive covert acquisition drive throughout Europe and North America.[126] The plant may yield up to fifty bombs' worth of enriched uranium a year after its construction is completed. The second Pakistani facility is a more modest pilot project, where enrichment has already begun.[127] Its size is only one-tenth of the Kahuta plant, but it is still large enough to yield enriched uranium worthy of a few bombs a year. Several hundred tons of natural uranium to be enriched in both projects have been acquired in Niger, directly as well as through Libya.[128] A fluoride plant, which transforms natural uranium to uranium hexafluoride gas, was purchased in West Germany: such a transformation is a prerequisite to the employment of the centrifuge method for uranium enrichment.[129]

The expectation that Pakistan's nuclear program may prove an avenue to Libya's efforts in this realm is based on various reports pointing to Libyan financial participation in Pakistan's program.[130] The aid is said to have been offered during Qaddhafi's 1974 visit to Pakistan and to have been agreed to during Jalloud's 1978 visit. In return, Libya is said to expect a sample of the future Pakistani bombs.[131] Other less reliable reports have indicated the planning of a joint Pakistani–Libyan nuclear test in the Libyan desert.[132] Libyan transfers to Pakistan of natural uranium purchased in Niger were a further indication of close Libyan–Pakistani cooperation.

If Qaddhafi really expected to receive Pakistani nuclear weapons, he was bound to be disappointed. Pakistan is unlikely to surrender control over mass-destruction weapons to a leader of such ill repute. The political costs likely to follow a possible intelligence penetration of this sort of transaction would be enormous. Yet a more modest Pakistani contribution to Libya's efforts could not be ruled out. For example, Pakistan could have been expected to provide Libya with reprocessing or enrichment services. Libya could thus obtain weapons-grade material, a significant shortcut to nuclear weapons. More recently, however, Pakistani–Libyan ties were reported to have deteriorated.[133] This has diminished—at least temporarily—the odds of nuclear technology transfers from Pakistan to Libya. Yet to some extent the Pakistanis have confirmed their intention to transfer nuclear technology to Arab states. In reaction to Washington's 1979 decision to cut off aid to Pakistan following that country's construction of the enrichment plant, Pakistan charged that the decision was "the outcome of Israeli efforts to stop Pakistan [from] sharing advanced nuclear research with fellow Islamic countries."[134]

The third focus of Libya's nuclear efforts was India. Economic cooperation between the two countries developed significantly during the mid 1970s. At that time, numerous Libyan civilian projects were contracted to Indian firms. When the Iranian revolution prevented the shipment of oil to India, Libya agreed to provide her with inexpensive oil. In exchange, Libya expected—in the framework of their bilateral nuclear cooperation agreement—to receive Indian technology for the construction of nuclear weapons. By late 1979 India had made it clear that her reading of their bilateral agreement was different from Libya's. Qaddhafi reacted by terminating the shipment of oil to India.[135]

The fourth focus of Libya's efforts is the Soviet Union, primarily in the realm of energy and scientific infrastructure. In 1975 the Soviets agreed to supply Libya with a 10-megawatt research reactor as part of a nuclear physics research center, and in December 1976 the two countries signed an agreement for the construction of a 440-megawatt Loviisa-type dual-purpose nuclear plant for power production and desalination.[136] Both reactors are unlikely to provide an immediate avenue to nuclear weapons acquisition, because the Soviets insist on applying tight safeguards to such reactors.[137] Nevertheless, the project would clearly provide Libya with the ability to train a generation of nuclear scientists. These would add to the substantial number of Libyans already being trained in the nuclear sciences in the United States, France, and the USSR.[138]

Finally, since 1977 Libya has accumulated hundreds of tons of natural uranium. Between 1977 and 1981 from Niger alone some 450 tons were purchased.[139] The rationale for this stockpiling remains unclear at the time of this writing.

Whether through a "quick fix" route or through the slow construction of an appropriate infrastructure, Egypt, Syria, Iraq, and Libya are all seeking to obtain a nuclear capability. The Middle East is no longer on the threshold of the nuclear era; it is now far beyond that point.

The discussion in this section points to three important conclusions: first, that the Arab states regard the possibility of Israeli nuclear weapons as so constraining that an Arab response is badly needed; second, that the proposed Israeli nuclear posture would eventually require the Arab states to adopt nuclear-deterrent postures of their own; third, that the perceived possibility that Israel might adopt a nuclear-deterrent posture is already propelling the major Arab states toward the acquisition of appropriate deterrents. This raises the further possibility that even if Israel chose not to adopt a nuclear posture in order to deter Arab massive or limited conventional attacks, it might eventually be forced to adopt such a posture in response to Arab acquisition of nuclear weapons. Hence one needs to study the impact of a multinuclear Middle East on Israeli security. The following section will discuss how the acquisition of nuclear weapons by a number of Arab states would affect the degree to which nuclear weapons would provide security for Israel.

Israeli Deterrence in a Multinuclear Middle East

The acquisition of nuclear weapons by a number of Arab states would alter significant elements in the previous analysis of the deterrent effect of the proposed Israeli nuclear posture. First, Israel would no longer have the exclusive capacity to inflict enormous punishment. Second, mutual capability to inflict punishment would affect Arab perceptions of the punishment they would suffer in a failure of deterrence. More important, it would affect their perceptions of the distribution of punishment. Third, the new distribution of punishment might affect their sensitivity to the costs of nuclear war—namely, their perceptions of the constraints imposed by these costs. Finally, the acquisition of nuclear weapons by a number of Arab states might affect the stability of Israeli nuclear deterrence by threatening its retaliatory capability.

Some have claimed that because the Arab–Israeli conflict is characterized by an asymmetry of vulnerability, the introduction of nuclear weapons throughout the Middle East would place Israel at a sharp disadvantage.[140] The assertion is based on the observation that Israel is a nation of three million, concentrated in three to five medium-sized cities, while the Arabs are blessed with a population of close to a hundred million dispersed in the wide region extending from Mesopotamia to Gibraltar. If the Arabs acquired the ability to inflict nuclear punishment on Israel, the disparity in area and numbers would allow the Arabs to win nuclear confrontations because they would be willing to run higher risks. The Israelis, being more vulnerable, would be self-deterred. Israeli nuclear deterrence in this case would be either ineffective, irrelevant, or simply too dangerous.[141]

Arab leaders, as well as members of the Arab press, have been most interested in advancing and supporting these views in an effort to induce Israeli self-deterrence. Thus Egypt's Minister of War, General Gamassy, stressed in an interview with *Al-Ahrām* that "while Egypt and the Arabs enjoy a numerical advantage over Israel, and can absorb an attack by these weapons, Israel will not be able to absorb such an attack."[142] This view was repeated in 1977 by President Sadat.[143] Syria's President Asad has voiced the same view: "If Israel has nuclear weapons it should sell them. . . . If Israel does get them then this is the worst evil for Israel. One can easily imagine that when both sides possess such weapons, it is Israel which won't be able to withstand a larger number of bombs."[144]

The importance of the numerical asymmetries is that they influence calculations of recovery rates. Thus President Sadat has attempted to convince Israel of superior Arab capabilities to recover from nuclear war. In 1977 he warned: "If a half a million Egyptians were to die, I could recover them. But if I respond . . . and half a million Israelis are killed, Israel would never be able to make up the loss."[145] In 1980, Syria's Minister of Defense Mustafa Talas expressed a similar view: "The Arab nation [may possess] tens of nuclear weapons of 20 kiloton size, while in order to terminate, once and for all, the third attempt to steal Palestine, only three bombs are required."[146] This perception was well formulated by the

Arab ~~deny~~ deter w/ Nukes

Saudi Arabian newspaper *Al-Yamama* (August 15, 1975): "At the level of nuclear confrontation the Arabs enjoy strategic depth, which Israel lacks. Should Israel use nuclear weapons, the Arabs will absorb the first strike, but any nuclear strike against Israel would be the first and the last."[147]

At first glance these arguments have compelling logic. Their force is much diminished upon examination, however. First, as our discussion of Israel's ability to inflict punishment has clearly shown, vulnerabilities in the Middle East are much more symmetric than what some Arab leaders would have us believe. The vast territory of a country is irrelevant if, taking Egypt as an example, a quarter of the nation's population may be found in her capital during business hours.[148] Second, even if it were true that the Arab world as a whole is less vulnerable than Israel, when making decisions on war and peace Arab leaders are likely to regard this as irrelevant. For each leader the important question to be considered is the vulnerability of his own state. The leader of any one Arab state will not be much comforted by knowing that other Arab countries will go unscathed. Nor would expectation of long-term recovery capability have a decisive impact on the decision-makers' calculations. The fact that their countries may have a better chance of recovering from a large-scale nuclear attack in twenty years' time is unlikely to induce these leaders to ignore deterrent threats. Political leaders have much shorter time horizons. As a recent Congressional study points out, "it seems unlikely that any national leader would take the desperate step of initiating nuclear war on the belief that after ten or fifteen years his nation would be in a position 'superior' to that of his opponent."[149] Decision makers will also remember that until their countries recover from the nuclear exchange they will be extremely vulnerable to a conventional takeover by third parties that did not take part in the exchange. Fourth, in comparing relative vulnerabilities it should be noted that in some measure the asymmetry is in Israel's favor. As Lawrence Freedman has pointed out, "[In the event of an Arab nuclear attack on Israel] the large Arab population in Israel would suffer, as would Arabs in refugee camps and the neighbouring territories. In addition, Israel contains many sites of great religious and traditional importance to the Arabs, as well as the homeland of the Palestinians, supposedly the point of the whole conflict. The nuclear destruction of Israel would also be the nuclear destruction of Palestine."[150] Fifth and last, there is some evidence that the Arabs themselves are becoming aware of these points. Two illustrations may be instructive. Hassan A'ah, a member of the Research Department in Egypt's Ministry of Culture, stresses that the density of Egypt's urban population is greater than Israel's and adds that the Arabs "must take into account the fact that the Arab cities lack Jewish inhabitants which might have otherwise constituted some constraint upon Israel's freedom of action."[151] Likewise, Amin al-Anfuri, writing in Syria's Al-Majalla Al-Askariyya (October 1975), reminds his readers that "there is a problem with respect to retaliation against the enemy at the depth of conquered Palestine. . . . Israel can attack any Arab target without reservation because the Arab states lack large concentrations of Jews which might otherwise have prevented her from doing so. On the other hand, in Palestine there are many Arab citizens, in proximity to the economic targets, and within the concentrations of Jewish population. This fact creates serious constraints on the means of Arab retaliation."[152] These views are shared by Lieutenant Colonel Hitam al-Ayubi.[153] The above quotations indicate that Arab elites are slowly developing the perception that in a multinuclear Middle East the ability to inflict punishment is in fact symmetric. With the open introduction of nuclear weapons, this socialization process is likely to be accelerated.

The discussion so far suggests that in a multinuclear Middle East all parties equipped with nuclear weapons will have the ability to inflict assured destruction on their adversaries. Furthermore, it is evident that some Arabs are beginning to realize that this will indeed be the case. Thus the first and second prerequisites for effective deterrence are met. I shall now address the strategic implications of the ability to inflict mutual destruction and argue that Arab challenges to Israel's

everything to loose — fight w/ everything

survival under such conditions are extremely unlikely to occur.

As I have said in the first chapter, a conflict between states equipped with the means to inflict an unacceptable punishment will be determined in favor of the party demonstrating greater willingness to absorb punishment. I further argued that the party acting to insure its survival has an enormous advantage because it will invariably demonstrate greater willingness to absorb punishment.[154] The greater the extent to which the defender fears that conquest is likely to result in his physical extermination, the greater the extent to which the balance of deterrence will tilt against the attacker. As formulated earlier, the prospects of unavoidable holocaust make Samson-like deterrent threats credible. In the Middle East context, if the Arabs threatened to launch a total conventional or nuclear assault endangering Israel's survival, she would have everything to lose and would therefore be willing to run risks greater than those of the attackers. Israel would have fewer incentives to refrain from activating her deterrent threats and the Arabs would have more reasons to hesitate. Israel's destruction would bring them little joy if they are destroyed in retaliation. The balance of deterrence would tilt sharply against the Arabs.

Impressive evidence suggests that some Arabs already perceive that if Israel's conventional defense becomes excessively difficult, she will become more willing to run risks, and that this makes nuclear deterrent threats more credible. Hasanayn Haykal has said that "Israel has nuclear weapons but will not use them unless she finds herself being strangled."[155] On another occasion he said that Israel would use these weapons "if she feels threatened and is willing to commit suicide."[156] Egypt's General al-Shazly, chief of staff during the 1973 war, would only say that "Egypt has always felt that Israel may use atomic weapons in certain circumstances."[157] King Hussein of Jordan, however, was willing to elaborate: "The Israelis in my opinion would not use atomic power—a nuclear device or devices—unless they were in mortal danger. In such an eventuality they would."[158]

Israel's particular historical experience adds credibility to any nuclear threats she might make, even when the threat is made to avoid defeat in a purely conventional war. With memories of the holocaust so vivid in the minds of Israelis, the prospects of military defeat are likely to induce even greater risk-taking than would normally have been the case. Israelis have been deeply affected not only by the gruesome experience of their parents' generation before and during World War II but also by the conviction that too little was done to resist. Regardless of the unfairness of this notion, for our purposes the important thing is that two generations of Israelis believe that more risks should have been run to resist the Nazis more effectively and that never again can Jews compromise themselves and place their fate in the hands of others.

There is so far only one example to indicate that the Arabs understand this point of view. In an article already cited, Lieutenant Colonel al-Ayubi argues that in the Israeli case nuclear threats are credible even against conventional threats in an environment of mutual acquisition of nuclear weapons. This credibility is a consequence of:

> the conviction of the Israelis (or at least the majority of them) that any military defeat would mean the destruction of the State and would pose Israel's society with the danger of extermination. Thus, the nuclear balance of terror, which is a consequence of the fear of the extermination resulting from nuclear war would not bring about the non-use of nuclear weapons in the instance that Israel faces the danger of a complete conventional military defeat. This is due to the fact that in the Israelis' opinion the result in both cases would be the same: extermination and physical liquidation of the State and its citizens.
>
> We are not going to debate here the "danger of extermination" which is deeply rooted in the hearts of the Israelis and is accompanied by complexes, imagination and feeling of inferiority. It surfaces when the Israeli is faced with danger. It was clearly revealed during the initial days of the October War . . . anyone reading *The Blunder* (Hamechdal) comes out with a deep impression that the enemy's society lived with a nightmare of extermination, at least through the first three days of the war.

Al-Ayubi goes on to say that this special Israeli sensitivity to threat creates an imbalance in risk-taking willingness that is to Israel's advantage: "Psychological differences influence the decision to use nuclear weapons or to execute the first strike. Israeli fears of conventional (nonnuclear) extermination gives them the incentives and needed justifications for making decisions in the nuclear field, while the absence of Arab fears of conventional extermination following defeat might delay taking such decisions."[159]

Whether or not the Arab states will in fact heed Israeli "general deterrent" threats in a multinuclear Middle East depends on two factors: first, the extent to which these states will be sensitive to the costs of nuclear war; and second, the extent to which they will come to realize that mutual capability to inflict punishment coupled with Israel's willingness to run higher risks once her survival is threatened exposes them to a high probability of nuclear disaster should they decide to challenge Israel's survival. Once nuclear postures are overtly introduced into the region, the socialization process that will follow their introduction is likely to bring about full comprehension of both factors among Arab elites. The net effect would be a recognition that in order to avoid nuclear punishment in a multinuclear Middle East, the Arab states would have to refrain from threatening Israel's survival through a massive conventional or nuclear attack. Israel's basic security would thus be achieved.

Some initial realization of the effect of overt introduction of nuclear weapons can already be found. These first discussions merely point to the general direction of the socialization process that can be expected following such overt introduction. A few illustrations may be instructive. Ahmed Samih Khalidi, a Palestinian, wrote in the *Middle East Forum* that "when Israel gets the Atomic Bomb there will be a 'stalemate.' Egypt will also get atomic weapons and then neither country will dare attack the other and the sands will have run out for the Arabs."[160] A commentator in Egypt's *Al-Akhbār*, Mahar 'Abd al-Fattah, wrote in 1975 that "[i]t is no secret that for some time Israel has been trying to secure its existence through nuclear weapons. Our answer, therefore, is to obtain the strength to counter it. Hence the balance of terror in the area will become synonymous with security. What will the result be? A mutual fear of total destruction potential that will inevitably freeze everything as it is now."[161] Muhammad Sayid Ahmad, the prominent Egyptian writer, asserted in 1976 that "it is correct to assume that the Arab–Israeli conflict is marching into the nuclear era with all its implications in the realm of diplomacy, politics and warfare. . . . Nuclear diplomacy has created what is called 'international detente' . . . [which] means the ability to control conflicts and contain them before they pass certain thresholds. International detente did not solve international disputes. Rather, it 'froze' them within certain controlled frameworks."[162] Sayid Ahmad's views are echoed by the anonymous Egyptian statesman cited earlier who stated in an interview given to the Lebanese Al-Sayyād (February 26, 1976) that "a balance of terror would begin to operate [in the Middle East] as it does between the U.S. and the Soviet Union. This is the origin of the feeling that there will be no solution to the Middle East conflict in the near future." Other examples go even further, indicating that in a multinuclear Middle East the Arabs will even be deterred from conducting violence at levels short of what might threaten Israel's survival. I shall save these to illustrate our later discussion of specific deterrence. So far I claim only that the balance of terror would provide Israel with security by deterring the Arabs from launching activities that might carry a possibility of Israeli nuclear retaliation. The degree to which this security will be stable depends on the extent to which the balance of terror will be stable. The issue will be taken up in the next section.

Israel's Second-Strike Capability

The issue of second-strike forces for small states is of critical importance. If Israel and her neighbors cannot be sure of the survivability of their forces, the result would be dangerous insecurity. If in addition they should cherish beliefs and hopes of effectively disarming their adversaries' forces, the consequence would be an enormous and constant temptation to preempt. In the absence of second-strike capabilities, a Middle East balance of terror would be extremely unstable.

Indeed, some have argued that a regional balance of terror in the Middle East is likely to be unstable.[163] Alan Dowty, for example, writes that "In a mutually nuclearized situation the vulnerability of both sides and the ease of delivery would provide a constant temptation to pre-emptive strikes."[164] Stanley Hoffmann adheres to the same view.[165] Yair Evron talks of vulnerability less as a constant factor than as something transitory: "The development of invulnerable nuclear capabilities is a difficult process and involves many uncertainties. Moreover, the development of such a capability takes a long time; in the transition period the two sides will have grave fears about first strikes launched by the other side."[166] Leonard Beaton and Alastair Buchan both point out the difficulties that small states face in attempting to achieve a stable and invulnerable nuclear force.[167]

Steven Rosen takes the opposite view. He wisely understates his conclusion, but the thrust of his argument is that a balance of terror in the Middle East can be stable. In his view, regional nuclear weapons will not undermine the stability of the Israeli nuclear deterrent because they would not significantly threaten Israel's ability to retaliate. Her capacity to strike back could survive an Arab preventive or preemptive attack, thus qualifying it as a "second strike" force.[168]

The truth about the vulnerability of small nuclear forces probably lies between these two extreme views. Although Rosen probably underestimates the difficulties of attaining a secure second-strike force, the spokesmen of gloom and doom probably overestimate the extent to which some measure of vulnerability would destabilize the system. Although Rosen's schemes for making Israel's deterrent secure often border on fantasy, Evron, Dowty, Aron, Hoffmann, and

Buchan do not seem to realize how extremely vulnerable a nuclear force would have to be to tempt an adversary to preempt.

A detailed and technical analysis of second-strike capabilities requires extremely specific assumptions about the relevant force structures. Too great a specificity in making such assumptions often carries analysts into the realm of pure speculation. Hence it may be wise to limit our discussion to general notions about how stable the deterrence of small states like Israel can be. The central proposition advanced here is that in a multinuclear Middle East, Israel is likely to enjoy stable deterrence despite the many difficulties. Although the nuclear forces of a small state like Israel will be much more vulnerable than the nuclear forces of a superpower or even a medium one,[169] decision makers will, nevertheless, remain uncertain about just how vulnerable those forces are. This will be enough to dissuade them from contemplating preventive or preemptive action and will provide the system of mutual deterrence with the required stability.

Generally speaking, seven different elements play a role in providing invulnerability to a nuclear force: variation in the means of delivery; number of weapons and delivery vehicles; mobility; hardening; alertness; dispersion; concealment and secrecy. Each of these elements contributes its share to complicate the adversary's efforts to achieve a disarming first strike.

Variation in the type of delivery vehicles used is important. Each type of delivery vehicle will require that the adversary develop a particular antidote. The more variation, the greater the difficulties. Most analysts assume that Israel will use a mix of aircraft and surface missiles for delivery. The aircraft most often mentioned in the past are the F-4 Phantom and the indigenously produced Kfirs. However, nuclear weapons may be delivered by other aircraft as well, such as Arava STOLS, Skyhawks, C-130s, and large helicopters. In the early 1980s delivery can be based on high-performance F-15s and F-16s as well. Delivery by missiles is based on the supposition that Israel will have developed a 280-mile-range Jericho surface-to-surface missile.[170] This appears to be a fairly vulnerable mix, particularly the aircraft and runways, which are useless without each other. It takes no more than two p.s.i. overpressure to destroy all parked aircraft.[171] This raises a question of vulnerability to an Iraqi strike, since Iraq is outside the assumed range of Israel's Jerichos. A successful Iraqi nuclear attack against Israel's airfields would leave Israel unable to retaliate. To be successful, however, would require that the Iraqis be correct in their estimates of the Jericho's range, and that they be absolutely certain of their ability to destroy all of Israel's airfields. Moreover, the vulnerability ascribed to Israel's delivery mix is based on assumptions that are likely to be outdated by the time the Arab states acquire enough nuclear weapons to begin to contemplate a first strike. The specter of Arab acquisition of nuclear weapons is still a few years away. It would take these states much longer to acquire such weapons in numbers sufficient for a first strike. By that time Israel could greatly diversify her delivery capability. A surface-to-surface missile with sufficient range to reach Baghdad could be developed; high-performance VTOLs could be acquired to reduce dependency on runways; the use of naval platforms could be developed. The naval option has particular appeal in the light of the fact that so many cities of the Arab world are on the seashore: Alexandria, Tripoli, Bengazi, Beirut, and Latakia, for example.

In order to achieve a first-strike capability, the Arabs would have to devise a specific antidote for each of these delivery vehicles. This promises to be an extremely complex task because each of these antidotes would have to operate perfectly to achieve a disarming first strike. Even if only a few of the antidotes work in less than perfect fashion, the Arabs would suffer nuclear retaliation.

The number of weapons that Israel could deploy would add to her invulnerability. Since an adversary cannot rely on the perfect operation of his counterforce weapons, he must send more than one weapon against each Israeli target. The average number of weapons an adversary must employ

IS advantage

against each Israeli target constitutes the attacker/target ratio. It also implies that a large increase in the number of Arab nuclear weapons would be required to offset each small increase in the number of Israeli nuclear weapons. This is likely to further complicate the Arabs' ability to conduct a disarming first strike.

Mobility is a further element of invulnerability. High mobility of Israeli weapons would make their precise location more difficult to ascertain and would hence decrease the danger of a counterforce attack and destruction. In the near future mobility could probably be enjoyed only in the air, possibly by round-the-clock flights of F-4s, Kfirs, F-16s, or F-15s. In the longer term, however, mobility could be gained on the seas and on land as well by the movement of naval platforms and surface-to-surface missiles and by the constant relocation of high-performance VTOLs. The need to locate mobile forces and destroy them would thus further complicate Arab efforts to disarm Israel's retaliatory capability. To be sure, some mobile systems will be detected by Airborne Early Warning systems (AEW), such as the Hawkeye E-2C, or by Airborne Warning and Control Systems (AWACS), such as the Boeing E-3A Sentry.[172] Such systems are already on their way into the region.[173] However, an AWACS cannot distinguish a delivery vehicle carrying nuclear weapons from one that is not. A first strike based on AWACS data would require that all detectable mobile vehicles be hit regardless of whether they were carrying nuclear weapons. Surely it would require an inordinate number of weapons to do this.

Israel could achieve greater invulnerability by hardening a few of her delivery vehicles. She would merely need a few perfectly survivable delivery systems in order to have a credible retaliatory force. Therefore, Israel might choose to implement Bernard Brodie's scheme for a sliding scale of protection for her retaliatory force. A small number of weapons may be extremely well protected, at almost any cost, "against the worst kind of enemy attack it is possible for us to imagine." Other portions of the nuclear force "may perhaps do with somewhat less protection, on the ground that the worst imaginable contingency is fortunately not the only likely one and may not be even the most probable one."[174] For example, if a handful of Israeli weapons are hardened to 2,000 p.s.i., an adversary attack using 20 kiloton weapons would have less than a 20 percent chance of destroying the Israeli delivery vehicles, even if the adversary's weapons are accurate to within 600 feet.[175] Or Israel may choose to harden a few more weapons to only 300 p.s.i., against which the single-shot kill probability of a weapon as large as 50 kiloton drops to 35 percent at a CEP of 1,000 feet.[176] Should the Arabs deploy weapons closer to the 20 kiloton range, the single-shot kill probability will drop more dramatically. Hardened silos would greatly complicate Arab efforts to achieve a first-strike capability.

Some writers question the long-term benefits of hardening. Steven Rosen argues that they would be negated by the introduction of long-range precision-guided munitions. In his view, hardening would not provide invulnerability for long since cruise missiles or glide bombs with a circular-error probability of 150 feet and a 20-kiloton warhead would have a kill probability greater than 95 percent even against a target superhardened to withstand 1,000 p.s.i. overpressures. Rosen also points out that a wide array of precision guidance technologies are now becoming available with accuracies better than 150 feet, "including laser designation, electro-optical, infra-red, and radar seekers, radar area correlation, distance measuring equipment, microwave radiometers, and satellite position fixing. With accuracies down to ten feet, it may be possible to destroy many hard targets even without nuclear warheads by using fuel explosives."[177] To modify Rosen's observations, I would like to point out that it is at this point doubtful that long-range PGMs would ever become a reality. Such ascribed accuracies (10 feet!) for long-range vehicles seem to belong to the realm of fiction. Furthermore, since the actual production of such weapons is at least some years off, it is safe to assume that countermeasures will appear at approximately the same time. Also, the more sophisticated these weapons would be, the more susceptible to various means of jamming them. Finally, at this point there are no indications that the Arabs are about to acquire long-range weapons with accuracies resembling those implied by the term "long-range PGMs." So far the elements of PGM technology that have entered the Middle East are all short-range. Should long-range PGM technology ever become relevant in the Middle East, hardening may indeed prove to be merely a short-term option. Until such time, hardening should be an important element in creating an invulnerable nuclear force.

Alertness can provide further protection from an incoming first strike. Aircraft and missiles can be launched as soon as an incoming attack is detected. An Arab disarming strike against thirty or forty dispersed point targets in Israel would have to be of a grand scale. This makes it easier for Israel to detect it early enough to launch some of her delivery vehicles. Given the extremely short flight-distances in the Middle East, however, protection by alertness would require almost instantaneous decisions. Since any signal of an enemy attack is likely to be somewhat ambiguous, this form of protection may be the least stabilizing of all. In view of this, Israel may choose to forego the option of "launch on warning," particularly for nonrecallable vehicles.

Dispersion may be another element in an Israeli effort to make its nuclear force invulnerable. The greater the dispersion, the larger the number of weapons the Arabs would have to deploy in a first strike. The dispersal of jet aircraft is limited, however, by the small number of airfields in Israel. Greater dispersal can be achieved with surface-to-surface missiles. By the time the Arab states reach nuclear capability, Israel may be able to disperse naval platforms as well, thus exploiting the vast seas. This would require the development or acquisition of a missile with an appropriate range. An additional future option already mentioned is the use of VTOLs. Future generations of high-performance Harrier-like aircraft may act in concert at times of ease but may be quickly dispersed to hardened or semihardened sites in the event of an international crisis. Their VTOL capability would allow them to carry out their mission even if Israel's airstrips were meanwhile destroyed. Their maximum dispersal would decrease the Arab states' confidence in their ability to achieve a successful disarming first strike. Furthermore, as both Rosen and al-Ayubi have pointed out, dispersion can be selective. Israel can place a disproportionate number of her launchers in the vicinity of Arab population centers. If these launchers are hardened or semihardened, an Arab first strike would require ground-bursting in order to obtain the necessary accuracy. Ground bursts, however, create fallout. "Radio-active fallout originates with the tons of soil, rock, and other material that would be melted or vaporized by the heat of such an explosion and mixed with its radio-active by-products. The debris would be carried to a height of some miles with the rising fireball. In the stratosphere the fireball cools and the larger particles would descend on the ground within a day or so as local fallout. The smaller particles would drift a great distance and eventually descend as global fallout."[178] The dispersal of Israeli launchers to the vicinity of Arab population centers would increase the likelihood that these populations would become victims of an Arab first strike. This would prove an extremely important attack constraint. As al-Ayubi had indicated, "Israel can bomb the Egyptian airfields and launching sites without hesitation while Egypt cannot do the same with respect to Israel. This is especially so if the enemy will place his launchers in proximity to the West Bank and the Gaza Strip [Jerusalem, Nablus, Gaza, Hebron, Rafiah], or in proximity to the Arab towns conquered in 1948 [Safed, Nazareth]."[179] The effects of fallout are bound to influence the cost–benefit calculation of any Arab leader contemplating a disarming first strike, since no one would like to suffer the inter-Arab costs involved in assuming the role of grand executioner of the Palestinian people. Furthermore, some hardpoint counterforce attacks would involve risking lethal fallout descending upon Damascus. For example, given an Arab nuclear counterforce attack employing three 60 kiloton weapons against hardened Israeli weapons deployed at the northern tip of Israel, lethal doses of fallout might reach Syria's capital.[180] This is likely to deter not only the Syrians but also other Arab states that may fear Syrian retaliation against the state responsible for such a calamity. Thus selective dispersal may present the Arab states with extremely difficult attack constraints. Israel's proximity to Arab populations may provide her with effective deterrence against an Arab disarming first strike. Selective dispersal aimed at exploiting this proximity will be an important element of Israel's second-strike capability.

As in the case of defense against an Arab conventional first strike, concealment and secrecy may yet prove to be the most effective protectors of the Israeli nuclear force. The Arabs are extremely unlikely to launch a first strike without perfect information as to the location of all Israel's nuclear weapons and absolute confidence in the reliability of that information. Target acquisition is probably the most serious attack constraint facing any state contemplating a nuclear first strike. As Admiral Noel Gayler has pointed out, "by quite simple ways of interfering with information about which hole has what in it, [it is possible to] penetrate that kind of targeting. It has nothing to do with the size of the attacking warhead or its accuracy; it is simply a targeting problem. If [one] does not know where to shoot [his weapons, one] cannot make [them] effective in killing weapons; [one] can stir up a lot of nuclear radiation and kill many people with the fallout, but [one] cannot kill the weapons."[181]

As mentioned earlier, the difficulties that Arab states currently face in trying to ascertain whether Israel does or does not have nuclear weapons are illustrative of the difficulties they would have in trying to locate Israel's weapons. Israel may further complicate such efforts. For example, by deploying dummies Israel could seriously confuse Arab attack planners. Were the Arabs to obtain information as to the location of Israel's real launchers, an unlikely prospect, the launching of a first strike would still require that they attribute perfect reliability to this information. How could they do this? Only the superpowers are capable of obtaining and supplying such information to the Arabs; and only the Soviet Union could be politically tempted to do so. Mobility, dispersal, concealment, and secrecy are all penetrable by superpower technology. Delivery vehicles, even if mobile and dispersed, are vulnerable to detection by satellites. Less is known for sure about their ability to detect warheads, but clearly here, too, Soviet support of the Arab forces would be of enormous help. However, that such support would be forthcoming is most unlikely. First, the Soviets are unlikely to hand such information to the Arabs because they do not want to increase the probability of a regional nuclear war. Second, the Soviets are unlikely to transmit such data because of the serious security problems involved. Its interception would reveal precisely what the Soviets are and are not capable of detecting; they are unlikely to depend on their Arab clients' capacity to protect such information. In fact, even at the height of Soviet–Egyptian cooperation, in the far more stable era of purely conventional weaponry, the Soviets refused to provide Egypt with satellite data.[182] In the nuclear era providing such information would be more destabilizing and therefore far less likely. Furthermore, even if the USSR gave out the information, the Arabs would not have absolute confidence in it because of their traditional suspicion of both superpowers and the love–hate character of Soviet–Arab relations. Hence the Arabs are unlikely to rely on such information enough to justify the possible cost of launching a nuclear first strike.

Some of the elements offering protection to a small nuclear force can be illustrated by considering a hypothetical situation raised often by scholars, namely: that Israel's adversaries "saturate" her with nuclear bombs even under conditions of imperfect intelligence.[183] The scenario assumes that Israel's delivery vehicles are limited to aircraft and dispersed missiles, and that the Arabs saturate her with nuclear bombs, making sure that her ability to retaliate is destroyed. The saturation possibility cannot be taken lightly. As noted earlier, no more than 2 p.s.i. overpressure is required to destroy any parked vehicle. Were Israel attacked by some six hundred nuclear weapons with a yield of 40 kilotons each, her entire territory would suffer such overpressure.[184] Furthermore, to

achieve such limited overpressure, the Arabs would be likely
to airburst their weapons. This would spare Syria, Jordan,
and the Palestinians the long-term effects of the fallout
caused by surface bursts. And yet, this course of action has
major drawbacks. First, no single Arab state is likely to be
able to mount such an enormous attack; a number of Arab
states would have to cooperate in such an endeavor. Since
in the absence of perfect operational reliability many more
than six hundred warheads would have to be sent, inter-Arab
cooperation would be an absolute prerequisite. Such cooperation, however, might compromise the attackers' ability to
achieve surprise. The more elaborate the coordination activities required, the higher the attackers' risks that their activities will become known to Israel's intelligence, triggering
Israeli countermeasures. Also, saturation of Israel's territory
will not destroy whatever portion of her delivery systems are
placed on constant air alert. Thus, it would not make the
attackers entirely immune to retaliation. In addition, the cooperating Arab states would face enormous logistical problems. The delivered weapons would have to explode in perfect dispersal to insure that the entire country suffer the
requisite overpressure. And the entire attack would have to
be executed simultaneously and perfectly. Otherwise, Israel
would launch some of her delivery vehicles before they could
be hit. If some of her forces were placed on a "launch on
attack" alert, the attackers would not escape retaliation even
if they managed to destroy Israel's central command and control facilities. Finally, even if they were to cooperate, it would
take the Arabs many years to assemble a force of sufficient
size for such an attack; by that time Israel could restructure
its own delivery capability to guard against it. A small number
of her surface-to-surface delivery vehicles could be hardened
and a similar number could be placed on naval platforms, for
example. Such basing would render saturation bombing impractical. Destroying the hardened delivery vehicles would
require surface bursts that would expose Israel's Arab neighbors to devastating fallout. The remaining naval platforms
could not be destroyed without saturating the high seas, a

proposition both far beyond the capacity of the Arab states and complicated by the presence of superpower naval forces in the area.

Could concealment and secrecy, dispersion and alertness, hardening and mobility, and the number and variety of delivery vehicles all guarantee that the majority of Israeli weapons and delivery vehicles would survive an Arab first strike? Hardly so. Suggestions to the effect that states like Israel, small in territory and nuclear force structure, can easily and cheaply provide themselves with a solid and stable second-strike capability are unconvincing. The variety Israel could introduce into her delivery vehicles would not be nearly as constraining as the structure of the American Triad; concealment, secrecy, and dispersion would all be limited by the small territory of the state; alertness would be limited by the short flight-distances involved; and hardening and mobility would be limited by serious cost constrains. Nevertheless, by the time the Arab states acquire nuclear weapons and delivery systems in sufficient numbers to begin contemplating a first strike, Israel could much improve its position. By the acquisition of VTOL aircraft and naval platforms she would be able to improve dispersion; by the development of a surface-to-surface missile with sufficient range to reach Iraq, the odds of an Iraqi attack on Israeli airfields would diminish; by the deployment of dummies, Arab attack planners might be confused. By doing the most she can in each of these realms, within the bounds of her size and economic capability, Israel could create in the minds of Arab leaders sufficient uncertainty that their disarming first strike would succeed in destroying absolutely all Israeli delivery vehicles. Israeli activity in the realm of concealment, secrecy, dispersion, alertness, hardening, mobility, and number and variety of delivery vehicles may not guarantee that the majority of Israeli weapons would survive an Arab counterforce strike; but the probability that a minority would survive would prevent Arab leaders from ordering the attack.

The stability of the regional balance of terror will not be obtained through assured second-strike capabilities. Rather stability will result from the fact that a perfectly successful first strike could not be guaranteed. The fact that deterrent weapons may operate in less than perfect fashion and still succeed in their object, while any effort to disarm them must be conducted perfectly, assures that the balance of terror will remain stable. Arab nuclear postures are unlikely to diminish the extent to which a nuclear posture would enable Israel to fulfill the five prerequisites to effective deterrence. Nuclear deterrence can grant Israel security in a multinuclear Middle East as well as under conditions of Israeli nuclear monopoly.

CHAPTER 3

Israel, Nuclear Weapons, and Peace

Shai's memos on dates

Can the general deterrence provided by strategic nuclear weapons be converted to specific deterrence? Can strategic nuclear weapons deter specific lower-level challenges? Or are tactical nuclear weapons required to deter challenges of lower magnitude? Can nuclear weapons not only enhance Israel's security but also promote peace? These are the questions to be addressed in this chapter.

My discussion will revolve around three central themes. First, general deterrence will more easily translate into specific deterrence if Israel withdraws to lines approximating those she held prior to the 1967 war. The closer Israel's borders are to the essential core of the country, the more likely she is to succeed in deterring lower-level challenges with strategic nuclear weapons. Second, the deployment of tactical nuclear weapons would be both unnecessary and detrimental to Israel's security. Finally, the adoption of an Israeli nuclear posture would help to reduce terrorist activity against Israel and lower the risks involved in the establishment of a separate Palestinian state.

From General to Specific Deterrence

What Alan Dowty calls "the issue of convertibility,"[1] converting general deterrence to specific deterrence, is a highly intricate one. As pointed out in chapter 1, effective general deterrence does not easily translate to equally effective specific deterrence. American–Soviet strategic relations since 1945 reflect these difficulties. American success in deterring a direct Soviet attack on the North American continent did not automatically convert to deterrence of a wide array of Soviet activities, ranging from the Berlin blockades of 1948 and 1961 through the invasion of Czechoslovakia in 1968 to the 1979 invasion of Afghanistan.

Difficulties of the superpowers in this regard have led some to despair about Israel's ability to deter specific Arab lower-level activities. Alan Dowty, for one, is of the opinion that "few things have been so over-rated as the usefulness of nuclear weapons in response to everyday non-nuclear threats or as a means of compelling one's foes to behave themselves. . . . Would Arab terrorists or Arab governments believe an Israeli threat of suicidal nuclear war, unless survival itself was at stake? Assuming that Arab states obtain matching nuclear capability, one could not credit such a threat in response to a border raid, limited military incursion, or even full-scale conventional attack like that of October 1973. The deterrent might not even be credible against a conquest that was carried out in very gradual stages, no one of which was in itself sufficiently threatening to make a nuclear counter-threat believable."[2]

Dowty's views are echoed by Egypt's Hasanayn Haykal. In 1976, Haykal argued that mutual acquisition of nuclear weapons would prevent the translation of general deterrence to specific deterrence. Arab acquisition of nuclear weapons would check the deterrent effect of Israel's nuclear arsenal; it would create a stalemate at the strategic-nuclear level, thus allowing the parties to wage war with conventional forces.[3] The Jordanian *Al-Sabāh* (July 24, 1974) questions Israel's ability to convert general deterrence to specific deterrence even during the period of Israeli monopoly over nuclear weapons: "Any Arab activity which does not escalate [into a threat on Israel's survival] will not cause Israel to turn to the nuclear alternative. This implies that Israel will not be

able to deter the Arabs from carrying out any military operation of limited purpose."

Dowty's and Haykal's views did not pass undisputed. Robert Tucker, for example, makes another assessment of the
issue of convertibility. In his opinion, there is always a danger
that hostilities, once initiated, would quickly escalate. In a
nuclear environment, the potential costs of such uncontrolled
escalation are likely to deter any type of provocation. Furthermore, uncertainty would play a positive role insofar as
"uncertainty over what is or is not peripheral and, accord-
ingly, over what action might or might not risk a nuclear
response, will itself have a deterrent effect."[4] Haykal's views
are similarly disputed by much Arab commentary, some of
which has already been cited. The other writers consider that
even if an Israeli nuclear posture were matched by Arab
nuclear postures, the Arabs would not be at liberty to continue waging conventional wars. Nuclear weapons are expected to bring about a complete stalemate; a freezing of the
conflict in its present state; pressure on the Arabs to negotiate
and coexist.[5]

Thus two schools dispute the issue of convertibility of general to specific deterrence. One denies it altogether; the other
not only believes in it but also regards it as automatic. The
following analysis takes the middle ground. It does not deny
that some deterrence converts from the general to the specific
fairly automatically. It argues, however, that the attainment
of effective convertibility depends on the ability to meet
some prior conditions. These conditions will be elaborated
and specified.

A limited measure of deterrence is likely to spill over from
general to specific automatically. When faced with a nuclear
state, an adversary will not only refrain from challenging that
state's survival directly, he will also think twice before taking
any step that might potentially escalate into such a challenge.
States are dissuaded from initiating limited acts of organized
violence against nuclear adversaries by their perception of
the horrors of nuclear punishment, and their recognition that
even the most limited act may eventually escape control. The

US | Soviet absence of violence

enormity of the potential punishment changes the very nature of states' calculations. In a nuclear environment, a state contemplating limited action cannot limit itself to estimating the chances of attaining its limited goals. Instead, the state is first compelled to estimate the chances that the situation will get out of hand. When faced by a nuclear opponent, each state must seek "to avoid unnecessary provocation, to try to minimize risk, to be above all prudent and cautious."[6]

This "new math" is in large measure responsible for the tranquility of the East–West frontier in Europe. The absence of a single skirmish between Soviet and American forces during a period of some thirty-five years best demonstrates the stabilizing effects of the nuclear calculation. The Soviets have refrained from firing a single shot across the border dividing the two Germanies for over three decades. They have refrained from doing so because, regardless of what the United States says, irrespective of what its doctrine and force structure in Europe are, there is an irreducible chance that any limited conventional operation would escalate, eventually leading to strategic nuclear war.[7]

Arab leaders are likely to make a similar calculation. The leaders of Syria and Egypt are bound to think twice before initiating limited warfare, whether of the mobile-conventional or the war-of-attrition type. Both types will elicit Israeli responses, to be met by Arab counterresponses, and so on; some risk of unintended escalation would be inevitable and the Arab leaders would have to consider these risks carefully before initiating such warfare.

However, thinking twice before initiating limited warfare does not imply that such warfare will necessarily be avoided. The Koreans and the North Vietnamese both fought a nuclear-armed America. Asad and Sadat would probably not have refrained from initiating the October 1973 war even if they considered Israel to be nuclear-armed at the time. Although general deterrence automatically converts to some measure of specific deterrence, this measure is sometimes not sufficient to deter specific challenges. Specific deterrence may become effective only under certain conditions. These con-

ditions must include the two elements determining the distribution of specific deterrence. As I proposed in the theoretical framework, a state's specific deterrent power consists of its ability to deliver punishment and its willingness to absorb punishment in order to win the specific issue at dispute. If both sides can inflict unacceptable punishment, the winner in a deterrent dispute will be the party more willing to absorb high costs. The relative willingness to absorb punishment depends on the degree to which each side cares about the issue at dispute. If both can inflict limitless damage while the issue is dramatically more important to one country, the other one has little hope of deterring the first.

For Israel, the ability to deter specific Arab challenges would depend on their nature—that is, on the extent to which the challenge would be limited in size and purpose. Two situations can be compared: first, one in which the issue at dispute would have been Israel's continued occupation of the territories it conquered in the 1967 war, while the purpose of the Arab challenge would have been to compel Israel to withdraw from these territories; and second, a situation characterized by Israeli forces being positioned along the pre-1967 lines, while the purpose of the Arab challenge is to harass Israel incrementally. An Israeli nuclear posture would probably fail to deter the Arab states from launching a limited mobile conventional war or a war of attrition designed to restore Arab sovereignty over the occupied territories. Prominent among undeterrable Arab actions may have been some versions of the 1969–1970 war of attrition as well as of the October 1973 war.[8] As long as the issue at dispute is control over the occupied territories, nuclear weapons will not have provided effective specific deterrence. Both of those wars demonstrated an impressive Arab willingness to absorb costs. Israel's occupation of the territories conquered in 1967 has placed her forces in the Arabs' backyard. Egypt found Israeli forces stationed along the Suez Canal, not much more than a hundred miles from Cairo; Syria found Israeli forces less than an hour's drive from Damascus. Both regarded the territory Israel occupied as their own sovereign territory and

were willing to take great pains to restore sovereignty over
it. Contrary to the situation in 1948, in 1970 and 1973 Egypt's
effort was aimed at getting Israel to leave *Egyptian* territory.
Contrary to what had been the case in 1948 and in 1965 (when
the Syrians attempted to divert the sources of Israel's water),
in 1973 Syria's effort was aimed at getting Israel to leave
Syrian territory.

Regardless of whether Israel has or does not have nuclear
weapons, most Arab challenges to the post-1967 lines would
reveal the same central feature: an asymmetry in the willingness to absorb punishment. Syria and Egypt would enjoy
a national consensus on the justification of restoring sovereignty over stolen territory, while in Israel the domestic
scene would uncover increased dissension over the usefulness and justification of Israel's continued control of these
lands. Even with a nuclear-armed Israel, Arab superior willingness to absorb punishment would probably override Israeli nuclear threats; most likely Israel's attempts at specific
deterrence would fail. If both Israel and the Arab states could
inflict unacceptable punishment, Arab superior willingness
to absorb punishment over the issue of the occupied territories would tilt the balance of specific deterrence in their
favor even more decisively. They would be more willing to
run high risks and would calculate that as long as the issue
is limited to the occupied territories, Israel would not be
willing to do the same. Arab ability to threaten counterretaliation would have self-deterred Israel; she would not risk
nuclear war over her occupation of Sinai, the Golan Heights,
or even the West Bank. Hence, under conditions of multiple
nuclearization, Israel's capacity to deter the Arabs from
launching a war of attrition or a limited mobile conventional
war along the post-1967 lines would be extremely limited.

Some Arab statements support the view that Arab efforts
to achieve the limited objective of pushing Israel back to the
pre-1967 lines could not be deterred by Israeli nuclear
threats. A key such statement was made in 1976 by Egypt's
Minister of War, General Gamassy, to the Saudi paper *Al-Madīna*: "Israel's possession of atomic weapons or the threats

being made by the Israeli enemy to use them will not force the Arabs to surrender their land or the rights of the Palestinian people."[9] President Sadat expressed the same view in 1975: "The existence of a nuclear weapon or the threat to use it will not force us to surrender as they tried to make us do before the October war by various ways of threat and psychological warfare. Their threats will not affect us nor will we give up our land or the rights of the Palestinian people."[10] This statement was later echoed by the Cairo daily *Al-Jumhūrīyya* (December 10, 1976): "In any case, the presence or absence of nuclear weapons in Israel will not influence the Arab demands and their conditions for a political settlement." In 1981, another Egyptian commentator, Ibrahim Nafi, noted: "Egypt entered the October 1973 war knowing that Israel had the capability to manufacture an atomic bomb, if it was not actually in possession of it, but this did not weaken its resolve or the resolve of its men."[11]

It is in the light of these statements that I interpret the more general statements by Sadat, for example, to the effect that his "country is not frightened by reports that Israel possesses nuclear bombs,"[12] or that "whether they [Israel] have atomic weapons or not, we shall not be scared,"[13] or that "it is not easy, not at all easy to frighten us, even if Israel does have nuclear weapons."[14] These statements reflected Sadat's view that Israeli nuclear threats lack credibility under the post-1967 territorial division. His view seems to have been that as long as the Egyptian–Israeli confrontation took place along the Suez Canal, Egypt's willingness to run higher risks would result in an overall greater deterrent power, the presence of nuclear weapons in Israel's hands notwithstanding.

The Syrians seem to reflect a similar view. An article published in the ruling Ba'ath party journal, *Tashrīn* (May 3, 1977), states: "The Arabs, who refused to concede their lands or their rights under the influence of their military defeat in 1967, when there wasn't one soldier to defend the road from the [Suez] Canal to Cairo, will refuse to concede their lands or their rights, whatever the threat may be, including the nuclear threat. . . . The Arabs are following Israel very care-

[handwritten: Arabs not retreat from Palestinian demands]

fully and take her threats very seriously. However, they will not retreat from two principles: a return of the conquered land and the return of the national rights of the Palestinian people as conditions for any settlement in the area."

Once Israel withdraws to lines similar to those she held before 1967, declaring at the same time that any significant crossing of these lines would meet nuclear punishment, Arab figuring will change dramatically. The balance of specific deterrence will then be to the Arabs' disadvantage and they are likely to realize this quickly. Following Israeli withdrawal to the pre-1967 lines, the general deterrence provided by a nuclear posture will deter the Arabs from launching serious challenges to Israel's survival. Under such circumstances any lower-level Arab military activity could be aimed at harassing the Jewish state. Arab reckoning would then have to take four factors into account: First, a major undertaking to dismember Israel would be prohibited by the likely nuclear retaliation. Second, small-scale Arab military activity would yield little benefit to the Arab states. Third, less limited Arab military activities would carry the danger of escalation, thereby increasing the prospect that nuclear weapons would eventually be used. Fourth, whereas low-level activities aimed at harassing Israel would yield little value to the Arabs, they would be a great nuisance to the Israelis. Fighting would then take place in Israel's backyard; the safety of her population would be involved; a national consensus with respect to the justification for fighting would easily emerge. The Israelis would care much more and be willing to run higher risks. Israel couldn't accept continued Arab harassment and would most probably answer in force in order to increase Arab costs. The Arabs would then have to calculate that if they respond by increasing the level of warfare, they would also be increasing the likelihood of escalation to nuclear war. The limited benefits which the continued harassment of Israel might yield could not possibly justify risking Israeli nuclear retaliation.

Following Israel's ascribed withdrawal to lines approximating those she held prior to the 1967 war, the options for

[handwritten in left margin: Arab will change if to pre '67]

It Is went pre '67 Syria

Syria should take into account a number of factors: First, the goal of withdrawal will have been achieved and most of the marks of what Syria calls "the aggression of 1967" will have been erased. Second, the goal of destroying Israel would be unobtainable without enormously high risks of deadly nuclear retaliation. Thus it would be impossible to erase the marks of "the aggression of 1948." Under such circumstances, only limited goals could be postulated: for example, harassment of Israeli civilian settlements in the northern tip of Israel (the area known as the Galilee's finger). The purpose of such harassment could be to force Israel to roll back its forces and civilian settlements from a strip that is at places no more than a few miles wide. This could be the first slice in an overall "salami" strategy. That Syria's president would embark on such a venture in a nuclear environment is unlikely for two reasons: first, the gains involved in obtaining a few extra miles will seem minuscule when compared with the risks involved in the likelihood, even a very small one, that the operation might get out of hand and escalate, eventually leading to a nuclear exchange. Even small probabilities of escalation to the horrors of nuclear war would provide ample deterrence. Second, Syria's president will have to take into account that only a tiny slice of the "salami" can be cut off before the probability of nuclear retaliation will rise dramatically. He will also have to consider that for many Israelis any slice of the pre-1967 territory is of significant value. Therefore, an attempt to conquer any such slice would cause an immediate and steep rise in Israeli willingness to run risks. Finally, Syria must reckon that once she crosses Israel's borders and violates her territorial integrity, there is no clear stopping point. Even if the territory involved was intrinsically insignificant, Israel would ask herself, "If not here, where?" Israel would run higher risks to deter any challenge to her national boundary because, as Thomas Schelling pointed out, no portion of a country can be conquered without tempting the attacker to go a little further.[15] Therefore, in Israel's eyes her national boundaries would constitute the "ultimate threshold." This means that to avoid the high probability of nuclear punishment, Syria's president would have to avoid not only challenging Israel's survival but also attempting to annex any of its pre-1967 territory.

Some evidence can already be mobilized to suggest that the Arabs are beginning to share the aforementioned conclusions regarding the effects of nuclear deterrence along the pre-1967 lines. One Arab writer who has come to a similar assessment is Muhammad Jabber al-Nasr. Writing in the Lebanese *Al-Anwār*, al-Nasr asserts that "if Israel is forced to accept the just peace which the Arabs seek actively, then nothing will compensate her for her strategic withdrawal and for her historical fears and psychological worries except for the atomic bomb; she will declare to the Arabs her ownership of this weapon and that she has brought to their region a balance of terror, and that they have no alternative but to accept a detente [in Arab–Israeli relations] as all conflicting parties had to accept a detente as a consequence of this 'balance of terror.'"[16] In his 1973 article, Hasanayn Haykal also provides support for the assessment that Israeli nuclear threats to retaliate against Arab crossing of the pre-1967 lines will be credible. He said, "[h]e does not believe Israel can use [nuclear] bombs in this age in view of the universal prohibitions, such as the world balance of power and the influence of public opinion, except in the case of an Arab penetration inside the pre-1967 territory which Israel could not stop."[17] Another Egyptian commentator, Ahmad Baha' al-Din, also implied that nuclear deterrence would provide Israel with sufficient security along the pre-1967 lines.[18]

Thus, Israeli nuclear threats along the pre-1967 borders are likely to be credible and will provide effective specific deterrence. Yet, there is nothing sacred about these lines; historical chance converged to bestow international legitimacy upon them. It also happens that the entire Israeli populace accepts the need to do everything required to defend Israel along the pre-1967 borders. A similar consensus has not emerged to engulf the lands acquired by Israel in the 1967 Six Days' War. However, that such an alternative consensus would not emerge was by no means self-evident. Had Israel's leaders decided, immediately following that war, that the territories acquired are an integral part of Israel, had they supported this decision by socializing the Israeli public to that end, and had they reinforced this decision by settling these territories with masses of Israeli civilians, a national consensus engulfing these territories might well have emerged. In such an instance, Israeli nuclear deterrent threats against Arab attempts to reconquer these territories could have enjoyed sufficient credibility. As it was, such steps were not taken, and the corresponding consensus has never emerged.[19] Effective specific deterrence remains along the lines Israel held until the 1967 war.

Faced by a nuclear Israel positioned along the pre-1967 lines, the Arabs would face the same basic dilemma that has characterized Soviet behavior in Europe during the last thirty years. Albert Wohlstetter portrayed it in the following manner: "From [the Soviet] standpoint, the problem of successful aggression in Europe is to find a level and kind of attack large enough to be useful, but small enough to be well below the threshold risking American nuclear response."[20]

The dilemma would be even more difficult to overcome for the Arabs because their threshold would be far lower than that of the Soviets. Israeli territory is much more important to Israel than West German territory is to the United States. Therefore, it would be more difficult for the Arabs than for the Soviets to find a level and kind of attack large enough to be useful yet small enough to be well below the threshold risking nuclear retaliation. Thus the dilemma seems to have no solution. From the Arab perspective, small-scale warfare would be ineffective and therefore both expensive and pointless while larger-scale warfare would present the likelihood of being met by an Israeli nuclear response. The insoluble nature of the dilemma would in all likelihood produce a Middle East detente. Continued hostility would be pointless and the Arabs would have no reason to avoid the benefits of such a detente.

From Israel's perspective, the strategic objective would be to see to it that the Arabs remain trapped indefinitely in the dilemma portrayed above. Just as the Arabs would experience the Soviet Union's European dilemma, Israel would encounter NATO's central problem. Quoting Wohlstretter again, "NATO's problem is to try to make sure the Russians cannot manage a useful attack without making it so large that it would be hard to distinguish from the start of a central war."[21] The difference between NATO and Israel is that to overcome this problem would be far easier for the latter; Israel has the conventional capability to deny the Arabs useful limited attacks. During thirty years of active defense, Israel has developed the ability to conduct surgical small-scale warfare. This capability has been demonstrated not only by the spectacular raids on Beirut airport and Entebbe but also by hundreds of operations across her borders. They demonstrate that Israel is capable of conducting small-scale warfare, that she can deny Arab success in this realm, and that she can constantly raise the level of warfare to assure Arab failure. The Arabs will calculate that if they react by raising the level of warfare any further, they will risk uncontrolled escalation.

The combination of Israeli nuclear capability and the capability to conduct effective small-scale conventional defense/offense might deter the Arabs from pursuing any form of warfare; small-scale would be ineffective while large-scale would be prohibited by the existence of nuclear weapons. Once the Arab objective is limited to harassing Israel, Israel's ability to promise that this harassment would either fail or eventually lead to nuclear retaliation is likely to prove a highly effective deterrent. An Israeli declaration that specific challenges along her pre-1967 lines will lead to nuclear punishment would provide credible deterrence whether only Israel had nuclear weapons or in a multinuclear Middle East.

Nuclear weapons in this deterrent role would only fortify patterns of behavior already developing in the Middle East. Egypt after 1956, Jordan after 1967, and Syria after 1975 have all avoided small-scale warfare. This was the outcome of a learning process: Arab states have discovered that benefits can only be derived from large-scale warfare. These benefits accrue, however, only if general war occurs at a time that is advantageous to the Arabs. Subconventional warfare, by contrast, produces the danger of escalation at a time disadvantageous to them. Egyptian efforts at small-scale warfare during the period following 1953 led to Israel's victory in 1956. Syrian efforts at small-scale warfare following 1964 led to Israel's victory in 1967. The care that some Arab states currently take in order to avoid escalation is best exemplified by Syrian behavior vis-à-vis Israel on the Lebanese front. When Israel embarked on the Litani Operation, placing Israeli units very close to Syrian units while the Israeli Air Force bombed sites in close proximity to Syrian forces, the Syrians were careful to avoid reactions that might eventually have escalated to general war.

With the odds on general war diminished by the nuclear deterrent, Syrian, Jordanian, and Egyptian reluctance to engage in futile warfare would remove almost all options for Arab military action. Thus nuclear weapons do hold the promise of converting effective general deterrence to specific deterrence.

Finally, it should be pointed out that there are also some technical–military reasons why general deterrence is likely to spill over to deterrence of lower levels of warfare. I shall give two examples of how Israel may facilitate such convertibility.

One possibility would be for Israel to communicate in advance to her adversaries, first that she had adopted a launch-on-warning posture; second that she was unable to distinguish the opponents' penetrating bombers carrying conventional explosives from those carrying nuclear weapons; and third that, this being the case, the adversary had better refrain from even limited conventional air bombardments because Israel would have to launch its nuclear forces prior to verification of the precise nature of the adversary's attack. The Arabs, it can be argued, might not see such a threat as entirely credible, since the consequences of counterretaliation are likely to be so grave as to deter Israel from unleashing her deterrent in response to what could have been a very limited Arab strike. To launch such an attack, however, the Arabs

converting general → specific deter

would have to be perfectly certain that Israel would not in fact carry out the threat. Lacking such perfect confidence, Arab states must believe that there was some probability that their limited conventional strike could lead to nuclear disaster. Taking such a probability into account, it is highly unlikely that an Arab state would ignore the threat.

Another method of converting general deterrence to specific is to make it clear that the requirements of general deterrence prohibit the conduct of limited war. For such a claim to be credible, Israel would have to explain that her nuclear retaliatory force depends on conventional means of delivery: missiles and aircraft. Israel must assure herself of sufficient delivery capability to be used if ultimate threats to her survival developed. Hence, she could not afford to expend her conventional weapons and particularly her delivery vehicles in a mutually reductive limited conventional war. Should that war become effective in reducing Israel's capabilities, Israel would at once be forced to use her nuclear retaliatory force for fear that if she continued to refrain from doing so she would remain without the ability to deliver the threat. An effective Arab conventional strike would be forestalled by Arab understanding that any conventional strike effective enough to reduce Israel's conventional capabilities would force Israel to launch her nuclear retaliatory strike. Once again, nuclear deterrence of ultimate threats to the state's survival would spill over to provide deterrence against lower levels of warfare.

One important policy question remains. If a nuclear posture would not provide effective specific deterrence to Israel along the post-1967 lines and yet could offer such deterrence along the pre-1967 lines, what would its effects be within geographical boundaries between these two extremes? Alternatively, one can pose the following question: how much farther can Israel position herself away from the pre-1967 lines and still expect to enjoy the benefits of specific nuclear deterrence? Or, how close to the post-1967 lines can Israel stay without losing the fruits of effective deterrence? The

Is there balance betw pre/post '67

Syria

answer to this question lies more than any other in the realm of speculation. Yet some intelligent guesses can probably be made, and are unavoidable since the reality of the post-1979 Egyptian–Israeli peace treaty is characterized by Israeli movement toward the pre-1967 lines. The changes on the southern front still remain unmatched on the eastern and northern fronts; yet this may not remain the case for long. The possibility that Jordan, Syria, and the PLO might follow the Egyptian initiative may not materialize immediately, but may do so in the longer run. In addition, having concluded an agreement with the Republic of Egypt, yet unable to get its other neighbors to conclude similar agreements, Israel might take a different approach on the remaining outstanding issues. She might, for example, reach an additional agreement with Egypt on a number of unilateral steps to be taken on the other fronts. On the Syrian front Israel could withdraw to some extent unilaterally, with the purpose of reducing Syrian motivation to go to war. As Israel backed away from Damascus, Syria's willingness to absorb punishment in order to get Israel's forces to evacuate the remaining part of the Golan Heights would be bound to diminish. If Israel's withdrawal was coupled with the adoption of a nuclear posture, the possible costs involved in forcing a complete Israeli withdrawal might be considered by Damascus to be prohibitively high. How much of the Golan Heights could Israel hold and yet expect to enjoy specific nuclear deterrence? How much of the West Bank? Jerusalem? What could it hope to deter on the Egyptian front?

On the Golan Heights Israel remains, despite the 1975 disengagement agreement, in a position that directly threatens Damascus. Consequently, Syria can be expected to run fairly high risks in order to obtain Israel's withdrawal. From Israel's perspective it would probably be strategically unwise and politically impossible to abandon the first line of hills overlooking Israel's agricultural settlements in the Jordan Valley. The geographic features there would make conventional defense exceedingly difficult. Since Israel would want

some capability to deny Syrian efforts to harass her settlements incrementally, it would be a mistake on her part to
abandon the heights entirely, but she may choose to withdraw
from parts of the Golan Heights. The parts she would probably wish to keep would consist of the first line of heights
and a strip, some six to eight miles wide, extending beyond
the first line. The strip's width would provide the minimum
area required for defense against a possible Syrian effort to
rush the forces stationed on the first line of heights. Israel
might see this also as her minimum requirement for the security of her northern settlements. Once Israel supported her
holding of the remainder of the Golan Heights with a nuclear
deterrent threat, the threat would be backed by a great deal
of will, and hence would be likely to enjoy much credibility.
The Syrian government will be sufficiently uncertain that
Israel will not carry out her threat. Syria's willingness to
provoke incidents that might escalate to a nuclear confrontation would be particularly diminished when the issue at
stake became a strip only a few miles wide, situated at the
far end of the Heights. Thus Israel would have an excellent
chance to obtain effective nuclear deterrence along such
lines. Her control of limited parts of the Golan Heights could
be stabilized once she adopted an overt nuclear deterrence
posture.

A few words are in order about the likely specific deterrent
effects of nuclear weapons in the Israeli–Egyptian context.
Clearly, the relationship between these two countries will
be affected by the 1979 Egypt–Israel Peace Treaty. The
treaty stipulates, with small exceptions, the complete demilitarization of the entire Sinai northeast of the strategic passes.
In the area southwest of the passes, Egypt is allowed to maintain only one mechanized division.[22] As our previous analysis
of the effects of nuclear deterrence along Israel's pre-1967
lines indicates, Egypt is unlikely to present Israel with general or specific challenges along these lines. The stipulation
of the 1979 treaty also imply that before issuing a challenge
to Israel along the pre-1967 lines, Egypt must first violate

[handwritten: Egypt calculations are 'off']

the demilitarization of Sinai. The question here is to what extent might Israel's nuclear deterrence extend beyond the pre-1967 lines and prevent Egyptian remilitarization of parts of Sinai. In a nuclear environment, the relevance of this question would likely be greatly diminished. Since Israel's nuclear posture would be likely to deter Egypt from challenging Israel in both general and specific ways along the pre-1967 lines, the question whether the Egyptians do or do not maintain conventional military forces along these lines would lose much of its significance. Egypt would thus be able to calculate that Israel would not care enough about this issue to invoke the nuclear threat credibly. Consequently Egypt might calculate that Israeli specific deterrence did not extend to the vast Sinai sands. According to this hypothesis, Israel would not be able to deter Egypt from remilitarizing the Sinai.

However, there is some reason to doubt that the case would be so clear-cut. Although Egypt could assume with a fairly high measure of confidence that Israel would not invoke her nuclear deterrent over the issue of Egyptian remilitarization of the area southwest of the strategic passes, it could not be sure that this assumption would be equally valid for the areas lying to the northwest of these passes. Egypt would probably fear that Israel might come to regard the remilitarization of the second area as indicating that Egypt intended to invade Israel; that Israel might become uncertain about whether Egypt's forces would stop short of crossing the international border; that Israel might overreact by a selective and demonstrative use of its nuclear deterrent either in a counterforce role against the advancing forces or in a countervalue role against an Egyptian city. Thus Egypt might well come to feel that in remilitarizing areas beyond Sinai's important strategic passes she might be risking enormous punishment. The closer the Egyptian remilitarization extended to the international border, the higher the risks. This consideration would constitute an effective deterrent. Thus, despite the fact that Israel's nuclear posture would probably fail to deter

Arabs not risk Nuclear for Palestinian - WB (handwritten)

the Egyptians from remilitarizing parts of Sinai, a measure of deterrence would be likely to spill over some distance beyond the international border.

With regard to the West Bank and Jerusalem, two types of problems are involved. First is Israel's ability to deter efforts by Arab states to make her withdraw from the West Bank and East Jerusalem; second is the effect of an Israeli nuclear posture on efforts by Palestinian Arabs to achieve such a withdrawal by either conventional guerrilla warfare or nuclear-terrorist means. I shall examine the first of these problems now. (The discussion of the effects of nuclear deterrence on guerrilla warfare and on nuclear terrorism will take place in other sections.) Israel's nuclear posture would be likely to deter Arab states from attempting to compel Israel to withdraw from the West Bank and East Jerusalem. Egypt, Syria, and Iraq would be likely to care less about the West Bank than Israel, in whose backyard the area is located. They are unlikely to risk Israeli nuclear retaliation against their cities and values on behalf of the Palestinian cause. No established Arab state, not even belligerent Libya, will risk its people and cities to gain Israeli withdrawal from the West Bank and East Jerusalem.

Israel could further decrease the willingness of Arab states to run risks on behalf of this cause by allowing them some footing in these areas. For example, by granting Saudi Arabia limited and symbolic sovereignty over important religious sites, Israel would further reduce Saudi willingness to support an Arab effort to compel Israeli withdrawal. Thus the deterrent effect of a nuclear posture, especially when coupled with some political concessions, would deter the Arab states from attempting to force Israel's hand on the issue of the West Bank. This does not imply, however, that Israel could hold onto the West Bank indefinitely. On the contrary, political pressures from the United States and Western Europe as well as from the West Bank itself may well make Israel's continued control of that area untenable. This assessment notwithstanding, Israel's nuclear deterrence, general and specific, could extend on her eastern front beyond the pre-

(handwritten margin notes: *IS Political concessions*; ** IS can not hold territory forever*)

1967 lines to deter Arab states from attempting to force Israel out of the West Bank by military means.

The Wisdom of Nuclear Defense

Md East Nuke defense?

The question that derives from the preceding discussion is whether it would be wise for Israel to supplement nuclear deterrence with nuclear defense. In terms of hardware, it is whether Israel should attempt to produce and deploy tactical and theater nuclear weapons. Two subquestions underlie the main one: first, would Israel's nuclear deterrent posture so lack credibility that it would have to be supplemented and reinforced? Second, could nuclear defense do this job and would the adoption of tactical nuclear weapons contribute to Israel's security? The discussion of nuclear defense will first refer to medium- and large-yield tactical nuclear weapons with a deployment and doctrine similar to that presently employed by NATO in Europe. Later an analysis will be made of the merits of deploying very small-yield mininuclear weapons as suggested by Robert Sandoval and Robert Shreffler.

Drawing from the debate on the role and effectiveness of American strategic nuclear deterrence in Europe, some military thinkers are likely to advocate the adoption of tactical nuclear defense in the Middle East. The case for nuclear defense in Europe was based on doubts about the readiness of the United States to risk the destruction of its cities on Europe's behalf, hence about the effectiveness of U.S. strategic nuclear threats in deterring possible Soviet conventional or tactical nuclear attacks on Western Europe. Arguments were advanced to the effect that U.S. general deterrence could not translate to specific deterrence in Europe. Specific deterrence requires specific weapons and doctrines. If the United States faced a Soviet invasion in Europe without specific means of defense and deterrence, it would have only one option: escalation to strategic nuclear war. Since the United States would not want to risk its cities on Europe's behalf, the choice would result in American paralysis. To avoid this, the United States must have some intermediate options—hence the need for theater nuclear defense. The conclusion drawn from this debate as it applies to Israel is that to deter limited challenges along its frontiers Israel would have to acquire and deploy tactical nuclear weapons.

The military rationale for the deployment of tactical nuclear weapons is that these weapons prevent a potential adversary from aggregating his conventional forces for an offensive. In order to overwhelm a well-prepared defense, a potential adversary must concentrate his efforts in a few sectors along the front. To do this he must aggregate his forces prior to the attack in a limited number of staging areas. Tactical nuclear weapons, being extremely lethal area weapons, enable the defender to preempt these forces in these staging areas. Thus tactical nuclear defense precludes the concentration of conventional forces. Since such concentrations are a prerequisite to the mounting of a successful offense, the net effect of nuclear defense is to prohibit the conduct of offensive warfare. This is the appeal of tactical nuclear weapons. The overall case for tactical nuclear defense is therefore based both on the proposition that strategic nuclear weapons provide insufficient deterrence on their own and on the proposition that the defensive advantage of tactical nuclear weapons enables them to fill the gaps in strategic deterrence.

Both propositions provide insufficient rationale for the adoption of tactical nuclear defense by Israel. In the last section I have shown that strategic nuclear weapons are likely to provide for effective specific deterrence under specified conditions. The perceived need for tactical nuclear defense is based solely on deductions from the problems facing the United States in Europe. These deductions are invalid because the two contexts—the United States in Europe and Israel in the Middle East—differ in a number of important respects. America has a significant yet limited stake in Europe. Soviet challenges to Europe's security would take place thousands of miles away from America's coasts. It would have significant repercussions for America's global position but would only indirectly and belatedly affect the well-being of the American people. Some argue that this would lead the Soviets to question U.S. willingness to risk its cities and population on Europe's behalf, and therefore raises doubts about America's ability to deter Soviet challenges in Europe by threatening strategic nuclear war. As indicated earlier, these apprehensions are largely unjustified. The Soviet Union is unlikely to develop the absolute confidence in U.S. nonresponse necessary to launch an attack on Europe. But even if such doubts could somehow be justified with respect to the American strategic umbrella for Europe, they would not be similarly justified in Israel's context. For her the stakes in challenges along her frontiers are far less limited. As her major population centers are situated so close to her borders, challenges to her security are more significant and meaningful to her citizens. Security threats along her frontiers have direct and immediate effect on the well-being of Israelis. Hence the credibility of strategic nuclear threats will be much less in doubt. In Israel's context, strategic nuclear weapons can well provide sufficient deterrence of specific and limited challenges.

In terms of the credibility of Israeli deterrence the adoption of tactical nuclear defense would probably be a net loss. While her strategic nuclear threat would consist of an effort to convince prospective opponents that Israel would punish them severely should they attempt to challenge her security, the adoption of tactical nuclear defense would signal precisely the opposite. It would betray a lack of will to carry out the threat to respond with strategic nuclear punishment.[23] Instead of enhancing deterrence, the adoption of tactical nuclear defense would be an invitation to war. A recent Congressional study correctly asks: "Does not the preparation to fight a limited nuclear war make such war more easily survivable, more 'thinkable,' and thus more likely? If so, then deterrence has been weakened, not strengthened."[24] Thus the proposed cure to perceived problems in the credibility of strategic nuclear deterrence would seem to increase rather than diminish the magnitude of the problem.

In addition, it is doubtful that a viable doctrine for the

tactical use of nuclear weapons in the Middle East could be formulated. The actual use of such weapons, in the 4- to 12-kiloton range if they are of Western design or 5- to 100-kiloton if they are of Soviet design, would cause immeasurable damage to the regional environment.[25] The effort to fill the gaps in strategic deterrence would thus consist of an invitation to regional destruction. In Europe too, efforts to formulate a sensible doctrine for the use of tactical nuclear weapons has met with enormous difficulties. This was well articulated by Alain Enthoven, who testified that he was "prepared to conclude that 20 years of efforts to find an acceptable doctrine for the use of nuclear weapons in the defense of Western Europe have failed because one does not exist. The planned first use of nuclear weapons for the defense of Western Europe simply doesn't make sense. It amounts to saying, 'we'll have to destroy this continent in order to save it.'"[26] For Israel such difficulties would be harder to overcome. The proximity of the likely battlefields to her essential core insure higher odds that tactical use of nuclear weapons would cause incalculable damage.

Furthermore, threats to wage tactical nuclear war would be less credible in Israel's case than in the case of the neighboring Arab states. Arab challenges would take place along Israel's borders, which are closer to Israel's core than to the core areas of the neighboring Arab states. Israel is likely to suffer greater and more meaningful collateral damage than the Arab states. Hence a signal to the effect that she would be willing to conduct such warfare would be detrimental to her interests.

In addition, there is the important issue of the asymmetric effect of high levels of casualties. A tactical nuclear exchange in the Middle East is likely to result in tens of thousands of casualties on each side. However, the effects of such levels of casualties will be different for each of the parties. For example, while 35,000[27] casualties would consist of nearly one percent of Israel's population (equivalent to three million Americans), a similar level of casualties will consist of only 0.07 percent of Egypt's population. Thus, under conditions of symmetric losses in absolute numbers, Israel may well be the loser in relative terms. It would therefore seem unwise for Israel to adopt tactical nuclear defense.

On purely military grounds there are additional reasons to doubt the rationale for the adoption of tactical nuclear defense. The proponents of TNWs base their optimism on the favorable cost-exchange ratio between a TNW and some concentration of conventional forces. However, what is often ignored is the overall effect of TNW in a situation characterized by mutual acquisition of TNW. What would be the effect of such weapons when two complex military systems, each consisting of a mix of conventional and tactical nuclear forces, faced each other in the battlefield? Would tactical nuclear weapons under such circumstances still favor the defense? Would the introduction of such weapons result in increased stability or would it instead make the front even more volatile? Are tactical nuclear weapons militarily useful? Can a credible doctrine for their use be formulated?

A look at the debate on the role of tactical nuclear weapons in Europe generates deep skepticism as to the ability to answer any of the above questions in a positive manner—indeed, to draw any conclusions from it. The degree of uncertainty that surrounds the issue is enormous and affects the ability to theorize on the possible usefulness of tactical nuclear weapons. Most of this uncertainty results from the fact that few if any have a clear conception of what a tactical nuclear war would look like. As Bernard Brodie has pointed out, "the fact is we do not even know yet whether armies can fight in a nuclear environment."[28] Philip Karber has understated the issue when he said, "it is not clear that if nuclear war breaks out any army really knows how to fight on a battlefield contaminated with not only prompt radiation but also the inevitable residual radiation that is likely to occur."[29] The result of this uncertainty is confusion over what role tactical nuclear weapons may play in an actual war. This directly affects the possible usefulness of these weapons because such confusion could well lead to paralysis. As Lawrence Martin has pointed out, "Ambiguity is not synonymous with

confusion, and there is considerable suspicion that the dis-
array in NATO thinking about tactical nuclear weapons is
not only excessive, but could easily inhibit effective action
in crisis."[30]

The advantages of tactical nuclear weapons for defense are
further diminished by a number of problems. First, there are
motivational constraints on the use of TNW. The wish to
avoid crossing the threshold between conventional and nuclear weapons will cause delays in ordering the use of TNW.
As Philip Karber has pointed out, "By the time the decision
to use is made it is unlikely to save the threatened sector."
Second, target acquisition would prove extremely difficult:
"because of multiple simultaneous penetrations and the high-
speed dispersed advance, it is difficult to acquire targets and
respond in time. Area saturation is not effective because the
tactical assault is too close to the defense and there is inter-
penetration in the defensive rear area."[31]

Finally, once both opposing military systems are equipped
with tactical nuclear weapons it is at least debatable that
these weapons would actually favor the defense. Some claim
quite the opposite. Karber determines that "the mutual possession of nuclear artillery probably favours the offensive,"
and stresses that this is likely to be the case especially in
desert warfare where "tactical nuclear forces would blow the
defense with large quantities of relatively low-yield nuclear
weapons."[32] Such advantages to the offensive would yield
incentives to preempt. This is reflected in Soviet nuclear
warfare doctrine, which, according to Jeffrey Record, "continues to emphasize theater nuclear preemption as a means of
carving out corridors for blitzkreig and of liquidating [the
opponent's] means of reinforcements."[33] A recent Congressional study of the role of theater nuclear forces in Europe
concurs that such forces place a high premium on preemption. "Because NATO theater nuclear forces pose a strong
threat to Soviet forces massed for the offensive, the paramount objective of Soviet nuclear strikes would be the destruction of NATO theater nuclear forces."[34] Hence instead
of fostering stability, tactical nuclear weapons are likely to

have the opposite effect. Thus the military rationale for the adoption of tactical nuclear weapons defense (to prevent the massing of forces) is deficient. It seems that on military ground alone there is sufficient reason for Israel to avoid initiating the introduction of tactical nuclear weapons into the Middle East.

There are also important financial and technological drawbacks for Israel to enter the field of tactical nuclear weapons. Contrary to countervalue strategic nuclear weapons, which can be crude and inaccurate and still extremely effective, tactical nuclear weapons require high accuracy of delivery and the miniaturization of warheads. This involves extremely sophisticated technology and enormous financial investments in the research and development of such technology. Furthermore, where a high premium is placed on accuracy and warhead sophistication, the technological race knows no limits. New warheads and delivery vehicles must be researched, developed, and produced constantly. Expensive tests must be conducted. The burden of this course on Israel's economy would be enormous.

In light of some of the above-mentioned problems, Robert Sandoval and Robert Shreffler have suggested that small states adopt a new type of nuclear defense, based on the acquisition and deployment of low-yield nuclear weapons. The "new nuclear force" calls for early and defensive use of "a guided missile of 100 km. range which is tipped with a subkiloton nuclear fission warhead."[35] The doctrine of the early use of such weapons has been advocated by Kenneth Waltz on the grounds that the early use of very small warheads may stop escalation while later use "is riskier because it appears as one more step in a crescendo of violence." Waltz points out that "the attempt to keep war conventional in its initial stage may guarantee that nuclear weapons, if used, will be used in a losing cause in ways that multiply destruction without promising victory."[36] Shreffler argues that the mininuclear force will be extremely effective in its primary task of defeating an aggressor, that it will minimize unwanted damage, that it will be quite invulnerable, and that it will require minimum logistic support. The mininuclear force is expected to provide effective defense and is seen as increasing stability.[37]

There are, however, important reasons to doubt that the introduction of mininuclear defense will have the beneficial effects that its proponents identify. First of all, the proponents derive most of the benefits by asking what effects the "new nuclear force" will have when faced with conventional forces. This is an interesting question but it is also of limited utility. If small-yield nuclear weapons come to be regarded as effective, both opposing parties would quickly opt for them. Therefore, a more realistic question is to ask what effects the adoption of mininuclear forces might have if both parties opt for a mix of conventional forces and mininuclear weapons. Under such circumstances, would the introduction of the mininuclear force still have a stabilizing effect? Would mutual acquisition of such forces still favor the defense?

The reply to both questions appears to be negative. Stability is unlikely to prevail once both opposing parties adopt doctrines calling for very early use of nuclear weapons. In times of crisis each party will fear that the other's early use doctrine will lead it to use its mininuclear weapons first. Mutual temptation to preempt will be considerable. Claims to the contrary rest on the proposition that the mininuclear force will be hardened and hence invulnerable. A hardened force, however, provides an extremely inflexible defense. It may be outmaneuvered if the front is wide enough. In addition, it could lead to a Maginot-Line mentality. Furthermore, the hardening of a large number of small-yield missiles, very expensive for a superpower, is prohibitively expensive for a small state. Finally, whereas it is theoretically possible to harden the missiles of the new nuclear force, other components of the force would remain extremely vulnerable, such as the forward observers and the fire-direction centers, the two critical elements for target acquisition by the new nuclear force.[38] By preempting these two elements through the use of heavy artillery, conventionally armed missiles, low-yield nuclear weapons, or larger-yield theater nuclear weapons, an opponent can neutralize the small-yield nuclear force entirely. The vulnerability of these two critical elements will result in overall system vulnerability. Hence the introduction of mininuclear forces will result in high temptation to preempt.[39] The consequence will be greater instability.

It is also far from certain, under conditions of mutual acquisition of mininuclear forces, that such a force would favor the defense. Steven Canby seems to imply that neither the defense nor the offense would benefit: "[T]he relative advantage of firepower tends to cancel out, and each side is merely likely to have higher casualties."[40] It is also possible that a defensive advantage of mininuclear forces at the tactical level will be exploited in support of an offensive strategy. An opponent might strive to achieve a breakthrough by springing a strategic surprise, using mininuclear and tactical nuclear weapons to preempt Israel's own mininuclear force.[41] He might then attempt to stabilize his gains by exploiting the defensive advantages of the new nuclear force at the tactical level. The overall effect would be to favor the strategic offense.[42] Hence small-yield nuclear weapons are neither stabilizing nor do they necessarily favor the defense. The adoption of the proposed new nuclear force would bring with it all the problems that would appear in opting for larger-yield tactical nuclear weapons.

To sum up, we may conclude that Israel should not attempt a tactical nuclear defense. It is not needed to supplement her strategic nuclear deterrence, and neither large- nor small-yield tactical nuclear forces are able to provide an effective defense. Their adoption would at best have no effect and at worst be detrimental to Israel's security.

Nuclear Deterrence and Terrorism

This section will examine the possible relation between an Israeli nuclear deterrence posture and the frequency and intensity of Arab, particularly Palestinian, terrorism. The

terrorism

term "terrorism" will encompass both field guerrilla warfare, which is commonly called guerrilla warfare, and urban guerrilla warfare, which is commonly called terrorism. I shall limit the discussion here to conventional terrorism. The relation between the adoption of a nuclear posture by Israel and the probability of nuclear terrorism in the region will be taken up in the fourth chapter.

Terrorism is a relatively unimportant issue for Israel. Whether nuclear deterrence increases, decreases, or does not affect its frequency and intensity is simply not very significant. Terrorism is unpleasant and sometimes painful, but in Israel's case it does not constitute a real threat to the state's security. For every Israeli victim of terrorism, five die in traffic accidents. One of the most common criticisms leveled against suggestions that Israel should adopt a nuclear deterrent posture is that such a posture will not provide an answer to terrorism.[43] But once nuclear deterrence is commonly assessed as providing effective deterrence of all other forms of warfare, its adoption would be well worth the investment regardless of its effects on terrorism. The discussion of the possible relation between nuclear deterrence and terrorism must therefore proceed from a balanced appreciation of the limited importance of the question.

The first possibility is that nuclear weapons will have no impact on terrorism. It is based on the general proposition that strategic nuclear weapons cannot affect activity at the subconventional level; the two realms are unconnected. One important possible reason for this lack of connection is that guerrilla or terrorist groups simply do not represent a sufficiently large target. As a consequence, nuclear threats against such groups cannot be meaningful. Such threats also would not be credible even if directed at host states instead of at the terrorist groups. This is likely to be the case precisely because terrorism does not constitute a problem of sufficient importance to merit the utilization of nuclear threats. Israel is unlikely to be willing to pay the political costs of using nuclear punishment over an issue that is of peripheral importance.

No Nuke Deter
Position

Indeed, the view that nuclear deterrence is irrelevant to terrorism is held by the leaders of the Palestinian guerrillas. Farouk Kadoumi, chief spokesman on foreign affairs for the PLO, stated in 1976 that "the Palestinians are guerrilla fighters. We do not care about atom bombs because we are working inside our occupied land."[44] In 1975 PLO leader Yassir Arafat expressed the same view: "We know that Israel possesses five atomic bombs. [However], the bombs do not frighten us [just] as the atomic and thermonuclear bombs of the United States had not frightened the Vietnamese revolutionaries."[45] The PLO's position was stated as far back as 1974 by the Voice of Palestine: "Whether the enemy has nuclear weapons or the technical capability and experience to produce them will not change the activities of our people and it will not make them deviate from their course or weaken their determination to continue the struggle until all the Palestinian soil is liberated."[46] Thus the leaders of the guerrillas facing Israel appear not to be deterred by the perceived possible presence of nuclear weapons in Israel's hands.

The second possible relation between nuclear deterrence and terrorism is that the former may actually result in an increase of the latter. The introduction of nuclear deterrence into the Middle East is expected to constrain the use of conventional capabilities by both Israel and the Arab states. Israel's vulnerability to terrorism would then multiply because she could no longer hit terrorist bases in neighboring Arab states: such punitive actions would be extremely dangerous in a nuclear environment. The net outcome might be that the introduction of nuclear weapons would supply the terrorists with the necessary refuge for a successful war of national liberation. This argument was raised, although not supported, by Fuad Jabber.[47] It seems difficult to dispute. Counterinsurgency operations, and particularly offensive operations involving penetration of enemy territory, are indeed likely to be constrained in a nuclearized environment by the fear of escalation. This seems to promise terrorist movements greater freedom of action.

This argument must immediately be qualified, however:

Maximize Counter
Deter Position

the adoption of a nuclear deterrent posture would both permit and encourage Israel to restructure her conventional forces in a way that would maximize her capability to conduct defensive counterguerrilla warfare. To counter guerrilla warfare is in Israel's case quite inexpensive if it is done surgically and not by saturation. Small increases in investment may yield large returns. If a nuclear deterrent posture can effectively decrease the danger of general conventional war, it would enable Israel to divert resources away from preparing to conduct conventional war and toward strengthening counterguerrilla warfare. Thus, even if Israel's ability to conduct offensive counterguerrilla warfare were constrained in a nuclear environment, her ability to devote more resources to defensive counterinsurgency warfare would be greater.[48] Israel would be better able to reduce the effectiveness of Palestinian terrorism once she adopted a nuclear deterrent posture.

While both types of relation between nuclear deterrence and terrorism may develop, I regard a third possible relation between the two as more likely: that an Israeli nuclear posture would reduce Palestinian terrorism. This would be the consequence of the likely reduction in Palestinian motivation to continue conducting terrorism in a nuclearized environment. A second cause is that Israel's neighboring Arab states would be likely to curtail the terrorists' freedom of action.

The assessment that an Israeli nuclear posture is likely to reduce Palestinian motivation to conduct guerrilla warfare is rooted in the special circumstances of the Palestinian movement, in comparison with circumstances that have characterized other guerrilla movements. Such a comparison shows, for example, that the Vietcong's and North Vietnam's fight against the United States was relatively easy. The preservation of the South Vietnamese government was worth a limited price to the United States; the Vietcong and North Vietnam had merely to raise the actual level of costs beyond this limited level. As it turned out, forty thousand dead, equivalent to six hundred Israelis, was America's limit. The task of the Jewish underground movement in Palestine in the 1940s

Palestinian goal: Israel
Replace

Strategy

was equally easy. The continued occupation of Palestine was worth a limited price to the British; the Jews had merely to raise the actual level of costs beyond that limit. There are more examples, but the lesson is clear: When the distribution of willingness to absorb punishment is uneven, it is fairly easy to win a dispute against the adversary who is less willing by increasing the costs of the conflict.

The Palestinians, however, do not enjoy such an advantage. Their strategic goal, as stated in the Palestinian Covenant, is the creation of a secular Palestinian state in the place of Israel. The importance for Israel of preventing the attainment of the Palestinians' goal is unlimited. There is no cost level beyond which it would not be worthwhile for Israel to oppose the PLO. It is as if the Vietcong aimed to replace not the government in Saigon but the government in Washington, as if the FLN's goal was not to liberate Algeria but to dominate France. From Israel's perspective, the PLO's goal is a matter of national survival. Therefore the PLO cannot simply apply guerrilla warfare strategy. They cannot hope to obtain their goal by simply raising Israel's costs, because there is no limit to the costs Israel would be willing to absorb in order to resist the Palestinians' goal. Faced with this dilemma, the Palestinian guerrilla movements have adopted a strategy that varies slightly from the classical model of guerrilla strategy. They opted for a strategy aimed at causing maximum nuisance to Israeli society in the hope of eliciting Israeli overreactions. These overreactions might hurt some Arab states and thus require their intervention. Thus classical guerrilla strategy was replaced by a catalytic concept of guerrilla war. The attempt to influence the adversary directly by raising costs was replaced by an attempt to involve third parties by inducing the adversary to overreact. The success of guerrilla warfare was no longer a function of the ability to raise costs. Rather, the success of the PLO would be measured by the extent to which it was successful in catalyzing a general Middle East war.

Given the special circumstances of the Palestinian guerrilla movements, Israeli nuclear deterrence could influence the prospects of guerrilla warfare. Once success becomes a function of the ability to catalyze a Middle East general war, Israel's ability to deter general war through nuclear deterrence would completely undermine the logic of Palestinian guerrilla warfare. Since the costs of nuclear war would make Arab states' involvement prohibitively expensive, the catalytic process would fail to develop.[49] The Arab states would be likely to refuse to participate in the game. Thus the Palestinian guerrilla movements would find themselves in an even worse dilemma than previously envisaged. The unlimited nature of their demands renders their attempts to apply classical concepts of guerrilla warfare ineffective. At the same time, nuclear deterrence would undermine the logic of an alternative catalytic conception of such warfare. The Palestinian guerrillas would thus find themselves in a "no-win" situation. Given the costs to themselves of guerrilla warfare, it is highly unlikely that their movement would continue a form of warfare that was a priori hopeless. The risks involved would render the continuation of guerrilla warfare not worth their while.

Paradoxically, because the only logic for Palestinian guerrilla warfare is the catalytic one, a high degree of success would prove an equally effective constraint to guerrilla activity in a nuclearized Middle East. The PLO would have to calculate that if they somehow catalyzed a general war, this war could escalate into a general nuclear war. They would further reckon that the greater their success the greater would become that possibility. In view of the proximity of the Palestinian population of Gaza and the West Bank to Israel, the PLO would have to calculate that Palestinians might suffer enormous casualties in such a nuclear exchange. Success in catalyzing war, thus raising the specter of a Middle East nuclear war, would be dangerous to the Palestinians.

It would thus seem that there is no end to the hopelessness of the Palestinian movements in a nuclearized Middle East. They are restrained from applying classical guerrilla strategy to Israel because the unlimited nature of their goals makes this strategy inapplicable. This is the case whether the region is nuclearized or not. If the Middle East were nuclearized, the catalytic route would also become closed. Palestinian motivation to continue pursuing guerrilla warfare would be much reduced in a nuclear environment because the odds that a catalytic process would develop are very small while the costs to Palestinians if it somehow succeeded might be enormous. Thus, the first reason that nuclear deterrence might reduce guerrilla warfare is that its introduction would decrease Palestinian motivation to pursue such warfare.

The second reason is that their introduction would induce the Arab states to curtail the terrorists' relative freedom of action. Israel's adoption of a nuclear posture would compel the Arab states to put the Palestinian guerrillas under complete control. In a nuclearized environment the possible costs of uncontrolled escalation are extremely high. The Arab states, wishing to avoid such costs, could not allow terrorist movements to operate freely. Thus the existence of Israeli nuclear weapons would compel the Arab states actively to enforce a reduction or total elimination of guerrilla activity against Israel for fear of a process of escalation to a full-scale nuclear war.

An elaboration of this thesis is to be found in the writings of Egypt's Hasanayn Haykal, who stated in 1976:

> Certain people may say that Israel's use of the atomic bomb would not solve its problem. With the bomb it can deter Egypt and Syria, each of which is concerned about its own safety. But what good is the bomb against the Palestinians who have nothing to lose? They have no cities, or factories, water reservoirs or anything at all. The answer is that if Israel can deter Egypt and Syria with the bomb or threaten them without actually using it, we could imagine a new situation in which Egypt and Syria would be afraid of Israel's [nuclear] deterrent force. The Palestinians would be afraid of the Egyptian–Syrian force of [conventional] arms. This would mean that Syria and Egypt would find themselves compelled to maintain Israel's security against the Palestinians. Thus, they would be transformed into a police force for Israel against the Palestinians in order to avoid incalculable tension which might lead to undesired involvement.[50]

Internal terrorism would remain [handwritten annotation]

Thus the second route through which nuclear deterrence may reduce the prospects of guerrilla warfare is compellence. The risks involved in undesired escalation in a nuclear environment would be likely to compel the Arab states to enforce a reduction of Palestinian guerrilla activity.

This discussion of the likely causes for a reduction in terrorist activity following nuclearization should be qualified by emphasizing that it pertains mainly to terrorist acts emanating from outside Israel and the occupied territories. Acts of urban terrorism in Israel, the West Bank, and the Gaza Strip, expressing the local Arab discontent over Israel's prolonged occupation, would likely remain unaffected by the nuclearization process. Israel's internal security forces would have to continue to take care of this problem, Israel's nuclearization notwithstanding.

A separate but related issue involves the relation between Israel's security, nuclear weapons, and a prospective Palestinian state in the West Bank and the Gaza Strip. The question is: to what extent might a separate Palestinian state endanger Israel's security once Israel adopted an overt nuclear posture? The issue is extremely complex and deserves a very thorough analysis. The following discussion will be limited to a few basic observations.

Palestinian state danger [handwritten annotation]

A separate Palestinian state could theoretically endanger Israel's security in four ways: first, the Palestinian state could attempt to construct a potent conventional force in an effort to challenge Israel's survival directly. Second, it could attempt to orchestrate guerrilla warfare against Israel, either in an effort to undermine Israel's very survival or merely in an attempt to induce her to make important concessions. Third, it could provide other Arab armies with a staging area from which to launch an attack against Israel. Fourth, it could acquire nuclear weapons and attempt to compel Israel to concede by threatening to use these weapons. The question to be addressed here is to what extent an Israeli nuclear posture might deter such negative developments.

I shall begin with the third of the dangers enumerated above: the use of the Palestinian state as a springboard for other Arab armies against Israel. The movement of Arab armies into the West Bank would clearly threaten Israel's survival. The presence of such forces so close to Israel's capital and main commercial and industrial centers would place the very existence of the state in extreme jeopardy. Israel would care a great deal about such a development and would take great pains to avoid it. Israel's willingness to run risks in order to prevent such a development would likely be impressive. Thus an Israeli threat to punish Arab states whose forces entered the West Bank should be credible. An Israeli nuclear posture could therefore deter other Arab states from using the territory of the Palestinian state as a staging area against Israel. Hence, the third of the enumerated dangers involved in a prospective Palestinian state would become much less worrisome once Israel adopted a nuclear posture. The implication of this is that in any effort by the Palestinian state to threaten Israel's security, the former would have to stand alone.

The first danger listed above is an attack against Israel by potent conventional forces of the prospective Palestinian state. This, again, would endanger Israel since the West Bank is located extremely close to Israel's essential core. An attack of this sort would threaten Israel's central nervous system. Israeli threats aimed at deterring such an attack are bound to prove extremely credible. Before sending its ground forces against Israel, the Palestinian state's government would have to consider that by conventional bombings alone the Israeli air force would be quite capable of leveling all the major towns and cities of the West Bank and Gaza. Once nuclear deterrence had effectively prevented other Arab states from coming to the Palestinians' aid, an air force that has only recently fought the combined strength of Syria and Egypt could easily destroy all of the important centers of a Palestinian state. The conventional imbalance of power between Israel and the prospective new state should therefore suffice to deter the latter from undertaking any action that might expose her. In the Israeli–Palestinian context, an Israel equipped with nuclear weapons would only underscore this dramatic imbalance. Israel would therefore be expected to be able to deter a Palestinian conventional attack against her once she had adopted a nuclear posture.

The analysis of risks becomes slightly more complex if a nuclear Israel is faced with a nuclear-armed Palestinian state. Each party would then be able to inflict unacceptable punishment on the other. The comparative will of each would be of paramount importance in any effort by the Palestinian state to compel Israel to concede vital matters by threatening the use of nuclear weapons.

Many Israelis are likely to regard the prospect of a nuclear-armed Palestinian state as unacceptable. This would surely influence that state's motivation to acquire nuclear arms: fear of Israeli preemptive action prior to such acquisition would be significant. However, in a world of sovereign states it would be exceedingly difficult to ensure that the Palestinian state would not acquire nuclear arms. Therefore, the strategic implications of such an occurrence must be addressed.

In the event that the Palestinian state would try to compel Israel to concede vital matters by threatening to use nuclear weapons, Israel would manifest great willpower as almost all issues between her and the prospective state would involve her vital interests. By the same token, the prospective Palestinian state would also be likely to demonstrate a great deal of willpower. The Palestinians would perceive the issues as involving their homes and land, and their struggle as aimed at regaining these. The distribution of wills is therefore likely to be much more balanced in this context than in the Israeli–Syrian or Israeli–Egyptian contexts. Nevertheless, a Palestinian effort to force a change in the status quo would meet greater Israeli willpower. While the Palestinian state would be trying to expand its territory, Israel's efforts would be devoted to ensuring the integrity of its own sovereign territory. The distribution of wills would therefore tilt in Israel's favor. Moreover, in any situation where extremely high stakes for both sides are involved, the status quo is guaranteed, because anyone contemplating a change in it would have to calculate that his opposite has extremely high stakes in main-

taining the status quo and would therefore be likely to retaliate. So a Palestinian state contemplating a change in the
status quo would be self-deterred by the high probability of
nuclear punishment.

What we are left with is the second of our enumerated
risks: that the Palestinian state might orchestrate guerrilla
warfare against Israel. Again, this risk would become far less
worrisome once Israel had adopted a nuclear posture. The
probability that the Palestinian state might undertake to conduct or even merely permit guerrilla warfare against a nuclear-armed Israel is very low. Such warfare would elicit an
Israeli response; the Palestinian state would have to react
and Israel would counterreact. Israel would enjoy superior
conventional capabilities and would therefore be able to raise
the stakes consistently. The possibility of uncontrolled escalation between Israel and the Palestinian state would be
very real, while the former's nuclear deterrent would prevent
other Arab states from coming to the Palestinian state's aid.
Aware of these risks, the Palestinian state would probably
refrain from taking the first step. In short, the imbalance of
power between Israel and the prospective Palestinian state
would be large enough to preclude the latter from presenting
serious challenges to the former. An Israeli nuclear posture
would only make this imbalance more dramatic. The leaders
of the new state would have extremely high stakes in maintaining the integrity of their new entity. The two parts of the
prospective state, Gaza and the West Bank, would be con-
nected by a free road, as are West Germany and West Berlin.
Israel's ability to halve the new Palestinian state by merely
blocking this road would deter any leadership interested in
maintaining the integrity of its statehood. Israel's nuclear and
nonnuclear forces would merely provide added weight to this
important deterrent. The extreme vulnerability of the Palestinian state, coupled with the dramatic imbalance of power
between her and Israel, would essentially compel the former
to coexist peacefully with the latter. The PLO's Abu Iyad
merely reflected a recognition of reality when he recently
stated that "subversive Palestinian activities would end on

the day we shall have a state to lead—and above all to maintain." He predicted that in such a state even rejectionists like George Habash would behave as respectable citizens.[51]

The role of Israeli nuclear weapons in deterring the prospective Palestinian state has been singled out three times by PLO leader Yassir Arafat. On the first two occasions he was asked whether such a state might not endanger Israel's security and both times he responded that it is the Palestinian state's security that would constantly be endangered. "We would live at peace with all our neighbors. But it is we who need protection, not Israel. Israel has 12 to 15 atomic bombs. I know."[52] On the third occasion, as late as September 1979, when Arafat was interviewed by ABC's Barbara Walters, he failed to commit the prospective Palestinian state to a coexistence with Israel. Walters attempted to summarize the discussion to the effect that the PLO indeed strives for the destruction of the Jewish state. Arafat interrupted her: "To destroy Israel? Israel has atomic weapons, twelve or fifteen such weapons. Israel is a great power in the Middle East. You must not forget that it is we who are the victims. You only worry about Israel's security and her borders. What about us?"[53] Arafat's statements thus reflect the perception that the distribution of power between Israel and the prospective Palestinian state would favor the former dramatically. This is likely to provide Israel with effective deterrence vis-à-vis the future Palestinian state.

Nuclear weapons' ability to provide Israel with effective specific deterrence has been the focus of this chapter. A number of points were made: first, that under specified conditions nuclear weapons would enable Israel to deter limited challenges such as limited conventional attacks or wars of attrition; second, that Israel would not need to deploy tactical nuclear weapons in order to deter specific lower-level challenges; third, that the most likely effect on guerrilla warfare of the adoption of a nuclear posture is that the frequency and intensity of the latter would diminish. Furthermore, nuclear weapons would also be likely to reduce the dangers involved in the creation of an independent Palestinian state. Thus on various levels nuclear weapons could provide Israel with effective specific deterrence. The adoption of a nuclear posture would hence be expected to reduce the danger of wars by deterring Israel's neighbors from initiating them.

Nuclear would provide deter

CHAPTER 4

The Risks of a Nuclear Middle East

The past two chapters have been devoted to the advantages of nuclear deterrence. It was argued that the adoption of a nuclear posture can offer Israel effective general deterrence. In addition, I stressed that under specified conditions the adoption of that posture might also provide Israel with effective specific deterrence. I shall now turn to some of the risks likely to originate from within a nuclear Middle East subsystem.

Critics of nuclear proliferation, and particularly of Israel's adoption of a nuclear posture, have been extremely insightful in pointing out the risks entailed in such a move.[1] I shall devote uneven attention to ten different risks. They are: first, problems resulting from the level of rationality in the Middle East; second, problems in the level of conceptualization about the uses of nuclear weapons; third, the danger that nuclear weapons may simply be included in present "war fighting" strategies; fourth, the danger that Israel might not be able to match the aggregate nuclear forces of a number of Arab states; fifth, the problem of controlling escalation in a system of many nuclear powers; sixth, the problem of calculation in a multinuclear Middle East, including possible ambiguity of the sources of attack; seventh, the possibility of "catalytic war"; eighth, maintaining adequate control of weaponry; ninth, vulnerability of command and control facilities; tenth, the possibility that nuclear proliferation might encourage small groups to conduct acts of nuclear terrorism.

Among the risks associated with the proliferation of nuclear weapons the one arousing the most widely expressed concern is that such weapons will be acquired and used by irrational decision-makers. Newcomers to the nuclear club are considered immature, hence both irresponsible and unpredictable.[2] Michael Mandelbaum recently asserted that "the farther the bomb spreads from the confines of the industrial circumference, the greater are the chances that it would find its way into the hands of persons who would not show the prudence that the guardians of existing nuclear stockpiles have so far displayed."[3] This concern was raised in the mid 1960s by both Raymond Aron and Stanley Hoffmann.[4] At the same time, some analysts associate high risks of irrationality with the present members of the nuclear club as well.[5] David Krieger, for example, produces possible situations involving irrational behavior by a new Chinese leadership.[6] The concern that irrational decision makers might level the Middle East with nuclear weapons is most widely expressed. Alan Dowty, for example, has pointed out that all theories of deterrence, including Mutual Assured Destruction, assume a steely cold rationality. Yet, asks Dowty, "who can say that one party, feeling war inevitable (as it often seems in Arab–Israel crises) and the use of nuclear weapons probable, will not strike a pre-emptive blow at the other's nuclear forces—even though he knows he cannot destroy them all?"[7] Yair Evron has stated the irrationality argument clearly: "The level of rationality of some of the leaders in the Arab world and the highly irresponsible behavior of some of the other leaders suggest that nuclear weapons in the Middle East, far from necessarily stabilizing relations in that troubled and tormented region, might in fact lead to the first full-scale nuclear war in the world."[8]

Little doubt should exist that enormous dangers are entailed in the irrational use of nuclear power. Nuclear weapons in the hands of a crazy leader, independent of control from

Hussain ?,

other echelons in the command structure, may indeed make for unmitigated disaster. The problem of irrational behavior cannot be easily dismissed. There are, however, some dubious assumptions underlying the question of irrationality. One such thought seems to be that underdevelopment is a cause of irresponsible behavior—else why would the likelihood of irrational behavior be greater in the Middle East than in the realm of Soviet–American relations? Yet the belief that underdevelopment is linked to irrationality is neither explicitly stated nor even minimally supported. Hence it is not very surprising that in the Third World it is both rejected and regarded as having racist connotations. As Sisir Gupta pointed out when the irrationality issue was raised about India some years ago: "No Indian can accept the underlying assumption, in many Western discussions of the dangers of proliferation, that there is necessarily a correlation between under-development and irresponsible behavior and that nuclear weapons in the hands of a new nation are like guns in the hands of juvenile delinquents."[9]

Second, assertions with respect to the particular irrationality of the people of the Middle East also remain unsupported by evidence. Proponents of the thesis have not made an effort to support it beyond mentioning that Nasser's behavior in the 1967 crisis is an example of irrational policy-making.[10] The single example of Nasser's miscalculations of Israeli intentions in 1967 will not sustain a strong association of irrationality with underdevelopment. Nasser was surprised by the Israeli air strike on June 5 and he did underestimate the strength of the Israeli defense forces. Nevertheless, he had taken the possibility of an Israeli attack into account. As Steven Rosen has already pointed out, "Nasser's 1967 miscalculation in Sinai may look no worse than Truman's misassessment of China's willingness to intervene in Korea, or Kennedy's groundless expectation that the Bay of Pigs incursion would trigger a popular uprising against Castro."[11] And, one might add, Nasser's mistake was no greater than Soviet misassessments of America's willpower as reflected in the Soviet decisions to place ballistic missiles in Cuba in

1962 and to challenge America in Berlin in 1948 and 1961. Nor is it greater than Israel's misassessment of the likelihood of war in October 1973, than Soviet misassessments of Hitler's intentions in 1941, than Britain's and France's misassessments of 1956 that led to the Suez fiasco, than Japan's misassessment of America's willingness to defend its interests in the Far East that led to the attack on Pearl Harbor. Geoffrey Blainey's *The Causes of War* is full of examples of miscalculations and misassessments made by the very nations that are now considered to be among the most advanced. There is no evidence that the Middle East is more prone to such mistakes than the more advanced European states.

A nuclearized environment may be as subject to miscalculations as a nonnuclear one. But the high price that is associated with mistakes in a sensitive environment also forces the parties involved to reassess their behavior constantly. Such reassessments have on occasion led states to pull back despite enormous loss of prestige. Thus the United States withdrew from the Bay of Pigs, the USSR eased the pressure on West Berlin and withdrew its missiles from Cuba; the French and British withdrew their forces from Egypt.

The third weakness of the irrationality hypothesis is that it is overused. It was applied again and again to societies that Western analysts found difficult to understand—first to the Soviet Union[12] and later to China and India,[13] but so far no evidence supports it. Instead, the evidence supports Bernard Brodie's comment of more than twenty years ago, that the allegation that "Soviet leaders, when faced with issues of peace and war, would be indifferent to the loss of individual cities and certainly of populations grossly distorts and exaggerates some undeniable and important differences between the Soviet system and our own."[14]

This leads us to a final point—to question whether rationality is required for successful deterrence. As the above examples indicate, it is quite possible that for purposes of successful deterrence a more modest demand that the parties manifest a *sensitivity to costs* may suffice. In fact, even Idi Amin (Dada) and Muammar Qaddhafi, two most fashionable

Irrationality still sensitive to costs

examples of irrationality, have demonstrated their sensitivity to costs. The former did his best to mock and discredit Britain but only until the sending of British troops became a distinct possibility. Despite his verbal bellicosity, Amin did not venture to conduct any crazy action against Israel in response to Entebbe. Qaddhafi's own sensitivity to costs, again despite impressive verbal aggressiveness, was reflected in 1977 in his quick withdrawal of the action against Egypt once a military invasion by Egyptian forces became more than a slight possibility. Nor did Qaddhafi react irrationally to Israel's downing a Libyan Boeing 707 commercial airliner in 1973. Even a more "advanced" leader might have reacted more violently than Qaddhafi did at the time.[15] In 1980 Qaddhafi sent his forces into Chad and in 1981 he began to harass the Sudan. He displayed a willingness to pursue such activities as long as they remained relatively cost-free. However, once the United States, France, Egypt began to threaten punitive action seriously, Qaddhafi quickly terminated the border clashes with Sudan and withdrew his forces from Chad.[16] Amin may have been cruel enough to slaughter members of disliked tribes, but he was sensitive to punitive actions that threatened his ability to rule. Qaddhafi may be as radical as he would like us to believe, but he is careful to shy away from any action that may undermine his support among the armed forces and population. Thus, to sustain a high level of profits Libya continues to fuel the "Western imperialists" with her oil.

Replacing the demand that decision makers be rational with the more modest demand that they be sensitive to costs may be justified by yet another reason—namely, that more perfect rationality may be counterproductive for deterrence. Deterrence in a nuclear environment may at times be the product of irrational fears of a nuclear holocaust, which cause paralysis even when rationality would indicate that action is possible and could be carried out with impunity. As Robert Jervis points out, "irrationality could also lead a state to passive acquiescence when rational grasp of the situation would lead to belligerence."[17] Similar notions have led Patrick

Morgan to prefer the term "sensible decision making." In Morgan's opinion, the sensible decision-maker considering attack is inhibited not as much by the prospects of large costs as by his inability to calculate the costs at all. "To attack is to step into the unknown where the consequences could be terrible not just if the worst happens but because it is not clear just what the worst is."[18] If sensitivity to costs is a sufficient substitute for the more complex concept of rationality, opponents to the adoption of a nuclear deterrent posture by Israel have a more difficult case to make. They must demonstrate that the Arabs are less sensitive to costs than are states presently possessing nuclear weapons. I see no such evidence. Although rationality and sensitivity to costs are difficult to prove, statements that those qualities are lacking in the Middle East deserve a great measure of skepticism.

A second cause of alarm about a nuclear Middle East is the assumed low level of conceptualization about the uses of nuclear weapons among the region's leaders. Alarm about this was first expressed by Robert Pranger and Dale Tahtinen, who feared that the worst outcomes might result from proliferation into a region that lacks a code for nuclear conduct. "The most dangerous element in nuclear proliferation among nations outside the realm of this web of policy, deterrence, technology and communication between Moscow and Washington is that beyond this almost ritualized, bilateral relationship there is no ritual, and in certain instances, not even bilateral relations. In the Middle East no significant formal or informal relationships between the Arab government and Israel exist, to say nothing of a code for nuclear conduct, should such weapons be introduced into this tumultuous setting."[19] The main point here is that if the proliferation of nuclear weapons is not coupled with the development of a doctrine for their use, the worst may result. In the absence of doctrines, the parties cannot develop a doctrinal dialogue, without which a mutually shared code for nuclear conduct will not emerge. If such a code does not emerge, there can be no agreement on thresholds and therefore, it is assumed, the task of controlling escalation may prove to be impossible.

To put these fears in proper perspective, three points must be stressed: first, as some of the quotations from the Arab press reveal, appreciation of the costs of nuclear war, of the distribution of these costs, and of the constraints imposed by these costs on Arab freedom of action is already developing.

Second, the development of weapons preceded the development of doctrine in all of the nuclear states. The present level of discussion in the Middle East is no less sophisticated than that which characterized the initial period following the nuclearization of other states. In the case of India, the newest member of the club, it seems that a doctrine has not been developed to this very day. In both French and British cases the development of doctrines appears to have been an effort to supply a rationale for the political decision to go nuclear. In neither country was the initial development of weapons associated with the identification of possible opponents.

Third, as has already been pointed out, socialization to the realities of nuclear life is likely to increase with the open introduction of nuclear weapons into the area. Probably the most important effect of the adoption of an *overt* nuclear posture would be the development of a code for nuclear conduct. The socialization of a large part of the political, military, and intellectual elites to the constraints imposed by nuclear weapons would be the greatest advantage of making the nuclear posture an overt one.

Finally, we should point out that Pranger and Tahtinen's assertion of the absence of formal and informal relations between Israel and the Arab governments is not entirely accurate. Informal meetings between Israeli and Arab leaders have periodically taken place. They have allowed for a frank exchange of opinions. Had nuclear weapons been openly introduced at the time, the discussion could have included their implications as well. Following the Israeli–Egyptian 1979 peace agreement, new opportunities for exchanging views are available. Formal and relatively open relations between the government of Israel and that of the largest of the Arab states have been established. The opportunities for mitigating the kinds of problems envisaged by Pranger and Tahtinen would henceforth increase dramatically.

A third source of risks associated with the introduction of nuclear weapons into the Middle East is the question of what impact traditional strategic-military patterns of behavior would have under the new circumstances. In contrast to the superpowers, in the Middle East nuclear weapons will be superimposed on a heated conflict with a tradition of thirty years of warfare. This is very different from the position of the United States and the Soviet Union. The two had no historical conflict between them much before the introduction of nuclear weapons. A fear often expressed is that the possibility that nuclear weapons will be used increases when such weapons are introduced into a traditionally volatile conflict. The second and related aspect of the historical problem is the impact of traditionally conflictive patterns of behavior on the likely performance of the respective bureaucracies. Yair Evron has suggested that the long tradition of war and violence may lead to the inclusion of nuclear weapons in existing "war-fighting" doctrines. As he puts it, "the military establishments, because of their inbuilt bureaucratic conservatism and because of the centrality of the war-fighting mission for the armed forces, may consider nuclear weapons as instruments for warfare rather than as deterrents."[20] Indeed, if the Mideast states, and particularly their military establishments, were to come to regard nuclear weapons as simply "more of the same," the probability of these weapons being actively used would increase almost to the point of certainty.

However, on both the general and the specific bureaucratic levels there are reasons to doubt that the risk of actual use of nuclear weapons is any graver in the Middle East setting. On the one hand it is an undeniable fact that in the Middle East nuclear weapons will be introduced into states that have already met each other at least five times in the battlefield. This obviously does have some impact on their approach and patterns of behavior. It clearly distinguishes this case from that of the United States and the USSR, who have never engaged each other in battle. Yet it seems unlikely that this would make enough of a difference to lead to actual use of nuclear weapons. Although it lacked duration, the Soviet–American conflict was extremely heated when nuclear weapons were introduced. The ideological cleavage was very intense, yet it had not led to the use of nuclear weapons. Furthermore, the United States, the Soviet Union, and France have all integrated nuclear weapons into their respective war-fighting strategies. The employment of nuclear weapons is a central feature of both NATO and the Warsaw Pact doctrines. Yet so far this has led neither to a nuclear war nor to the adoption of a "more of the same" attitude about nuclear weapons. During both wars the United States has fought since becoming nuclear, the Joint Chiefs of Staff have not submitted a single request to use nuclear weapons. At one point during the Korean War, the critical December of 1950, General Douglas MacArthur demanded that strategic bombing of China be carried out. However, he did not explicitly demand that China be bombed with nuclear weapons. MacArthur was in desperate trouble at the time; yet it is not clear whether he had intended that strategic bombing would include the use of such weapons.[21] What is clear is that the Joint Chiefs of Staff never asked the President for permission to use nuclear weapons during the Korean War. The same applies to the Vietnam War. Brodie reports that during the latter war "there was no real consideration of using nuclear weapons."[22] This is directly relevant to the bureaucratic-politics level as well. Although the United States, the Soviet Union, Britain, and France have all participated in two world wars in this century, the patterns of military-strategic behavior acquired did not induce them to take a "more of the same" approach when integrating nuclear weapons into their war-fighting strategies. A recent testimony of the military bureaucracy's position indicates that "the [U.S.] Army does not advocate reliance on nuclear weapons and does not want a nuclear war but does believe that nuclear weapons will have to be there for deterrence, and the deterrence comes from our being ready to use them."[23] Similarly, the reality of nuclear war-fighting as an integral part of Soviet "military science" has not lead the Soviets to the actual employment of nuclear weapons. Neither did it lead them to regard nuclear war in a cavalier fashion. In a recent official statement, they flatly reject the notion that a nuclear war can be fought and won: "[T]he Soviet Union holds that nuclear war would be a universal disaster and that it would most probably mean the end of civilization. It may lead to the destruction of all mankind. There may be no victor in such a war, and it can solve no political problems."[24]

A psychological explanation has also been offered for the lack of enthusiasm by military bureaucracies about nuclear war, even a limited one: military men do not like dirty weapons.[25] Nuclear weapons are ill-fitted for satisfying the generals' quest for victory. In the first place, military men have an aversion to anything that threatens to make the battlefield messy. Thus, armies that participated in World War I emerged from it convinced that chemical warfare is not the way to fight. None used chemical weapons during World War II. Second, military leaders are bothered by uncertainty as to how the individual soldier is likely to behave amid nuclear explosions. Their aversion to the use of nuclear weapons seems to be based on both these notions.

A similar attitude toward nuclear weapons is bound to develop in the Middle East. My own survey of Arab verbal and written statements since the October 1973 war about nuclear weapons does not yield the slightest indication that Arabs would regard these weapons as simply more of the same. On the contrary, almost all references to the possible introduction of these weapons into the area imply realization of the profound change they bring. The common denominator of almost all references to the introduction of such weapons is a statement made in 1975 by Egypt's then Minister of War, General Gamassy, to the effect that "the introduction of nuclear weapons into the area *will create a new* and dangerous *situation*."[26] President Sadat also observed that the introduction of such weapons will create "a completely new situation,"[27] and on another occasion stressed their deterrent, not war-fighting, role: "I stated my position. I said I am not going to use the atomic weapons in any war except as a retaliation."[28] Egypt's Chief of Staff, General Muhammad Ali Fahmi, discussed nuclear weapons in terms of their "deterrent power,"[29] while its Minister of Defense, General Ahmad Badawi, emphasized their deterrent role.[30] References of this sort by the men in charge of the Egyptian armed forces from 1974 to 1981 hardly support the proposition that nuclear weapons will be regarded as simply one more war-fighting weapon. Almost all references to nuclear weapons in the Arab press during the period surveyed refer to these weapons, either explicitly or implicitly, in terms of deterrence. The argument predicting their inclusion in existing war-fighting strategies is simply not strong enough.

A fourth risk sometimes associated with the introduction of nuclear weapons into the Middle East is that Israel would find itself confronting Arab nuclear coalitions. Yair Evron suggests different types of nuclear coalitions that might evolve. He further suggests that Israel might not be able to match the aggregate nuclear forces of a number of Arab states.[31] The risk is that the asymmetry in military and financial capabilities would result in Israel losing the nuclear arms race. However, it is doubtful that the aggregation of nuclear forces will be meaningful strategically. In addition, it is questionable that such aggregation would occur.

In both their countervalue and their counterforce roles, the achievement of numerical superiority through aggregation is not very significant. In their countervalue or deterrent role, nuclear weapons are relatively nonadditive. Because only a small number of weapons is required to cause unacceptable damage in Israel, they are likely to be acquired by *each* of the nuclearized Arab states. To combine their nuclear forces would not improve the Arab position; multiplying their overkill capability would not materially add to their deterrent power. The marginal utility of additional warheads declines in view of the finite number of important military, industrial, and civilian targets that a force must be able to destroy with confidence.[32] The fact that all parties would be able to inflict unacceptable damage is extremely important for the achievement of effective deterrence. That some parties would be able to multiply their overkill capability does not substantially reduce mutually effective deterrence. This is likely to be reflected at times of crisis as well. As John Steinbruner has argued, "in crisis the technical details of the balance are irrelevant to decision makers; they can attend only to the mass destructiveness of only a few nuclear weapons. The decision maker would make very conservative assumptions in attack planning and would not be concerned with the degree of the retaliatory threat; he would simply expect retaliation or not expect it and that is all that matters for deterrence."[33] Therefore, as long as Israel maintains a survivable deterrent, relative balance does not matter much.

In a counterforce role, the number of nuclear weapons at each side's disposal matters only if the disparities are enough to provide one of the parties with a first-strike capability. Numerical superiority in nuclear weapons is meaningless unless this superiority is so dramatic that the state's retaliatory capability can be seriously threatened.[34] As we have seen in the second chapter, Israel's retaliatory force would be secured by a number of mutually reinforcing elements. It is unlikely that numerical superiority alone would be sufficient to erode this security. Since the achievement of a first-strike capability would be technologically unfeasible, numerical superiority would not matter much, whether for deterrence or for counterforce. This is expressed in Henry Kissinger's well-known lament, "What in the name of God is strategic [nuclear] superiority? What is the significance of it politically, militarily, operationally at these levels of numbers? What do you do with it?"[35]

The Arabs are likely to refrain from combining into nuclear coalitions for another reason: They would face enormous difficulties in structuring such coalitions. Nuclear retaliation requires almost instantaneous decisions. But a nuclear coalition implies that decisions must be made by conference. A deterrent, to be of any force, would have to be operable in

Arab coalition? of Nationalistic [handwritten annotation]

hours, and certainly not in days.[36] The present reality makes the prospect of a quick political decision in the Arab world unlikely. Furthermore, each Arab state would require a veto power over the decision to use nuclear weapons. In the light of the enormous consequences such use might have, it is extremely doubtful that any Arab states would be willing to forego such veto power. The creation of a nuclear coalition also requires that the participating states would reach agreement as to how the decision to use nuclear weapons will be taken. By a majority vote? By all or a majority of a subcommittee? Any suggestion would raise the most acute questions of national sovereignty. States that have consistently resisted delegating authority on economic matters to supranational bodies are extremely unlikely to delegate the authority to decide whether or not they would continue to exist. Arnold Toynbee expressed this vividly by suggesting that states would proclaim "No annihilation without representation."[37]

Nuclear sharing implies physical sharing in strategic weapon systems, political sharing in strategic decisions, and specialized command and control arrangements. Arab states are extremely unlikely to reach agreement on any of these three. The difficulties that NATO countries have encountered in attempting to devise some form of nuclear sharing indicates how grave are the problems involved.[38] In the more fragmented Middle East such nuclear sharing would face even greater difficulties. Indeed, the most probable outcome of Mideast nuclearization is further fragmentation and a large measure of mutual disassociation. If anything, the most likely result of regional nuclearization is the obsolescence of alliances. The price of nuclear war "is so horrendous that no country can afford to take the risk unless its own vital interests are at stake."[39] Hence, the likelihood that the introduction of nuclear weapons would lead the Arab states not to unite against Israel, but to develop even greater rivalries among themselves.

A multinuclear Middle East is unlikely to lead to greater inter-Arab cohesion. Some indications of this can already be found. Since 1979 press reports appeared to the effect that

Iraq's nuclear program is causing substantial anxiety in a number of Arab countries. Saudi Arabia and the United Arab Emirates were reported to have expressed their opposition to the Iraqi–French nuclear deal, while Syria, Iran, and Egypt "have all made appeals to Paris to put dampers on Iraq's development of nuclear energy—and arms."[40] Syria's first ventures into nuclear energy were reported to be motivated by concern over Iraq's nuclear program.[41] Similarly, Saudi Arabia's willingness to provide financial support for Pakistan's nuclear program was reported to be aimed at preventing Pakistani–Libyan or Pakistani–Iraqi nuclear cooperation.[42] Yet there is little ground for expecting that the greater fragmentation likely to result from nuclear proliferation would lead to inter-Arab nuclear exchanges. Rather, a system of mutual nuclear deterrence would be likely to characterize the multinuclear Middle East. This is illustrated by a statement made by Egypt's Minister of Defense, General Ahmad Badawi, in 1980: "The day that [Libya's leader Muammar] Qaddhafi obtains a nuclear bomb, we shall also acquire such a weapon, not in order to use it against Libya, but rather in order to deter him from using it against us."[43] At any rate, we see that the aggregation of a number of Arab states' nuclear forces would not significantly affect the stability of Israel's nuclear deterrent, and that such aggregation is also unlikely to occur.

The fifth and sixth problems presented by the specter of multiple ownership of nuclear weapons are highly related. The difficulty of precise calculations and the danger of uncontrolled escalation have much in common. The first was elaborated by Stanley Hoffmann: "The dominant factor [in a system of many nuclear states] is the increasing difficulty of adequate calculations in a crisis. The more nuclear powers there are, the more uneven will be their stage of nuclear development, the more complicated calculations will be, the more dangerous yet likely misperceptions will become."[44] The Middle East is a multipower subsystem. Once four or five of the region's states acquire nuclear weapons, the subsystem's characteristics of eighteenth- and nineteenth-century Europe will be superimposed by nuclear weapons. Could such a system be stable? Could escalation be controlled in such an environment? The debate on the relation between the number of powers in the system and its stability is not new.[45] It seems that stability decreases with every increase in the number of powers in the system. The reason for this is that the larger the number of powers, the greater the problem of achieving a stable balance of forces and the greater the difficulty of controlling escalation.

Balancing becomes more difficult in a multipower world for two reasons: first, the attention a state can give to each of the other states decreases with every increase in the number of states possessing the capability to threaten its survival and security.[46] Each state's intelligence community must divide its attention among a larger number of objects and must spread its work more thinly. As a result, military developments, even breakthroughs, may go unnoticed and dangerous imbalances may occur. States may very well be tempted to exploit the temporary imbalance. Decreased attention would thus create instabilities, sometimes leading to war.

The second reason why balancing becomes more difficult the greater the number of powers in the system is that in a system of two large powers most of the balancing is internal. Each superpower attempts to balance the military developments of the other by developments of its own. When one power develops a weapons system, the other reacts by developing a similar system and/or a countervailing system. Such developments are usually slow, a matter of years even in the techno-electronic era. Hence they are vulnerable to detection by intelligence. Timely detection allows for the development of countermeasures before hopeless imbalances are created. In a multipower world most of the balancing is done externally, by constantly shifting coalition partners. This may occur much faster since shifting coalition membership merely requires a political decision that can be swiftly implemented. Thus an imbalance may be created and exploited before countervailing measures can be adopted by other states. Given the temptation of states to exploit imbalances by war, a system of many powers must be regarded as less stable.

An increase in the number of powers also increases the difficulty of controlling escalation, for a number of reasons. First, as mentioned earlier, the degree of attention each power can allocate to each of the other powers decreases with every increase in the number of powers in the system. The consequence of this is that reduced capability of states to monitor each other's action, leading to more uncertainty, would create a tendency to overreact. Escalation may occur more quickly; its control is likely to be more difficult.

Second, in a system of many nuclear states, escalation is likely to be accelerated by the party possessing the most rudimentary nuclear force. The reason for this is that a state possessing a small number of weapons as well as primitive delivery systems would lack "flexible response" options. The threat of being disarmed would provide an incentive to use its maximum strength early. The wish to maintain the ability to retaliate against the adversary's cities would dictate that weapons not be "wasted" on his forces. The primitive state would have few, if any, counterforce options and would necessarily escalate quickly to countervalue retaliation.

Third, even though nuclear coalitions have been discounted, states enjoying close relations might be able to involve each other in nuclear war. Such a relationship implies that an escalatory step taken by one state may commit a large number of states. States are likely to take balancing or bandwagoning measures, in both cases escalating the overall level of conflict. Controlling escalation would thus become more difficult. Both the second and the third points are demonstrated by the purposes of the French nuclear strategy. It is based on the assumption "that the French nuclear force could serve, in case of an extreme provocation against France or Western Europe, as a 'trigger' of the American nuclear arsenal."[47] One hypothetical situation has the United States and the Soviet Union limiting warfare to the battlefield. As France gets tired of observing Europe annihilated by theater nuclear weapons, it launches a demonstrative countercity attack. This elicits a chain of American and Soviet reactions. In such a context, restraints carefully developed by other states prior to hostilities would be to no avail; efforts at control would fail once a single party perceived a need to retaliate against its adversary's cities.

Difficulties of controlling escalation in a world of many nuclear states would only add to the inherent difficulties of controlling nuclear war. Some analysts are optimistic, stressing that men and states have often found ways to limit war. They claim that there is little reason for concern that failure of nuclear deterrence would necessarily bring catastrophe.[48] Alain C. Enthoven believes that the ability to limit nuclear war "depends on our will to make it so."[49] The statement may be valid; yet even if there is the will, there are good reasons to doubt that it would be easy to limit a nuclear war once initiated.[50]

To qualify the optimistic view we should point out that although it is true that most wars throughout history were limited, the reason may have been that the resources mobilized by the parties to the conflict prior to the initiation of hostilities were limited. Far more rare are the instances of war being kept limited by refraining from use of existing capabilities.[51] In the nuclear era, the indiscriminate effect of nuclear weapons, coupled with the sheer size of the destruction created by the individual weapon, will make it very difficult to keep war limited. True, nuclear weapons can be miniaturized almost to conventional dimensions, but that makes it even less likely that a war can be fought without becoming nuclear. As Pierre Gallois has pointed out, the miniaturization of nuclear explosives and the enlargement of the destructive power of conventional weapons has created a long continuum. "From the machine gun to the thermonuclear ballistic missile, each side possesses the complete scale of the means necessary to obliterate the other." A continuum implies the absence of clear thresholds. Each side fears that should it take the first step up the ladder there would be no clear place to stop. As Gallois put it, "The destructive power of the opposing panoplies has three characteristics: it is graduated, continuous, and infinite. To make use of it, starting from any stage of destruction, means to risk one by one the steps which lead to the irremediable."[52]

Finally, the essential element needed for war limitation—clear saliences that permit each party to know what the other has refrained from doing—will be extremely difficult to obtain under the conditions of nuclear war. The demands such a war would place on the nerves of the command and control echelons and on the operation of the communications system will be enormous. Decision-makers at all levels would be overtaxed by the shock and confusion of nuclear explosions. Under such conditions decision-makers are likely to find it exceedingly difficult to discover salient thresholds. The speed with which nuclear war is likely to be waged will further tax decision-makers by reducing the time available for thought and the discovery of saliences.[53] The technical problems involved in verifying whether or not a threshold has been crossed are also likely to be enormous. For example, it would be extremely difficult to verify whether an adversary has exploded 4-kiloton rather than 6-kiloton weapons.

In the Middle East, a war between nuclear-armed states would be conducted on these states' territory, rather than on the soil of some peripheral proxies. Such a nuclear war would be extremely difficult to control because the pressures on decision-makers just described are likely to be far greater once direct attacks are involved. It is noteworthy that most expressions of optimism regarding the ability to control nuclear war between the United States and the Soviet Union assumed that such a war would avoid the territories of the two giants. Few were optimisitc about the ability to control a nuclear war on the European continent and fewer assumed that such a war could involve Soviet and American territory and yet remain limited.[54] Brodie wrote that limited war "practically always connotes a war in which there is no strategic bombing between the United States and the Soviet Union. . . . [A] situation which admitted some strategic bombing with nuclear weapons would be simply too near the blow-out point where restraints of any kind are abandoned."[55] When more than two states are involved, the probability that a nuclear war could be controlled is even smaller. Brodie once said that "it takes only one to start a total war, but it take two to keep a war limited."[56] In a system of many nuclear states it would take many more to keep the war limited. The failure of one will be the failure of all.

To sum up, if war occurs among states armed with nuclear weapons, its costs would inevitably be greater than those associated with a war of conventional defense. If war occurs and limitations fail between nuclear deterrent-armed states, the consequences may be horrifying. That states would fail to limit a nuclear war is far from certain, but the danger that it would rapidly escalate to an unlimited war is hardly negligible. When more than two nuclear states are involved, the danger that a nuclear war will escape control is very real.

The considerations elaborated above all point to the conclusion that an increase in the number of nuclear powers significantly complicates the task of achieving a stable balance of forces and controlling escalation. This would support the proposition that an Israeli nuclear posture, leading to a multinuclear Middle East, may be detrimental to Israeli security.

Fortunately, however, a number of factors mitigate this grim conclusion slightly. The first is that in the realm of nuclear forces the importance of precise calculations of capabilities is diminished with the reduced importance of precise balance. In the realm of conventional weapons a small advantage may be exploited to produce a large victory. To threaten a first nuclear strike, however, a state would need a tremendous imbalance of forces in its favor. Only with a dramatic imbalance may one enjoy partial immunity from retaliation. As long as one does not suffer a dramatically negative imbalance, the capability to threaten retaliation credibly is assured. The fact that precise balancing is less critical in the nuclear era is reflected in the development of American strategic thinking. It was first thought that a preponderance of nuclear forces is necessary to ensure security. Later, "parity" became the slogan, only to be replaced by the more moderate demand for "essential equivalence." Lately, it is commonly accepted that a situation of "rough equivalence" adequately provides stability.

Second, swift shifts in coalition membership are less likely to create critical imbalances in the realm of nuclear weapons. As a consequence of the relative nonadditivity of nuclear weapons, the movement of a nuclear state from one coalition of nuclear states to another is less able to undermine stability than had been the case in the era of purely conventional weapons. Since the nuclear force of a given state will not significantly add to the total deterrent power of the coalition it joins there is little fear of dangerous imbalance.

Finally, in the realm of nuclear weapons the cost of uncontrolled escalation will be enormous. This will create strong incentives for states to disassociate themselves from each other's actions. This likely disassociation will reduce the chance that an escalatory step taken by a single state would commit a whole group of states, thus resulting in catastrophe. A strong interest would emerge among the large number of moderate nuclear states to isolate the few more reckless. Disassociation, the opposite of coalition formation, would diminish the prospect of bilateral conflicts escalating to systemic war. Nuclearized Egypt, Saudi Arabia, Jordan, and even Syria would be likely to disassociate themselves from each other and particularly from Libya and Iraq. To reduce the possibility that the latter two would involve them in a suicidal war with Israel, the former four are likely to threaten at least tacitly that a Libyan or Iraqi strike against Israel might result in a nuclear retaliation of their own.

Nevertheless, the risks of uncontrolled escalation cannot be eliminated easily. The horrifying costs of nuclear war are precisely what makes nuclear deterrence so effective. But the enormity of the consequences of a possible failure of nuclear deterrence cannot be lightly dismissed.[57] Thus the risk of uncontrolled nuclear devastation should be taken very seriously. This is true particularly for the Middle East, where more than two nuclear states are likely to be involved.

Some serious attention should also be given to the possibility of catalytic nuclear war. The problem is to an extent a subrisk of the general problem of controlling escalation in a system of many nuclear states.[58] Evron regards catalytic warfare as a very real possibility in the Middle East. He notes that the behavior of some of the Mideast states, such as Syria, Libya, and Algeria, have always had many catalytic features, and that the preconditions for catalytic warfare exist in the Middle East. There would be, he says,

> strong motivation among some Arab states to initiate military confrontations between Israel and a third Arab country, [and] the short distances involved would make detection and early warning less reliable than in the superpower context. One relevant scenario could be the proliferation of relatively small missile boats carrying short-range (up to 100 miles) nuclear missiles. With missile-bearing ships of many different nuclear states operating in the Eastern Mediterranean, if a nuclear missile were launched at Tel Aviv, it would be very difficult to determine who was responsible. Moreover, a ship belonging to one state might be taken over by agents of another, or by an underground organization.[59]

With further use of the imagination, it would not be too difficult to come up with additional equally frightening catalytic situations. Even if the probability of catalytic war were not very high, the fact that it is larger than zero should be a cause of concern, to say the least. Just how large the probability is, however, will continue to be a subject of some debate.

I find only one reason to doubt that a catalytic nuclear war could occur, but it is a compelling one. As distinct from the probability of uncontrolled escalation, the particular problem of catalytic war requires that a specific party be interested in initiating a process that would eventually lead to general war. But the realities of nuclear war reduce the likelihood that any party might embark on such a venture. The logic of becoming a catalyst of war is that it is an inexpensive strategy for the achievement of desired outcomes. During the long months preceding the 1967 war, Fatah could hope that its behavior would act as a catalyst to bring about a war between

Israel and the Arab states and that the desired outcomes would result without prohibitive costs to the Palestinians. Although with a lower probability for success, the Syrians could hope for the same. Success in this case could be measured not only be whether or not a catalytic war occurred but also by the extent to which the catalyst survived the venture without incurring prohibitive costs. Catalytic behavior is typical of a party that is sensitive to costs. The catalyst of war is the thrifty one who devises cheap ways to produce desired outcomes. The catalyst cleverly attempts to shift the costs to the other parties. His motives are to receive the benefits without bearing any of the costs. Seen from this perspective, a catalytic nuclear war, especially in the Middle East context, is a contradiction in terms. An Arab–Israeli general nuclear war is likely to involve very high costs to both Syria and the Palestinians. The latter would suffer even if Israel did not retaliate. The odds that under such circumstances Syria or the PLO would catalyze a nuclear war are very small indeed.

Iraq, Libya, and Algeria would remain candidates for catalytic behavior. Regardless of their verbal bellicosity, however, all three have very limited stakes in the conflict. All have contributed financially to the confrontation states and Iraq has contributed a limited number of forces as well. Her actions seem to have been directed more by the wish to improve her position in the Arab world than by any real direct interest in the conflict with Israel. Yet, before embarking on any sort of catalytic behavior, an Arab state would have to consider that there is a probability, even if a small one, that the initiator of the catalytic process would be identified. Detection would expose such a state to nuclear retaliation not only by Israel but also by a neighboring Arab state in revenge for being involved in nuclear war against its own will. *Any* real probability that this could in fact occur should be sufficient to deter a thrifty party from embarking on the catalytic road. The enormity as well as the indiscriminate nature of the costs of nuclear war contradict the essential logic of catalytic behavior. A small probability that such costs might result would be enough to deter a potential catalyst.

This minimizes the likelihood of a catalytic nuclear war in the Middle East.

The eighth problem associated with the acquisition of a nuclear force is that of weapons safety. It is often asserted that the requirements of dispersal reduce the capacity to maintain control of weapons. Reduced weapons safety raises three disturbing sets of possibilities: first, accidental or unauthorized launching of nuclear weapons;[60] second, infiltration and takeover of a nuclear weapons facility by a terrorist group; and third, nuclear weapons being taken over by a domestic group, possibly a certain section of the armed forces, in an effort to win political power. Clearly these risks should not be taken lightly. Furthermore, efforts to minimize their effects should be pursued. At the same time, factors limiting these risks should be recognized.

Let us begin with the problem of accidents. The probability of accidental launching is often taken to be a function of the number of states possessing nuclear weapons. Alternatively, I would argue that it is a function of the number of weapons deployed. The United States and the Soviet Union together deploy over 40,000 nuclear warheads. In Europe alone some 12,000 tactical nuclear weapons are now deployed.[61] A nuclear Middle East might add a few hundred weapons to this arsenal. There is no reason why this addition should dramatically raise the overall probability of accidental war unless the assumption is that Mideast states will be equipped with more primitive technologies of control than those of France, India, and China. Even if we accept this assumption as valid, there are three factors that mitigate its effects. Because the states of the Middle East would be equipped with relatively small nuclear forces, the span of control will be much shorter. Second, as Steven Rosen has pointed out, "once a state comes into possession of nuclear weapons, it is in the interest of the entire international community that it also possess the means to manage them safely. It may be in the higher interest of the great powers, however opposed they may be to proliferation itself, to pass along weapons-security technologies that will reduce the chance of accidents and unauthorized detonations as well as disable weapons that fall into the hands of terrorists or fanatical insurgent groups."[62]

The superpowers might raise two objections: first, that by promising to make nuclear forces secure they would be encouraging proliferation,[63] and second that by supplying weapons-safety technology they will be compromising their own security. The secrets may leak or be passed on; the classified information may then be used in ways threatening to the superpowers' own weapons. As to the first objection, weighing the risk of nuclear weapons going off accidentally against the less immediate risks involved in more rapid proliferation, the superpowers are likely to respond to the more immediate and more terrifying threat at the expense of faster proliferation. They are likely to prefer greater security for existing nuclear forces at the risk that by making them more secure they might encourage proliferation. The need to provide a response to the immediate risk is likely to overshadow future expenses. As to the risk of compromising their security, the superpowers may implement policies similar to the ones they adopted in the realm of conventional arms transfers. Just as they at times produced weapons systems strictly for export purposes (e.g., F-5 aircraft), the superpowers can develop security measures and arrangements, for export purposes, different from the ones they currently deploy and yet equally effective. It is thus likely that the superpowers would eventually come to agree with Lewis Dunn that prudence "might require assisting future proliferators to develop more stable and controllable nuclear forces."[64] The third factor to lower the risk of primitive controls is linked to the fact that the technology required for the safe management of nuclear weapons is mainly in the field of electronics. The science of electronics is one in which Israel is blessed with impressive achievements. The possibility that Israel will develop technologies for ensuring weapons security and will then export them to other Mideast states, to ensure overall regional weapons safety, should not be ruled out.

Once the problem of accidental detonation and launching is reduced to the level of safety of the two superpowers, only the problem of weapons seizure remains. Weapons may be seized either by terrorists or by a section of the armed forces during a struggle for power.[65] A seizure by terrorists is highly unlikely. Since Middle East states are bound to have only a small number of weapons it will be relatively easy to assign enough troops to guard them against terrorist attempts. Dunn takes seriously the possibility that nuclear weapons will be seized in an attempt at a domestic coup d'etat. He thinks nuclear coups may occur "in the many politically unstable future proliferators with their previous histories of military interventions in domestic politics." He expects "efforts by military factions with future coup-vulnerable proliferators to seize control of nuclear weapons."[66] Dunn's predictions are debatable. A section contemplating a coup d'etat would require troops, a few tanks, armored personal carriers, some machine guns, submachine guns, and a few pistols. Armed with such weapons the rebels could head for the palace, the ministry of defense, the general staff, and the nearest radio and television station. Nuclear weapons would be of little use in conducting such a venture. What could the group threaten to do once it seizes these weapons? Surely they would not threaten to blow up the nation's capital. First, their own relatives would most probably be residing there. Second, they are least likely to be happy with the task of managing the country following a nuclear catastrophe. Third, they would have no chance of acquiring or maintaining popular support following a disaster of this sort. Without the ability to threaten to use nuclear weapons, a group or section of the armed forces attempting a coup would have no incentive to seize them. A coup would not undermine the safety of such weapons through seizure. Nevertheless, one should not ignore Schelling's argument that nuclear weapons might be involved in domestic struggles simply because no faction would want to concede them to the others. In his words, "when Moslems are fighting Christians within a country, or officers fighting enlisted men, the Navy fighting the Army or French paratroopers marching in Paris, even those who would find plutonium an embarrassment may have to race for it and fight for it simply to keep it from falling into the wrong hands."[67] However, this in no ways implies that a faction would do something crazy with nuclear weapons once it seized them. Seizure might have no strategic consequences.

The ninth risk inherent in a world of many nuclear states is the vulnerability of command and control facilities.[68] The problem of maintaining a protected and responsible center for assessing ambiguous indications and making decisions to respond in an appropriate way is sometimes regarded as insurmountable. The difficulty of assuring that this center of assessment and decision would survive attack is enormous. Hence, the parties are apt to adopt a policy that implies automatic launching of delivery vehicles once the center for command and control is destroyed. The adoption of such a posture would invite preemptive escalation and would therefore be highly destabilizing. However, the relationship between vulnerability of command and control and stability can be made to yield the opposite result: the asserted sources of instability might turn out to be stabilizing; elements identified as sources of instability might enhance deterrence.

If the command and control facilities are located in Israel's capital or its largest city and Israel's doctrine implies automatic launching once these facilities are destroyed, the threat would enjoy a large measure of credibility. After all, what would Israel's nuclear force be designed to deter if not a major attack on the state's largest cities? It is not as if the destruction of the center of assessment would increase the likelihood that a limited attack would be misconstrued as a total attack. The attack that destroys the center of assessment so located will *indeed* be total (should the United States consider a Soviet attack that destroyed Washington, D.C., as anything less?) and should be so interpreted. A threat of total retaliation in response to such an attack would be entirely credible; if it were not, nothing would be. One should also add that even if the center for command and control is not destroyed, the problem of assessing the precise nature of a nuclear attack and its immediate effects is still enormous. It would also be extremely difficult to devise an appropriate response, i.e., one that does not constitute an unnecessary overreaction. The very difficulty of assessment may at the same time produce highly effective deterrence. The perception by Israel's adversaries that any nuclear attack on Israel would create enormous chaos; that this would undermine the government's ability to arrive at measured assessments; that this, in turn, would increase the chances of an Israeli overreaction is most likely to deter them from launching any such attack. Given the costs of a possibly wild Israeli overreaction, uncertainty as to how Israel might interpret a nuclear attack, even a limited one, would produce a strong positive deterrent effect. In this way vulnerability could also enhance deterrence; in the nuclear realm weakness is very often a source of strength.

The final problem is that of nuclear terrorism. A risk with enormous potential consequences is that Palestinian terrorists would acquire nuclear arms and then use or threaten to use them against Israel. The risk, coupled with the intangible nature of the problem, requires that we devote to it more attention than we have given to other risks involved in the proliferation of nuclear arms into the Middle East.

Among analysts there is general agreement that the actual detonation of a nuclear device by terrorists would have serious consequences. Roberta Wohlstetter calculates that the detonation of a .1 kiloton device would kill about 37,000 people in Cairo and about 9,000 in Tel Aviv.[69] Thus one terrorist incident might cause three times the total casualties Israel suffered in the Yom Kippur War. Analysts also agree that nuclear terrorism is both conceivable and technically feasible.[70] But this does not tell us how likely it is to occur. Two levels of probability should be considered. First, the likelihood that terrorist groups would obtain nuclear weapons and threaten to use them unless specific demands are met. Second, the likelihood that terrorist groups would actually detonate a nuclear device. In both cases there are two determining factors: capability and intentions. Capability may be acquired through a number of alternative routes—

one of them could be by theft. Terrorists might attempt to steal a nuclear weapon from the arsenals of one of the nuclear-armed states.[71] Safety measures taken by all nuclear states, however, though far from perfect, would make such an attempt rather difficult. The second possibility is that terrorists would obtain nuclear arms from a supporting sovereign state. Libya is often mentioned as a country that might supply terrorists with nuclear weapons once she obtains them.[72] This scenario, however, is even less likely. From the sovereign state's perspective such a transfer would involve the loss of control over a tool of enormous unforeseen consequences. Libya would have to consider that there was some probability of Israeli intelligence penetration somewhere along the chain between her and the terrorist group; that there was some chance that the source of the nuclear device would be discovered; and that there was some chance that as a result she would suffer deadly retaliation. In fact, Libya might consider that she could suffer retaliation even if the weapon's source were not discovered. Israel might retaliate in extreme anger and frustration against all radical elements suspected as being the possible source of the terrorists' device. In addition, Libya would have to consider the possibility that the terrorists might turn around and and use the nuclear device in an act of extortion against her. Even Libya would be reluctant to expose herself to such an extreme threat, particularly so in light of its often stormy relations with the PLO.[73] For the Soviet Union a transfer of nuclear arms to terrorists is entirely out of the question. The Soviets are almost religious about the issue of control. They are not likely to equip terrorist groups with the means of involving them in escalatory and catalytic processes over which they might have no control. In general, odds are that a superpower intent on making meaningful gains within a generally stable international system would not support groups that might run wild with the means of mass destruction. Thus the probability that terrorist groups would be supplied with nuclear devices by a sovereign state seems very low. A third possibility is that terrorists would produce nuclear weapons themselves. However, the

development and production of nuclear devices is a prolonged process and requires considerable resources. The
route to a nuclear threat involves five stages: the obtaining
of fissionable material; the designing of the bomb; the production and assembly of the weapon; the delivery of the
bomb to the target; and the setting off of the device or the
staging of the threat.

To carry out the first three stages requires specialists in at
least half a dozen different disciplines.[74] Financial resources
and freedom of action within the confines of a certain territory
are necessary. In addition, the terrorist group must manifest
a determination to complete a task lasting a number of years.
The final two stages demand that the group have a fairly
elaborate organizational infrastructure. These requirements
are not easy to meet. First, fissile material is very well controlled and hence difficult to obtain. Second, "the fabrication
of a nuclear explosive is a complex matter, especially if the
weapon is expected to be reliable."[75] It is questionable
whether a large enough group of people "with the requisite
skills for serious nuclear terrorism could be assembled to
achieve utterly mad objectives."[76] Third, "dealing with near
critical masses of fissile material is very dangerous. Amateur
weapon designers, which would include most Ph.D. physicists, are likely to be killed if they were to attempt to make
a nuclear weapon."[77] Fourth, the length of the process as
well as the need to recruit specialists of various kinds is likely
to expose the terrorist groups to penetration by the intelligence networks of prospective target states. Fifth, for some
of the same reasons that will dissuade supporting states from
providing nuclear arms to terrorists, host states are unlikely
to provide terrorists with the requisite freedom of action.
Fear of nuclear retaliation by the surviving victims of the
terrorists should be particularly effective. Finally, few groups
have either the organization infrastructure or the time horizon
needed to persist in such a lengthy and elaborate enterprise.
Thus, in terms of the requirements for skills, resources, territorial freedom, time, and organization infrastructure, a terrorist organization must be "almost a state" if it is to design

and produce nuclear weapons.[78] The PLO would probably come closest to meeting this description.[79] The organization enjoys much support from one sovereign state, Libya, and relative freedom of action in another, Lebanon. It can meet the financial burden through aid from Saudi Arabia, Iraq, and Libya. Furthermore, it is at least symbolically already "in the game" by virtue of the fact that it enjoys an observer's status at the International Atomic Energy Agency (IAEA). This status also allows the PLO direct access to material concerning the security of nuclear installations.

Yet terrorist groups that could possibly meet the prerequisites for atomic capabilities are also the ones least likely to attempt nuclear terrorism. Serious motivational constraints exist to dissuade the PLO from exploding a nuclear device. One is the possibility of retaliation. There would be reasonable fear that the leaders of the target population, in this case Israel, would retaliate against the population on whose behalf the terrorists operate. For a terrorist organization which is almost a state the possibility of retaliation will act as an important constraint. An organization that sees itself entrusted with responsibility for its nation, the PLO would have to weigh the odds of Israeli retaliation against Palestinians carefully before opting for nuclear devastation. From a more general perspective, terrorist organizations that are almost states constantly strive for legitimacy. Hence they are less likely to take actions that threaten to undermine their public and international standing. Having labored for legitimacy in the world arena for some years, the PLO is unlikely to pursue a route that would gain them so much contempt.[80] Third, the actual detonation of a nuclear device would not serve the terrorist goals. It would reverse rather than move forward the attainment of the terrorists' objectives because of the enormous hostility it would generate.[81] As Brian Jenkins put it, "terrorists want a lot of people watching, not a lot of people dead. . . ."[82] The acquisition and use of nuclear weapons by a terrorist organization would complicate its relations with the supporting superpowers, supporting states, and fellow terrorist groups. Nuclear weapons in the hands of a terrorist

organization would create extreme fear among its various supporters that they might be implicated in unintended and undesired consequences. Traditional supporters are apt to disassociate themselves from the terrorist organization. The
PLO would have to consider the possibility that its traditional
supporters, such as Iraq and Syria, would move to prevent
Palestinian acquisition of nuclear weapons.[83] More than that,
fear of the possible consequences to their own national security might lead Syria and Iraq to move to exterminate the
PLO following serious signs that the latter was about to construct a nuclear device.

Finally, it is not at all clear that terrorists have already
reached the limits of their existing nonnuclear capability.[84]
So far they seem to feel that they can accomplish much with
relatively simple weapons and tactics. The PLO may feel that
it is on the right track even without resort to nonconventional
means. As long as this perception persists there is little reason
to expect attempts at nuclear terror. Even if the PLO were
to acquire a nuclear device, being "almost a state" means
that the organization is unlikely to use it in a wild fashion,
but rather as any state would. As Schelling puts it, terrorist
organizations capable of producing nuclear weapons are also
likely to be "very much like nations in the way they set their
goals and conduct their diplomacy." Consequently, Schelling
asserts that if a terrorist organization were to resort to nuclear
terrorism, it "would probably look more like diplomacy than
terrorism."[85]

From the terrorists' perspective nuclear terrorism is much
more attractive as a threat than as an action.[86] But in order
to present a credible threat, terrorists must demonstrate that
they possess adequate quantities of fissionable material; that
they are able to construct a nuclear device; and that they are
able to set it off. Providing evidence of this will not be easy.
Inability to do so will reduce the credibility of the threat. In
addition, the threat's credibility will be somewhat diminished by the constraints on actual detonation. However, to
be effective the threat need not be fully credible. A national

government faced by terrorists threatening to explode a nuclear device will not be completely sure that the threat is a bluff. This uncertainty can give the terrorists enormous leverage. The incentives for terrorists to attempt nuclear threats may in the future become considerable. Terrorists may reach the conclusion that their current level of activities no longer inspires fear nor produces the desired publicity. Also, the climate of opinion may change so that the public no longer prefers governments to meet the terrorists' demands. Already the last few years have given rise to a general consensus not to give in to terrorists' demands. Thus the terrorist organizations may come to believe that they must escalate the level of threat dramatically if they are to restore public pressure on governments to meet their demands. In such a context, creating a nuclear threat might seem particularly appealing to a terrorist group.

The effectiveness of the threat will have a number of causes. First, the terrorists' demands may be perceived as minuscule in comparison to the damage threatened. Second, the greater the threat, the greater would be the direct involvement of the public. As a consequence, there would be more effective public pressure on the government to meet the terrorists' demands. Third, nuclear threats are of a nature to discourage government responses other than compliance. The elements of surprise, fear, lack of preparedness, and lack of suitable methods to deal with such a situation are bound to slow down the government's reaction and reduce the efficacy of its reponse. Finally, the terrorist organization performing such an act would achieve publicity much beyond what terrorists could hope through the usual acts they have conducted in the past. Yet these incentives are not without problems. The usefulness of nuclear threats will have some severe limitations. As Brian Jenkins has pointed out,

> even with a nuclear device, terrorists could not make impossible demands. They probably could not permanently alter national policy or compel other changes in national behavior. To do so would require

at a minimum that they maintain the threat and it is not clear how long this can be done without discovery or betrayal. They could not create a homeland, at least not without offering the victims of the blackmail a future set of hostages to retaliate against. They probably could not persuade a government to liquidate itself. They could not realistically expect to be given more nuclear weapons by claiming or even demonstrating that they had at least one. They could not easily collect billions of dollars of ransom, even if it were paid.[87]

The probability of nuclear terrorism must be determined from the balance between these various incentives and disincentives, possibilities, and constraints. In sum total it seems that nuclear terrorism is feasible but that its likelihood is not very high. It also seems that nuclear terrorism is more apt to appear in the form of threat than as a plain nuclear detonation. Nuclear terrorism in the form of threats would look much like nuclear diplomacy. It might be very effective for some purposes but not for others. If aimed at forcing positive changes, nuclear terrorism would encounter many of the difficulties that states would face if they attempted nuclear compellence. Finally, it should be emphasized that there is no necessary connection between nuclear terrorism and Israel's overt nuclearization. The PLO might attempt nuclear terrorism even if Israel did not adopt a strategy of overt nuclear deterrence. Israel must take such a possibility into account, study it, and prepare for it.

To conclude, the proliferation of nuclear arms involves a significant measure of risk. Some of the dangerous aspects are more worrisome than others. Among the less worrisome are the possibility of irrational behavior; the possible consequences of the lack of proper conceptualization about the uses of nuclear weapons; the danger that a more-of-the-same attitude about them would be adopted; the concern that Israel might not be able to match the aggregate forces of a number of Arab states; the possibility that a catalytic war could occur; the problem of maintaining adequate control over weaponry and ensuring invulnerability to the command and control facilities. Each of these involves a measure of risk but that is often mitigated by countervailing forces. Other areas of risk remain quite worrisome. The problem of calculations in a multinuclear environment as well as that of controlling escalation remain a source of concern. The possibility of nuclear terror cannot be written off. Despite their low probability these risks are significant because of the high costs involved. They can by no means be ignored.

CHAPTER 5

The Superpowers' Response to a Nuclear-Armed Israel

Within the structure of the present international system, Soviet–American nuclear relations constitute the highest ring.
No other set of relations supersedes it in importance. Consequently, a Middle East regional nuclear balance will
merely constitute a realm within a realm, existing in the shad-
ows of the central nuclear balance. This involves a major risk:
namely, that the parties to the central balance might act to
cancel whatever advantages can be gained by establishing
a regional balance. Primarily two types of dangers can be
identified from Israel's perspective. First, the superpowers
might make a negative response to the act of disclosure described in the first chapter. In other words, the Soviet and
American responses to the adoption of an overt nuclear posture by Israel could vastly offset whatever advantages might
be gained by such a step. Second, the superpowers might
produce a prohibitive response not to the act of disclosure
itself but rather to the first instance of use of a nuclear threat.
The concern here is that the superpower would move in at
that point to neutralize the threat's effectiveness. Possibly
this might take the form of a joint intervention to disarm
Israel.

I shall first consider the likely Soviet reaction to Israeli
overt nuclearization. I shall analyze alternative Soviet responses to the act of disclosure. Some of these responses may
be particularly important once Israel actually attempts to

threaten nuclear punishment. The likelihood of these alternative Soviet responses as well as their strategic implications will be addressed. I shall then attempt a similar analysis of the probable American response to Israel's adoption of an explicit nuclear deterrent strategy. Finally, the likelihood of a joint Soviet–American response will be considered.

The Soviet Response

The disparity of forces between the Soviet Union and a nuclear Israel will continue to be sharply asymmetric. With its enormous nuclear capability, an elaborate system of surveillance and detection, an impressive long-range precision weapons technology, and an elaborate air defense system, the Soviet Union is assured of a first-strike capability. Since Israel is unlikely to have more than a few delivery vehicles capable of reaching southern Russia, a massive Soviet nuclear attack promises to destroy Israel's ability to retaliate.

Much opposition to the suggestion that Israel might adopt a nuclear posture has revolved around the possible Soviet response. Alan Dowty bases his objections, among other things, on the prediction that "an Israeli nuclear force would be neutralized immediately by Soviet counter-threats or transfer of weapons to Arab states." Dowty further suggests that "one possible response [to the adoption of a nuclear posture by Israel] would be to deepen Soviet involvement rather than curtail it," and predicts that "certainly one clear result of Israeli nuclearization would be pressure on the Soviets from its Arab client states to do exactly that."[1] William Bader believed that "Tel Aviv knows that such action [the overt production of nuclear weapons] would not only provoke an attack by the Arabs but probably force the Soviets to station atomic weapons in Egypt or to give the Arabs a security guarantee."[2] Bennett Boskey and Mason Willrich have commented that "the fact that the Soviet Union might react by making nuclear weapons available to the Arabs—even though the Soviets would doubtless keep custody and control over the weapons—would certainly be a strong deterrent to an Israeli decision to go nuclear."[3] The Soviet threat was also articulated by J. Bowyer Bell. In his opinion "Russia quite obviously has the capacity, if Moscow so desired and the international situation so permitted, to impose a final solution." What form might such a solution take? In Bell's view, one possibility is a "prohibitive nuclear attack on Israel."[4] In sifting through the various opinions it becomes evident that there are six different ways in which the Soviet Union might react to Israeli nuclearization: (a) by conducting a preemptive or preventive nuclear first strike against Israel; (b) by providing nuclear weapons to some Arab client states such as Syria, Iraq, and possibly to Egypt if the latter could not get these weapons elsewhere and thought Israeli acquisition of them justified returning to the Soviet camp; (c) by providing a number of Arab states with guarantees against Israeli first use of nuclear weapons; these guarantees might or might not be accompanied by the stationing of Soviet nuclear weapons in some of the Arab states; (d) by increasing the level of her political and military involvement in the Middle East without necessarily devising a *nuclear* response to Israeli nuclearization; (e) by doing nothing at all except to continue present practices at the political and conventional-military levels; and (f) by increasingly disengaging from the Arab–Israeli conflict area.

The first alternative, that the Soviets would move to neutralize the Israeli deterrent by conducting a preemptive or preventive first strike, is extremely far-fetched. The Soviet Union considers her interests in the Middle East to be vitally important. At the same time, Soviet behavior in the region reflects great sensitivity to costs. The Soviets have stayed away from full-scale military interventions of the kind conducted by the United States from Korea to Vietnam; for example, when four of their pilots were shot down over Egypt by Israel's air force in 1970, the Soviets carefully avoided escalation. Overall, their behavior in the region indicates that they have important but limited stakes in the Middle East.[5] A Soviet nuclear first strike against Israel would therefore be inconsistent with everything we know about Soviet behavior in the region so far. This is particularly in view of the enormous costs to the Soviets of a nuclear first strike against Israel, such as the risk of a superpower nuclear confrontation and the almost certain breakdown of detente coupled with the loss of all its fruits. The political costs resulting from the nuclear execution of three million Jews might include the complete discrediting of Euro-communism, violent—possibly suicidal—reactions inside the Soviet Union by Soviet Jews, and increasing difficulties in Eastern Europe. In addition, a Soviet strike could bring death and destruction to Arabs in Israel, the West Bank, and the Gaza Strip; it would cause the destruction of Moslem religious sites; it could result in nuclear fallout threatening parts of Jordan and Syria. The Arab world and the rest of the world would be antagonized for years. In conclusion, not only would a Soviet first strike result in far higher costs than Soviet interests in the region would justify, but also the execution of such a strike would undermine these very interests.

The second possible Soviet response to an Israeli nuclear posture is to supply nuclear weapons to one or more of the Arab states. To do that would not threaten Israel's nuclear posture. Anyway, the Soviets are not apt to choose this option. Students of the Soviet Union consider the possibility that the Soviets might transfer nuclear weapons to any state under any circumstances very implausible.

The Soviets' approach to nuclear proliferation is very pragmatic. On the one hand they have been opposed to nuclear proliferation fairly consistently ever since China exploited Soviet nuclear assistance for military purposes.[6] On the other hand the Soviets are unwilling to bear heavy costs to achieve nonproliferation goals. As Gerhard Wettig has noted, the Soviets have carefully refrained from creating too much noise about nuclear proliferation.[7] This probably stems from their reluctance to antagonize Third World countries. It also demonstrates what the Soviet Union's priorities are. Soviet interest in nuclear nonproliferation was predominantly an outcome of their concern about possible German rearmament.

The Soviets have repeatedly stressed that under no circumstances would they allow West Germany to acquire nuclear arms. After West Germany agreed to sign and ratify the Nuclear Nonproliferation Treaty, Soviet interest in nuclear proliferation has much receded.[8] The Soviet reaction to the Indian nuclear explosion of 1974 was extremely mild; in its aftermath the Soviets maintained both their formal and their informal linkages to India.[9] In fact, immediately following the Indian detonation the Soviets quickly moved in to replace Canada as India's primary supplier of heavy water.[10] Later, the Soviet Union criticized the United States for exerting pressure on France to cancel her agreement to sell a nuclear reprocessing plant to Pakistan. The Soviet *Socialisticheskaya Industria* stated: "This problem cannot be solved by unilateral bans, with one prohibiting to another what one does oneself."[11] The Soviets also showed a mild reaction to the German–Brazilian nuclear deal. *Pravda* commentator Yuri Kharlanov noted that "one can hardly oppose the use of new forms of energy, including atomic energy. However, it is essential that the provisions of the Nuclear Nonproliferation Treaty be strictly observed."[12] When a Soviet satellite spotted South Africa's preparation to conduct a nuclear test in the Kalahari desert, the Soviets rolled the problem of dissuading the South Africans over to the United States.[13] At the same time, the Soviets would also not risk a Libyan overture to the West for nuclear technology. Preemptively, they decided to provide Colonel Qaddhafi with a power reactor themselves.

Nevertheless, the Soviets have consistently refrained from doing anything that might accelerate nuclear proliferation. Bertram Goldschmidt reports that "the Russians have never transferred to their present satellites, who are all parties to the N.P.T., enrichment and reprocessing technologies and would certainly not allow them to acquire and develop independently these steps of the fuel cycle."[14] Moreover, the Soviets have forced the Indians to agree that full safeguard would govern the use of the heavy water they supplied.[15] They refrained from supplying Libya with the 440-megawatt reactor until she ratified the N.P.T.[16]

The Soviets have likewise consistently avoided doing anything that might be regarded as changing the global distribution of power to both the superpowers' disadvantage. The evidence points to the conclusion that the Soviet Union would not transfer nuclear arms to Arab states. Nuclearization would make the Arab states much more independent, whereas the advancement of Soviet interests requires quite the opposite. It is therefore even less likely that the Soviet Union would supply the long-range precision weaponry and the intelligence data required to pose a serious threat to Israel's retaliatory capacity. The odds of a Soviet transfer of first-strike capabilities to the Arabs are extremely low precisely because the recipients might use these capabilities. The Soviets would then face the prospects of a regional nuclear war, involving a very real danger of escalation to a superpower nuclear confrontation.

Admittedly, one piece of unconfirmed evidence would at first glance seem to contradict the assessment that the likelihood of any Soviet transfer of nuclear arms to the Arabs is low. It is the alleged introduction of nuclear weapons by the Soviet Union into the Middle East toward the end of the October 1973 war. Little information is as yet available on this episode and some unconfirmed press reports must be handled with care to avoid unjustified conclusions. Ze'ev Schiff and William Quandt have provided the most elaborate accounts of the affair.[17] In his *Decade of Decisions*, Quandt reports that on October 25, 1973, an "intelligence report has been received to the effect that a suspicious Soviet ship had arrived in Alexandria. While transiting the Bosphorus on October 22, the ship had given off neutron emissions, indicating the possible presence of nuclear weapons on board."[18] The story indicates possible Soviet willingness to supply nuclear arms to an Arab confrontation state. However, this conclusion would be highly premature for a number of reasons. So far very little evidence has been produced to the effect that a ship carrying radioactive material had in fact arrived in Alexandria during the October War. Even less evidence exists that any radioactive cargo was unloaded. It is more probable that, if such a ship ever headed toward the Middle East on the relevant dates, the Soviet intention was to send a message to Washington rather than to send nuclear weapons to Egypt. As Quandt has pointed out, "if the Soviets intended to send nuclear weapons to Egypt, they presumably would not send them by ship. If, however, they were engaging in a dangerous form of psychological warfare aimed at making the Americans worry about the possibility of nuclear weapons in the area, they might have chosen to send such weapons through the heavily monitored Turkish Strait."[19] The matter of the Soviet nuclear ship has since been subjected to a thorough analysis by two officers of Israel's Defense Forces. In an article published by the I.D.F.'s *Ma'archot*, Lieutenant Colonel Avi-Shai and Major Yishai Kordova point out the questionable and highly conflicting character of the reports that have surfaced so far about the affair. They regard the possibility that the Soviets have stationed nuclear arms in Egypt during the October War as very unlikely, particularly in light of the fact that the Soviets attempted to dissuade President Sadat from initiating that war. The authors also provide persuasive evidence to support their claim that the Kissinger–Nixon administration intentionally propagated reports about the arrival of Soviet nuclear weapons in Egypt. They hint that the entire affair was an American fabrication aimed at exerting pressure on Israel in order to induce her to adopt a more flexible political position.[20] Thus the story of the mysterious nuclear ship does not refute our basic proposition, namely that the Soviet Union is unlikely to furnish an Arab state with nuclear weapons.

A third Soviet option would be to offer to some of the Arab states guarantees against an Israeli first use of nuclear weapons. This option would seem best suited to serve Soviet interests assuming there is willingness to run the risks associated with any kind of political–military involvement in a nuclearized region. The deterrent effect of an Israeli nuclear posture vis-à-vis the Arabs, coupled with the deterrent effect of Soviet guarantees vis-à-vis Israel, will have three beneficial outcomes for the Soviet Union. First, the Israeli counter-

Arab deterrent and the Soviet counter-Israel deterrent would together contain the conflict without actually solving it. Consequently, Soviet guarantees would continue to be required and the Arabs would not be able to dispense with a measure of Soviet support. Soviet influence in the region would thus enjoy stability and assurance of continuity. Second, mutual deterrence would assure that Soviet influence would be largely immune to the danger of periodic eruption of warfare characteristic of a conventional balance of forces. Thus the price tag on Soviet influence in the region will have been reduced. Third, Arab perceptions of the threat of an Israeli nuclear posture are apt to result in their attaching great importance to the Soviet guarantees. This would increase their dependence on the Soviet Union, thus enlarging Soviet influence in the region. A Soviet nuclear guarantee to a number of Arab states would not undermine the deterrent effect of an Israeli nuclear posture because that guarantee is unlikely to be open-ended. As Lawrence Freedman has pointed out, "While the Soviet Union may be prepared to offer protection against Israeli offensives, it is very doubtful that she would be prepared to provide nuclear cover for the consequences of all Arab adventures."[21] The Soviet guarantee would probably be extended only against Israeli offensive uses of nuclear weapons. Odds are that the Soviets would not promise to counterdeter any and all Israeli efforts to deter Arab conventional or nuclear attacks. In fact, in pursuit of minimizing possible costs to themselves, the Soviets would be likely to condition the granting of guarantees on strict Arab adherence to a system of mutual consultations in advance of any activity that carried the slightest probability of escalation.[22] Should the Syrians, for example, accept such guarantees, it is their flexibility that would be curtailed.

As noted earlier, some reports indicate that the Soviets have already chosen this option with respect to Syria. Syria's Minister of Defense, Mustafa Talas, said he counted on the Soviet Union to bail Syria out in case of an Israeli nuclear threat. Another report claimed that a nuclear guarantee was included as a secret clause to the Soviet–Syrian Treaty of

Friendship of 1980. However, there is reason to question the authenticity of the latter report as well as to ask whether Talas was expressing more than wishful thinking. Past experience indicates that the Soviets are reluctant to provide any kind of nuclear guarantee. Throughout the late 1960s the Soviet Union refused repeated requests by India to grant her an explicit guarantee of support in case China ever threatened nuclear blackmail.[23] Syria has previously approached the Soviet Union about a possible counter-Israel nuclear guarantee, but the Soviets are reported to have shown great reluctance to commit themselves.[24] As Benjamin Lambeth has noted, "Soviet leaders have given every indication that they have no intention of becoming entangled in any regional defense commitments which, in a nuclear crisis, might limit their flexibility and their options. . . . [The] Soviets are apt to be doubly wary of getting themselves caught in some future situation where they would stand to have their own interests compromised."[25] All this points to the conclusion that if the Soviets ever extended a nuclear guarantee to some Arab states following Israeli disclosure, the guarantee would be conditional. A guarantee of that sort might in fact have a stabilizing effect. As Robert Tucker pointed out, "if the guarantee applied to an offensive war on Israel's part, it might have a stabilizing influence in that it would serve to reduce Arab fears that Israel might use nuclear weapons for expansionist purposes."[26]

The fourth Soviet response to Israeli nuclearization might be to increase the level of their political and military involvement in the Middle East without necessarily devising a nuclear response to Israeli nuclearization. As mentioned earlier, Alan Dowty has predicted that "certainly one clear result of Israeli nuclearization would be pressure on the Soviets from its Arab client states to do exactly that."[27] I tend to doubt that such pressure would arise. On the one hand, an Arab client state that can find its own means to create a nuclear deterrent would not wish to ask the Soviet Union to increase her level of political and military involvement. The particular Arab state would not make such a request because an increase in

Soviet involvement would decrease its own flexibility without providing a corresponding gain in security. On the other hand, an Arab client state that cannot find the internal means to create its own nuclear deterrent may need to present the Soviets with far-reaching demands: "Either supply us with nuclear weapons or provide us with nuclear guarantees or get out." An increase in Soviet involvement that lacks any real reply to the Israeli *nuclear* threat is not likely to be requested, or even accepted.

A mere increase in political and military involvement would not be useful from the Soviet perspective either. Rightly or wrongly, the superpowers think that the risks involved in a nuclearized Middle East will be quite high. It is not likely that the Soviets would increase their involvement without first attempting to reduce these risks by confronting Israel with a Soviet deterrent, in the form of a conditional guarantee to the Arabs. The purpose of this guarantee would be to contribute to regional stability by reducing the likelihood that Israel might take some type of action that could place the Soviets in the compromising position of having to decide between doing nothing, thereby losing political clout in the Arab world, or reacting with great force, thereby running all the risks associated with nuclear war. The guarantees would also contribute to stability by reducing the Arabs' sense of insecurity. It is not logical that the Soviets would react to Israeli nuclearization by increasing involvement without confronting Israel with such a deterrent. As elaborated earlier, such a guarantee would reduce neither the utility of an Israeli nuclear posture nor the stability of a Middle East balance of terror.

Finally, it should be noted that increased Soviet involvement in the Middle East, while contrary to the regional and global interests of the United States, would not necessarily decrease Israel's security. In fact, a highly visible Soviet conventional involvement in the region could strengthen Israel's position by making the need to support her more apparent to the United States. Israel's ability to retain such support is strongly related to her ability to present herself as the Free

World's front line of defense against the Soviet Union. Thus, the period of 1970–73, the peak of Soviet intervention in the area, was also characterized by the greatest intimacy in Israeli–American relations.

I shall now discuss the fifth possible Soviet response to Israeli nuclearization: to do nothing in particular about it. On the one hand this is a somewhat distant option in view of the demands that Arab clients are bound to place on the Soviet Union. On the other hand, it is a likely option considering that the Soviet Union will not be happy about such demands. In Freedman's words, "the Soviet Union would be unhappy if the problem of how to deal with an Israeli nuclear capability became a key factor in determining the level of Soviet intervention in the Middle East. In being forced to define the limits of her support for the Arabs more specifically than ever before, she could end up either dangerously overcommitted, or, by playing it safe, disappoint her Arab friends."[28]

At least one prominent Arab commentator believes the Soviets will prefer to play it safe and do nothing even if this disappoints Arabs. Writing in 1976, Hasanayn Haykal offered his view of the Soviet reaction to Israeli nuclearization:

> People might say that Israel's use of the atomic bomb would expose it to fearful reaction from the Soviet Union and perhaps other powers. But the question is: What is the extent of this reaction? What would the Soviet Union do? Would it launch its rockets against Israel? What would the United States do? Would it let the Soviet Union do that, or would other balances come into play with the matter coming to an end with loud and noisy protests against Israel and with resolutions condemning it, but the fait accompli becoming a fait accompli?[29]

But the Soviets could hardly afford to show no reaction. Their interest in various Arab states would persist; the Soviet Union would continue to seek influence in the area. It is very doubtful that the Soviets would be able to maintain and improve their position in the area without showing their clients that they are capable of providing a response to Israel's nuclear posture. Again, the minimally acceptable response is likely to be the limited guarantee discussed above.

Soviets unlikely to react under ~~cut~~ IS

A final possibility that should not be ruled out is that the Soviets would choose the sixth option, of disengaging from Arab–Israeli conflicts. This might happen if the Soviets decided that the payoffs they derive from their involvement in the Mideast conflict are not worth the costs and risks of continued involvement once the region becomes nuclearized. This would be be in line with Raymond Aron's prediction that "once nuclear arms make their appearance in the area, a diplomatic subsystem would automatically detach itself from the global system."[30] This formulation may be changed to say that it is more likely that the global system would detach itself from the diplomatic subsystem. The odds of superpower disengagement are, however, very low. A Soviet departure of this type would imply the willingness to lose all leverage and influence in the Middle East, which is a region of great importance to them. As Waltz has put it, "The United States and the Soviet Union will continue to have interests in various parts of the world for all of the old political, economic and military reasons. In a region where nuclear powers are locked in dispute, the great powers will move cautiously but not move out."[31]

On balance, then, a more than casual analysis of possible Soviet responses to Israeli nuclearization seems to indicate that the USSR is very unlikely to opt for any of the options that may undermine the utility of the Israeli deterrent or jeopardize Israeli security. These are the very options that carry greater risks for the Soviet Union. Nothing in past Soviet behavior indicates that the limited Soviet interests in the Middle East would justify the assumption of such grave risks.

Two important reservations should be raised against this comforting assessment of the likely Soviet response. First, to a large extent the assessment rests on the premise that we can predict from the past about the future, but new factors might emerge to challenge past practices. An example may be in order. If Israeli disclosure occurred soon after the next Soviet succession took place, Moscow's new leaders might seize the opportunity to assert their global authority. They might consider that a strong reaction was needed to demonstrate that the Kremlin is still an important address. Furthermore, to satisfy the desire for an immediate international success, the new Soviet regime might see a forceful reaction to Israeli disclosure as a possible vehicle for a reinforcement of its position in the Middle East.[32] Under such conditions, the granting of a less conditional guarantee, with or without the actual stationing of Soviet nuclear forces in the Middle East, becomes a distinct possibility.

The second important reservation in our benign portrait of the likely Soviet reaction to Israeli disclosure is that it assumes that the Soviets would consider the possible costs of alternative responses to Israeli nuclearization in the context of their regional interests. As long as they do so, they are unlikely to take a step as politically costly as a nuclear first strike against Israel. They might consider such a strike only if they first came to regard Israeli nuclearization as threatening the Soviet Union's own security, in the case that Israel adopted a nuclear deterrent posture aimed primarily at the Soviet Union. J. Bowyer Bell and Avigdor Haselkorn have both suggested such a posture.[33] The logic of both is that Soviet conventional military intervention would constitute a last-resort situation for Israel. Haselkorn has gone so far as to suggest that the Soviet intervention in 1970 has already created such circumstances, at least in the minds of Israeli decision makers.[34] Both Bell and Haselkorn think the possibility of Soviet intervention requires that Israel develop a nuclear capability to deter such action. Bell argues that "if Russia is to risk the ultimate threat, so defined by the Israelis, then the ability to raise the price for such a step beyond the willingness of Moscow to pay solely for a slightly more comfortable position in the Middle East is a highly desirable asset. An atomic capacity and the ability to deliver a punitive strike on Russia consequently would narrowly limit the extent to which Russia might be willing to threaten Israeli security."[35]

How would Israel be able to raise the Russian price? One suggestion is that Israeli F-4 Phantoms carrying nuclear weapons could conduct a one-way suicidal journey to south-central Russia, bombing some of the major cities of the region, such as Odessa and Tibilisi, as well as the Baku industrial region.[36] As Dowty has pointed out, there is a slight problem with this suggestion in that it overlooks "the fact that the Soviets have the densest air defense system in the world, with 5,000 surveillance radars, over 2,500 interceptors and about 12,000 surface-to-air missile launchers."[37] The proponents of a counter-Soviet deterrent have also failed to remind us that in time of crisis all this system would be searching intensely for the few F-4s. The suggestion that these F-4s might evade the net "by overflying weakly defended areas at tree-top levels"[38] would seem to ignore the fact that Israeli intelligence covering Soviet air defense systems is not likely to be all that accurate and that the Soviets have been extremely active in recent years in devising an air-defense system that is effective against low-flying objects. This system was developed to respond to the challenge presented by U.S. cruise missiles, but it is likely to work much more effectively against low-flying F-4s, F-16s, and F-15s.

For Israel to adopt a counter-Soviet nuclear posture has no merits, but it does have three important disadvantages: it would be infeasible, unnecessary, and highly detrimental to Israeli security. That it is infeasible has been argued in the preceding paragraph. That it is unnecessary needs some elaboration. According to its proponents, the counter-Soviet deterrent would stop the Soviets from intervening to impose a "final solution" in the Middle East. However, the Soviets would in any case have to consider that the United States might intervene on Israel's behalf. During the past two major Middle East wars the United States has effectively deterred the Soviets in precisely this way.[39] The American commitment to the security and survival of the state of Israel, vague and uninstitutionalized as it is, has been upheld by many presidents. As George Kennan demonstrates in his recent *A Cloud of Danger*, this commitment is now embraced even by some who, in the late 1940s, were opposed to the creation of the Jewish state.[40] The strength of the American commitment, regardless of its vagueness, is enough to deter the Soviet Union. Recall Albert Wohlstetter's argument against the building of independent deterrents by European states:

> It is sometimes argued that the small power need not be able to offer much of a probability that damage will occur at all. Even a very small probability of retaliation—a mere "shadow of incertitude," it is suggested—will be enough to deter, especially because a nuclear war might escalate and lead to almost "boundless" harm.
>
> . . . But even the strongest enthusiast for an independent deterrent should concede there is some finite probability that the United States would fulfill her commitments, and the harm done to the enemy by an undamaged American strike force, if not boundless, is at least as great as that to be inflicted by a damaged national strike force.[41]

Although Wohlstetter had European states in mind, his statements apply as well to Israel. The risks of a superpower confrontation escalating to a nuclear war are so grave that the Soviets must be absolutely certain of American nonintervention before intervening anywhere themselves. Washington's reactions so far have shown the Soviets that they cannot gamble on American nonintervention even when the stakes have been relatively minor and U.S. security has not been directly threatened.[42] In Israel's case at least, the Soviets would have to calculate that between the response of the United States and of Israel to a full-scale Soviet intervention, the American response would be costlier. In comparison the Israeli nuclear threat would seem rather irrelevant.

In addition to its infeasibility and irrelevancy, a counter-Soviet nuclear posture would also be highly detrimental to Israeli security. It would produce enormous anxiety in the Soviet Union. The Soviets would fear that Israel might misperceive and misinterpret Soviet behavior and launch some Samson-like action. Such anxieties, and only such anxieties, might conceivably drive the Soviets toward a preemptive nuclear attack on Israel. Only such anxieties could conceivably justify a Soviet attack of this sort in the face of the obvious costs involved. With little hope of acquiring a second-strike capability vis-à-vis the Soviet Union, Israel would not be able to deter such a prohibitive Soviet attack.

Therefore, Israel would be wise to shy away from any thought of contriving a counter-Soviet deterrent. Israeli nuclearization would have to include diplomatic steps to assure the Soviet Union that in no shape or form is the Israeli nuclear deterrent designed against her. Although diplomatic moves can mitigate the problem, however, they cannot solve it. Israel may be able to reduce Soviet anxieties but some Soviet fears will persist. These irreducible anxieties will have two sources. First, to some extent Israel's nuclear force will be threatening regardless of what Israel chooses to say. The Soviets are likely to weigh Israel's capabilities more heavily than its declared intentions. Unfortunately, just by being there the Israeli force would constitute a direct threat to the southern part of the Soviet Union.[43] The second cause of Soviet anxieties would be the increased difficulties of calculating sources of possible nuclear attacks on the Soviet Union. P. R. Chari has pointed out that "the Eastern Mediterranean is utilized by the United States for the deployment of its sixth fleet. The French navy also operates in this region. Attack vectors can be visualized from this geographical area upon the Soviet Union which could lead to confusion regarding the identity of the aggressor. The intrusion of another nuclear power would add to Soviet difficulties in locating the attacker and taking retaliatory measures."[44]

To conclude, the two reservations mentioned here demonstrate that Soviet reaction to Israeli disclosure involves a measure of risk. Under some conditions the Soviet reaction may go beyond benign neglect. What is most probable, however, is that Soviet behavior following Israeli disclosure would be characterized by what Michael Nacht has called "adaptive continuity."[45] The Soviets may grant some Arab states a conditional guarantee against Israeli offensive uses of its nuclear capability. None of the more extreme predictions regarding the possible Soviet response to Israeli nuclearization is apt to materialize.

The American Response

The costs Israel might incur as a result of disclosure primarily involve American–Israeli relations.[46] Because of its strong opposition to nuclear proliferation, the United States is likely to react in a strongly negative fashion to Israel's adoption of a nuclear deterrent posture. The extent of a possible forceful American reaction must be seriously considered before disclosure is made. A totally negative American reaction, such as terminating all U.S. aid and arms sales to Israel, would jeopardize Israeli security, conventional as well as nuclear. However, I shall contend that while there are excellent reasons to predict a harsh American response to Israeli overt nuclearization, this reaction will be somewhat constrained by a number of countervailing considerations. To a considerable extent America's reaction will be determined by the precise *context* in which disclosure is made and by the *manner* in which it is presented.

Much opposition to the suggestion that Israel adopt an overt nuclear deterrent posture has revolved around the possible American reaction. The concern that the United States might react by cutting off her aid is to some an effective deterrent against it. Dowty for one strongly believes that "the political costs of establishing such a [nuclear] force will be enormous, particularly regarding the impact on U.S.–Israel relations."[47] Evron also believes that among other factors the "concern about American political reaction . . . [has] considerably affected the Israeli decision not to 'go nuclear.' " Evron adds that "the strong political opposition of the superpowers to nuclear proliferation in the past is one of the reasons why it has been averted in the past. . . . It can be assumed that the superpowers, probably with the cooperation of other nuclear powers, will again become more active in taking measures to halt proliferation of nuclear capabilities and in applying more stringent safeguards to the use of nuclear material."[48]

To state the obvious, the United States enjoys great influence over Israeli foreign policy. Israel's dependence on the

United States both financial and military, has increased dramatically during the past decade. Nuclearization is not likely to release Israel from this dependency. Israel would still need a measure of financial support as well as the military hardware required to maintain a capability to meet intermediate and low-level military threats.[49]

To be sure, as Israel moves from defense to deterrence, the financial burden imposed by its current posture, as well as the need for enormous quantities of sophisticated conventional weapons, would decrease. Proportionately, Israeli financial and military dependence on the United States could also be reduced. Nevertheless, one cannot ignore the possibility that at least in the short run a negative American reaction to Israeli nuclearization could have detrimental effects on Israeli security. If, as Dowty predicts, nuclearization would result in "undercutting U.S. assistance to Israel," this would indeed accelerate the deterioration of Israel's conventional capabilities.[50]

American opposition to nuclear proliferation is based on a number of hypotheses about the probable effects of such proliferation. First, it is believed that the spread of nuclear weapons increases the likelihood that nuclear wars will be fought, partly because proliferation increases the chances of accidental war. The wish to avoid such wars is one motive for opposing proliferation.[51] Second, it is believed that using nuclear weapons in war will make them legitimate, thus threatening to involve the entire globe in nuclear warfare. Third, it is believed that increased proliferation will require the United States to intervene more often in local conflicts so as to ensure that they do not escalate to nuclear confrontations. President Kennedy noted that as nuclear weapons diffuse there would be "an increased necessity for the great powers to involve themselves in otherwise local conflicts."[52] Fourth, the United States and the Soviet Union believe that the consequence of nuclear proliferation will be a global redistribution of power which would be to their disadvantage. As William C. Foster put it in 1965: "[the U.S.] should not lose sight of the fact that widespread nuclear proliferation would mean a substantial erosion in the margin of power which our great wealth and industrial base have long given us relative to much of the rest of the world."[53] In line with Foster, Alastair Buchan explains that U.S. nonproliferation policy

> [was] the product of an American consensus, which has its less highly evolved counterpart in Soviet policy, that the stability of international relations is governed by the bipolar balance; if the two superpowers can moderate their adversary relationship to the extent of agreement to control the obvious dangers which technology, or geography or faulty communications present to it, then not only are the prospects of general peace maximized but the two superpowers can, by concurrent if not coordinated action, keep a reasonable degree of control over the pattern of events in the world at large.[54]

Thus, nuclear weapons proliferation should be opposed on the grounds that it would cause an erosion of this sort of "duopoly of the superpowers."[55] Recently, fear of such an erosion has received a new label in the United States— namely, "the loss of control." In the wake of events in Iran and elsewhere, some believe that America is losing its ability to influence events abroad. The acquisition of a nuclear capability is assumed to allow small states to resist external pressures better. Nuclear proliferation is therefore regarded as adding fuel to the progressive deterioration of America's global position.

Another motive for opposing proliferation is the fear of catalytic war. Americans fear that small nuclear states may involve them in a superpower nuclear war against their will. As a member of the U.S. House of Representatives put it, "more likely than an all-out war beginning between superpowers is a nuclear exchange between small countries, and a nuclear war anywhere has to be assumed to risk escalation to superpower involvement whether by deliberate intervention or by miscalculation, bluff or panic."[56]

The final motive for opposing proliferation is the perception that the acquisition of nuclear weapons by small states could undermine the logic of American strategy. The United

State has for some years invested great resources in developing the option to conduct a limited, primarily counterforce, nuclear war. The prime motive behind this development is to contain destruction should deterrence for some reason fail. However, if a nuclear-equipped small state reacted to a Soviet move with counter-city retaliation, all efforts to limit war and destruction would fail. This danger elicited Malcolm Hoag's complaint against the French nuclear force: "could our strategic forces fulfill their promise if concurrently the French strategic force were doing what it presumably [is] designed to do—namely to destroy Soviet cities—while American forces are taking pains to avoid them?"[57] The problem would obviously apply to other nuclearized small states as well.

Despite the strong motives for pursuing a tough antiproliferation policy, the execution of this policy has always been equivocal. The United States did take a position opposing nuclear proliferation almost immediately after having let the genie out of the bottle. In November 1945—some three months after Hiroshima and Nagasaki—President Harry Truman joined the Prime Ministers of Great Britain and Canada in signing a declaration promising to prevent the disclosure of information, even about "the practical industrial application of atomic energy," before an international system of control was set up.[58] The following year, in the form of the Bernard Baruch plan, the United States "envisaged the creation of an International Atomic Development Authority under the United Nations which, in addition to control of the world's nuclear raw materials, would have managerial control of all atomic energy activities considered potentially dangerous to world peace, as well as the power to inspect and license all other atomic installations."[59] However, these visions did not last long. By 1953, President Eisenhower launched the Atoms for Peace program, which had the opposite effect. Under its auspices much technical information pertinent to the production of nuclear weapons was released.[60] The resultant Atomic Energy Act of 1954 called for making available to cooperating nations the benefits of peaceful applications of atomic energy "as widely as expanding technology and considerations of the common defense would permit." The Act authorized the Atomic Energy Commission (AEC) to negotiate cooperation agreements without Senate approval.[61]

In the following years, the U.S. government facilitated the participation of American industry in atomic power activities abroad. Under "Atoms for Peace," twenty-six American research reactors were installed in other countries. The United States organized large conferences to transmit technical know-how; it licensed foreign firms to produce and sell American reactors; and it shipped materials abroad to help other countries move ahead in nuclear technology. Between 1954 and 1979 some 13,456 foreign researchers from non-Soviet block nations have received training in the nuclear sciences in the United States. Of these, some 3,532 were from nations that did not sign the 1968 Nuclear Nonproliferation Treaty.[62] "All told, [the U.S.] spent hundreds of millions of dollars on spreading nuclear technology abroad."[63]

There are three main reasons for the inconsistency of the American nonproliferation policy. The first has to do with the nature of the "good" resulting from a successful nonproliferation policy. The security provided by a successful ban on nuclear proliferation is a "collective good." All states, including those that invested nothing in the efforts to halt proliferation, would enjoy the fruits of this ban should it succeed. Since it is a "collective good," the United States, consistent with Olson's Collective Goods theory, has a tendency to underinvest in it.[64] She lacks an incentive to wage an all-out fight against nuclear proliferation, thus bearing a predominant share of the costs, in pursuit of a good that benefits all.

Another reason for the equivocal execution of the antiproliferation policy is a pessimistic assessment of the chances of success. The sources of pessimism include, first, the belief that "as far as technical knowledge is concerned, the genie is out of the bottle."[65] Moreover, the other advanced nuclear states cannot be persuaded to invest in nonproliferation efforts. Thus, in defense of the Atoms for Peace program Secretary of State Dulles testified that America could not hope to set up an effective "dam agains the flow of information, and if we try to do it we will only dam our influence and others will move into the field with the bargaining that that involves."[66] Two and a half decades later this argument had acquired even greater merit. As the Honorable Clarence Long has put it, "the countries with the ability to supply technicians, reactor hardware, and nuclear fuel have so many conflicting and even devious interests, that any anti-proliferation agreement must be at the mercy of the lowest common proliferator, with long delays and more loopholes than anti-proliferation clauses."[67] The third source of pessimism is the belief prevailing in Washington that should a state acquire a motivation for developing a nuclear force, nothing the United States could do would successfuly prevent it from achieving its goal. Evidence for this belief may be found in a key testimony given by former Secretary of State Henry Kissinger before a Senate Committee to the effect that "the causes of proliferation are too deep to be substantially influenced by any actions that the superpowers alone might take."[68] Leslie Gelb wrote in 1976 that the administration's perception is that "to many nations, their real rivals and enemies are neither Moscow nor Washington, but their own neighbors. . . . In the last analysis the decision to go nuclear will be made on the basis of whether local rivals go nuclear or seem to be going nuclear, or because of internal power struggles and the quest for prestige. The United States probably has little influence over these considerations. Thus, the deep pessimism of many arms controllers."[69] The motivation to absorb costs in pursuit of a collective good is usually quite low. In the case of nuclear proliferation the motivation is even lower because such small odds are given for the possibility of success.

The third reason for the equivocal nature of American efforts in this area is that U.S. interest in the nonproliferation of nuclear weapons must compete with a variety of other U.S. national interests. One example is the maintenance of good relations with America's allies. It is due to this competing goal that the Atoms for Peace program was devised. It was launched in response to criticism by America's allies that the

United States was pursuing a highly discriminatory policy by preventing others from enjoying the fruits of atomic energy. Thus, in the hope of mitigating criticism, the United States compromised her nonproliferation policy. Later, America's nonproliferation policy was compromised by other competing national interests, which caused the United States to refrain from initiating a nuclear test ban during the late 1950s. The competing interests included the priorities of America's own testing program, deference to the sensitivities of Great Britain, which had not yet completed her own testing series, and finally the wish to share America's nuclear knowledge and weapons with her allies in the hope of offsetting what was perceived as a Soviet advantage achieved by the Sputnik.[70]

It became obvious that U.S. policy with respect to nuclear proliferation was "not entirely negative, merely selective."[71] In 1957 the U.S. was willing to compromise her nonproliferation policy in order to strengthen NATO's deterrent capability. Secretary of State John Foster Dulles announced an American plan to participate in a NATO atomic stockpile system in Europe "to assure that nuclear warheads will be readily available to NATO forces in the event of hostilities." He also indicated that in order to strengthen the NATO deterrent, the "United States was prepared to make available to other NATO countries intermediate-range ballistic missiles, for deployment in accordance with the plans of SACEUR."[72] In 1958 the United States opposed French acquisition of nuclear weapons, but compromised her ability to pursue this opposition vigorously by simultaneously fostering a special nuclear relationship with Great Britain.[73] William Bader maintained that this compromised "international confidence in the sincerity of [the U.S.] nonproliferation stand and embittered one of [the U.S.'s] staunchest allies."[74] In order to make possible the special agreement with Britain, the antiproliferation McMahon Act of 1946 had to be further amended. The amendments legislated in 1958 compromised the principles of America's nonproliferation policy by authorizing "the transfer of technical information and material help for the manufacture of nuclear devices to countries that had already made 'substantial progress in the development of atomic weapons.' "[75]

The United States further compromised its nonproliferation policy in 1958 by voting against an Irish proposal for a United Nations nonproliferation resolution. "The reasons given for this position were artfully obscure. On a non-transfer proposal the United States could not 'accept any obligation, the observance of which could not be verified.' "[76] The decade of the 1960s, especially until 1968, continues with a similarly compromised American nuclear nonproliferation policy. Initially, the Kennedy administration determined "that opposition to the proliferation of nuclear weapons should be a fundamental tenet of American nuclear policy."[77] However, this general principle was soon compromised. Bader reports that "the contradictory elements in President Kennedy's policy were most painfully manifested in the short and unhappy life of the Atlantic multilateral force. Here the President simply was unable or unwilling to determine his priorities, and consequently ended up with a policy of attempting to blend the unblendable, that is, a continuation of the 'special' relationship with Britain, an almost theological position that 'all' nuclear spread was bad, and hints of support for the formation of a European nuclear force."[78] Furthermore, despite its opposition to an independent French nuclear force, the Kennedy administration decided to sell France a dozen KC-135 jet tanker planes, to be used to refuel the Mirage IV bombers of the French *Force de Frappe*.[79] At one point the administration even offered to sell France a nuclear submarine.[80] All this further contributed to the general confusion about America's nonproliferation policy. At the end of Kennedy's short tenure the United States succeeded in negotiating with the Soviets a Nuclear Test Ban Treaty, which was ratified by the Senate on September 24, 1963. However, since it did not bind third parties, the ban did not impose a barrier to nuclear proliferation.[81] During the second half of the 1960s President Johnson "made the attainment of a nonproliferation treaty a national jihad."[82]

In an effort to avoid offending America's NATO allies, however, the United States drafted its proposals in a way that
was completely unacceptable to the Soviet Union. Finally,
the Nonproliferation Treaty (N.P.T.) was concluded in 1968.
It aimed "at dividing the world between the five nuclear
weapon powers, which undertake not to assist any country
to manufacture a nuclear explosive device, and the other
states, which undertake not to proceed with such a fabrication
and agree to submit all their installations to IAEA safeguards."[83] However, the Treaty did not erase a legacy of an
American policy that was both inconsistent and equivocal.
This ambivalence was manifested clearly during the
Nixon–Ford administration.

Secretary of State Henry Kissinger's pessimism about the
odds of curbing proliferation was apparent in his implementation of the nonproliferation policy. On one hand, some significant measures against nuclear spread were taken, notably
the ban on the export of reprocessing technology. Also, an
effort was launched to prevent other states from exporting
such technology. The Symington amendment attached to the
1976 International Security Assistance and Arms Export Control Act promised to cut off military assistance or FMS credits
to recipients that either import or export a reprocessing plant.
In August 1976 Kissinger used this provision to discourage
Pakistan from purchasing a reprocessing plant, "informing
the Pakistani government that the United States might not
provide the A-7 aircraft Pakistan wanted if it acquired the
reprocessing plant."[84] In 1975 the Ford administration forced
South Korea to terminate its embryonic nuclear weapons program and in 1976 she was similarly persuaded to cancel the
planned construction of a French-made reprocessing plant.[85]
On the other hand, U.S.–Indian relations remained un-
scorched by the 1974 Indian nuclear explosion; the United
States did not terminate its nuclear supply relationship with
India and shipments of enriched uranium to that country
continued;[86] U.S.–Pakistani relations remained unaffected
by Pakistan's Ali Bhuto's statement that his country would,
if necessary, "eat grass but produce the bomb";[87] the Ger-

many–Brazil nuclear deal was neglected and ignored until very late;[88] an attempt to dissuade France from selling the nuclear reprocessing plant to Pakistan was rebuffed;[89] finally, in the name of a competing interest, i.e., improved relations with Middle East states, 600-megawatt nuclear power reactors were offered to both Israel and Egypt. Significantly, the Nixon–Ford administration did not require that the two countries sign and ratify the 1968 Nuclear Nonproliferation Treaty as a precondition for the sale. Indeed, Kissinger's appreciation of competing American national interests was reflected in his response to suggestions that the United States should apply sanctions against potential proliferators by withholding aid from states that refuse to sign the N.P.T.: "Of course, we strongly support the Nuclear Nonproliferation Treaty, and we hope that the maximum number of countries will sign it. On the other hand, we have to ask ourselves whether the security of the countries that we are assisting is in our interest, and if it is in our interest, then cutting them off from American support is against our interest."[90] Some of these possibly competing interests involve America's national security. For example, American interest in the dispersal of its nuclear forces required that they be stationed in various parts of the globe. As a consequence, the United States has refrained from embracing proposals for the establishment of Nuclear Weapons Free Zones.[91]

No American president took as strong a position against nuclear proliferation as did President Carter, who reiterated time and again that "the need to halt nuclear proliferation is one of mankind's most pressing challenges."[92] His strong position showed itself on various fronts. He was the first to call for a worldwide moratorium on the commercialization of plutonium fuel. Central to his approach was the administration's decision, announced in April 1977, to defer indefinitely the commercial reprocessing and recycling of plutonoum; to restructure the U.S. breeder program and to suspend plans for the demonstration Clinch River breeder-reactor project; and to continue to embargo the export of enrichment and reprocessing technology.[93] Second, the Carter administration exerted much pressure on the Japanese, British, French, and West German governments to rescind their plutonium reprocessing and fast-breeder reactor programs. The French were particularly pressed to cancel the planned reprocessing plant sale to Pakistan, while the West Germans were asked to forgo the export of a similar plant to Brazil. Furthermore, the Carter administration was the first to introduce legislation stipulating clear sanctions against potential proliferators, namely the Nuclear Nonproliferation Act of 1978.[94] The Act "provided that non-nuclear-weapons nations wanting U.S. enrichment services, nuclear fuel and equipment, and sensitive nuclear technology must agree to have all their nuclear facilities open to international inspections ('full-scope safeguards') and grant the United States 'consent rights' over reprocessing and transfer to other countries of their spent reactor fuel. This included U.S. supplies of enriched uranium fuel under new or amended nuclear cooperation agreements, as well as non-U.S.-supplied fuel used in U.S.-supplied reactors."[95] Existing agreements for nuclear cooperation between the United States and other countries had to be renegotiated to meet these requirements. Also, the Carter administration had been the first to officially apply sanctions against a potential proliferator. When Pakistan's acquisition of a uranium enrichment facility became known, the administration invoked the Glenn amendment to the International Security Assistance Act of 1977 and proceeded to cut off all aid for economic development granted to that country.[96] Finally, the administration initiated the convening in October 1977 of an International Fuel Cycle Evaluation (INFCE), which with the participation of a large number of nuclear suppliers and recipients undertook to conduct a $2\frac{1}{2}$-year study to investigate alternative fuel cycles that might keep down risks of diversions to weapons production.[97]

However, the uncompromising fervor that characterized the Carter administration's rhetoric as well as its actual pursuit of nonproliferation goals in early 1977 soon receded. What changed was not the direction of the policy but rather the intensity. True, the administration continued to demonstrate a willingness to strain relations with America's allies, Germany and France, while pressing them to withdraw their nuclear deals with Brazil and Pakistan. And the policy met some success in that in 1978 the French-Pakistani deal was canceled.[98] Yet, there had continued to be a gap between the administration's rhetoric and its actions. One one hand proliferation was characterized as the greatest danger to mankind; on the other there was a lack of willingness to cut off diplomatic relations with states that developed a nuclear capability. Rhetorically, the halting of proliferation was said to have top priority; in reality nonproliferation goals often gave way to competing national interests. The President's April 1977 antiproliferation guidelines were formulated mildly, to avoid a break with America's allies, after more restrictive earlier drafts raised "a lot of hell" among them.[99] Similarly, the Nuclear Nonproliferation Act legislated a year later was less restrictive than alternative pieces of legislation that were offered in both the House and the Senate.[100] The sanctions contained in the Act are limited to the realm of nuclear relations. A state found to be in violation of the law can expect no worse than a cutoff of nuclear exports by the United States. Moreover, in a clear attempt to avoid a clash with America's allies, Carter continued to ship nuclear fuel to EURATOM despite the West Europeans' refusal to renegotiate their nuclear cooperation agreements with the United States as required by the Act.[101] His ambivalence was also manifested in that the far more restrictive Glenn amendment to the International Security Assistance Act of 1977, offered by Senator John Glenn, was not endorsed, but merely "not opposed" by the administration.[102] This lack of enthusiasm was justified on the basis of competing national interests that merit the continuation of foreign aid, nuclear proliferation notwithstanding. As Undersecretary of State Lucy Benson said, "The difficulty with cutting off foreign economic or military aid is that there may be a time when this would for other reasons not be in the interest of our national security or in the interest of our long-term foreign policy objectives. The nuclear objective is only one of our foreign policy objectives. There are

other objectives to which foreign military assistance is fre-
quently directed."[103]

Carter's position on breeder-reactors demonstrates the nature and dynamics of his retreat. Strongly opposed to such
reactors, the President expressed his convictions in the April
1977 guidelines. However, in order to obtain Senate support
for his natural-gas bill a year later, Carter agreed to spend
$1.55 billion on breeder-reactor "research."[104] In 1979 he
suffered another setback when the final INFCE report
backed the European and Japanese view that fast-breeder
reactors will be needed to meet the world's energy needs.[105]
By election time in 1980 President Carter produced a letter
stating that "Throughout [his] Administration, [he has] maintained consistent support for a healthy, vigorous research and
development program for the liquid metal fast breeder reactor."[106]

The influence of competing interests was also reflected in
the way the Carter administration pursued its nonproliferation goals abroad. Thus, U.S. interest in inter-NATO cohesion
has set a limit to pressure exerted on Germany with respect
to its planned sale of a spent-fuel reprocessing plant and a
uranium enrichment plant to Brazil, as well as with respect
to its later planned sale of a natural uranium reactor to Argentina;[107] U.S. interest in Japanese economic cooperation
has set a limit to pressure that could have been exerted to
dissuade Japan from constructing a reprocessing plant and
breeder-reactors;[108] U.S. interest in French–NATO cooperation as well as in French–U.S. economic cooperation has
set a limit to pressure that could be exerted on Paris with
respect to its nuclear deal with Iraq; a similar interest limited
U.S. pressure on Italy regarding its own sale of "hot-cell"
simulators to Iraq; and the wish to avoid jeopardizing Switzerland's neutrality constrained possible U.S. pressure to prevent her from selling a sensitive heavy-water plant to Argentina.[109] This constant diplomatic maneuvering led Michael
Brenner to conclude that "Washington simply is not prepared
to risk a break with its allies over differences of approach to
the proliferation problem."[110]

The case of India was illustrative of Carter's ambivalence. Although India broke past promises, undertook a nuclear explosion, refused to sign the Nuclear Nonproliferation Treaty, and refused to submit her nuclear installations to full-scope safeguards, the Carter administration continued nuclear cooperation with her.[111] Violating the 1978 Nuclear Nonproliferation Act, India could not be provided with nuclear fuel. Yet, in 1978 and 1979, precisely when he tried to obtain European consent not to export sensitive reprocessing technology, President Carter utilized the grace period provided for in the 1978 Act and ordered the shipment of nuclear fuel to India.[112] Although the grace period ended in March 1980 and despite the absence of any change in India's position on full-scope safeguards, Carter decided in May 1980 to waive the provisions of the 1978 Act once again and to provide India with 38 tons of enriched uranium nuclear fuel. The President did this despite a unanimous negative recommendation by the U.S. Nuclear Regulatory Commission and in the face of much Congressional opposition;[113] in September 1980 a resolution to override his decision carried the House by a vote of 298 to 98 and was only narrowly defeated in the Senate (48 to 46).[114] Its competing interest in avoiding a dispute with India "in the wake of the Soviet drive into Afghanistan and the political turbulence in the Middle East and South Asia" compromised the administration's nuclear nonproliferation policy.[115]

Carter's handling of Pakistan's acquisition of enrichment facilities has had a similar outcome. The administration first tried to persuade Pakistan to commit herself not to produce nuclear arms in exchange for conventional arms supply.[116] Later, by invoking the Glenn amendment, Carter proceeded to cut off $40 million of A.I.D. funds intended for Pakistan. However, the larger $80-million food grant program, under Public Law 4-80, was not affected.[117] The ambivalent message could hardly have elicited the desired Pakistani response. Finally, in the wake of the December 1979 Soviet invasion of Afghanistan, President Carter asked Congress to lift the ban on aid to Pakistan. In stark violation of the spirit of its antiproliferation policy, the administration announced on December 30, 1979, its intention to provide Pakistan with artillery, night-vision devices, communications equipment, transport planes, and helicopters.[118] Carter included a pledge for such aid in his January 1980 State of the Union message to Congress.[119] Thus only nine months after having established the precedent of applying sanctions against a potential proliferator, the Carter administration established the further precedent of proposing to grant the first exemption from these sanctions. Pakistan's Zia el-Haq characterized Carter's two-year $400 million package as "peanuts" and rejected the administration's offer.[120] Eventually, therefore, there was no need to exercise the Glenn amendment's presidential escape clause. Yet, Carter's willingness to provide Pakistan such a waiver further diminished the credibility of his antiproliferation policy.

By failing to conclude a Comprehensive Test Ban Treaty and to obtain Senate ratification of SALT II, the Carter presidency further compromised its nonproliferation goals. These failures also eroded the policy's moral standing and made it vulnerable to objections that the United States was itself in violation of article VI of the N.P.T.[121] The article stipulated the obligation of the nuclear powers to take measures toward nuclear disarmament. Objections regarding superpower noncompliance with these stipulations were raised forcefully by numerous Third World countries during the Spring 1980 Nuclear Nonproliferation Treaty Review Conference.[122]

Finally, in its last months in office, the Carter administration further eroded the moral basis of its nonproliferation policy by considering an expansion of its own plutonium production capacity. The requirements of America's own nuclear weapons program, and her plutonium shortfall at the time, created the need to increase plutonium production.[123] Thus, the perceived imperatives of vertical proliferation undermined the efforts to limit horizontal spread.

The Carter administration's growing ambivalence was also partly due to the fact that only gradually did its members learn that one cannot predict how various antiproliferation measures might fare. Its officers became increasingly uneasy with exclusive reliance on punitive measures; they began to fear that by adding to small states' sense of insecurity, such measures might accelerate proliferation instead of halting it. As was the case with the Human Rights policy, the change of mood toward greater pragmatism occurred about a year after the administration took office. Furthermore, it gradually reached the conclusion that too much emphasis had initially been put on the energy route to proliferation and that not enough attention had been given to the security needs and threat perceptions of the would-be proliferators. This exaggerated emphasis has since been termed "the technology fix." As a consequence of this overemphasis, opportunities to slow down proliferation by fortifying Pakistan, India, Taiwan, and Korea's sense of security have been overlooked often. For example, following India's nuclear detonation, Pakistan sought international guarantees—a kind of nuclear umbrella—"that would bring other nuclear powers to its rescue were it to be subjected to 'nuclear blackmail.'"[124] Pakistan failed to receive such guarantees and had no choice but to push an indigenous nuclear program. Another example is the case of Taiwan. The Carter administration announced on December 16, 1978, that the U.S. was abrogating its Defense Treaty with Taiwan in order to obtain diplomatic relations with the People's Republic of China.[125] In doing so the administration either neglected to consider the effects that such a step might have on Taiwan's motivation to develop nuclear weapons, or did consider such possible effects and decided to put closer American–Chinese relations above its own nonproliferation goals. Both possibilities reflect an ambivalent approach to nuclear nonproliferation.

In the course of its tenure the Carter administration also developed a greater sensitivity to the costs incurred by the United States as a consequence of her nonproliferation policy. In part these costs were reflected in the loss of control over the international nuclear trade market. While the United States controlled 100 percent of the international nuclear trade in 1966, her share had dropped to 16 percent in 1976 and 0 (zero!) percent in 1977.[126] The Soviet Union has moved in to take America's place. By 1977 the Soviets were supplying 55 percent of the enrichment services required by Western Europe.[127] Thus while the United States pursued her environmental and nonproliferation goals, the Soviet Union has managed to reverse the direction of East–West interdependence in at least one critical field. The correct assessment of these trends is said to have led members of the Carter administration to have second thoughts about America's nonproliferation policy.

With the advent of President Ronald Reagan, America's nuclear nonproliferation efforts have undergone a shift in priorities. As a Presidential candidate, Reagan manifested a lack of interest in nonproliferation matters, insisting that the problem was "none of [America's] business."[128] Shortly after assuming office, Reagan let it be known that he intended to ask Congress for major changes in the 1978 Nuclear Nonproliferation Act.[129] His transition team endorsed the reprocessing of plutonium in "reliable" countries, recommending specifically that Japan and Western European nations be permitted to reprocess spent nuclear fuel. A subsequent administration review recommended that restrictions on nuclear exports also be eased.[130] Later, President Reagan approved a six-year, $3.2 billion economic and military aid package to Pakistan, and a separate $1.1 billion sale of 40 F-16 fighter-aircraft.[131] The administration also asked and received Congressional consent to exempt Pakistan from the stipulations of the Glenn amendment to the International Security Assistance Act. America's nonproliferation policy was compromised not only by the President's decision to waive the legislation's requirements, but particularly by his decision to do so while failing to obtain a clear Pakistani commitment not to develop a military nuclear capability and in the face of increasing evidence that Pakistan's efforts in the nuclear realm were proceeding with great vigor.[132] Despite much evidence that Iraq was planning to produce and separate plutonium, the United States cosponsored a United Nations resolution condemning Israel for the June 1981 bombing of the Iraqi nuclear reactor.[133] Following the raid, the administration made no visible effort to influence France's willingness to provide Iraq with an alternative reactor, the type of reactor to be supplied, or the conditions and safeguards attached. Likewise, no visible effort was made to obtain France's retreat from its plans to provide fuel rods for South Africa's nuclear power reactor. The latter's previous dependence on the United States for the supply of nuclear fuel provided America with the only leverage it had on South Africa's nuclear program.[134]

On July 17, 1981, President Reagan announced his administration's policy for preventing the spread of nuclear arms. The "new" guidelines, however, constituted no more than a pro-forma restatement of the virtues of non-proliferation and of America's intention to work to reduce states' motivation to acquire nuclear arms. Reagan also promised to widen adherence to the N.P.T., to strengthen the International Atomic Energy Agency, and to "[d]iscourage the transfer of sensitive nuclear material, equipment and technology and seek a requirement for adherence to international safeguards as a condition of any new nuclear supply commitment to nations not having nuclear weapons."[135] In practice, however, these guidelines were soon ignored. Contrary to past attempts to discourage uranium enrichment and spent-fuel reprocessing, Japan was permitted to continue to reprocess U.S.-supplied fuel in her pilot reprocessing plant, and with fewer restrictions attached.[136] In October 1981 Vice President Bush announced that the United States had made a "special-case exemption" to allow Brazil, which had not signed the 1968 Nuclear Nonproliferation Treaty, to purchase fuel for its nuclear reactor.[137] It also decided to increase by more than 70 percent America's own production of plutonium and tritium, thus accelerating a trend initiated by the Carter administration.[138] Also contrary to the spirit of its July policy guidelines, the Reagan administration decided in October to ease restrictions on nuclear exports. This was done in response to much initial criticism by America's nuclear industry that President Reagan was not "the good friend" it had hoped for.[139] In line with this new liberalism, Reagan decided in

November 1981 to offer Australia access to highly classified centrifuge technology to enrich uranium, technology that had not been previously shared with other governments.[140]

Thus, America's commitment to curb nuclear arms has been in constant retreat since April 1977. Of what was a forceful attempt to prevent further proliferation, only a distant echo remains. By late 1981 the United States continued to express concern about the prospects of further nuclear spread; in practice, however, indifference to proliferation was more often manifested.

America's reaction to the adoption of an overt nuclear deterrence posture by Israel is likely to reflect her general anti-proliferation policy. The United States is firmly opposed to Israeli nuclearization. This has been clear ever since the early 1960s when the Eisenhower, Kennedy, and Johnson administrations applied the carrot and stick technique. On the one hand they warned Israel against "going nuclear" in a very blunt and direct manner. The issue was first raised by the lame-duck administration of President Eisenhower, when Secretary of State Christian Herter summoned the Israeli ambassador to express the administration's "deep concern" about the nuclear reactor being assembled in Dimona.[141] In early January 1960, the administration took up the issue directly with Foreign Minister Golda Meir and Prime Minister David Ben Gurion in Israel. The exchange of views was sharp.[142] Later, President Kennedy sent Prime Minister Ben Gurion at least one strong warning against any thought of going nuclear.[143] The then Secretary of State, Dean Rusk, told this writer of at least one instance when he had warned Foreign Minister Abba Eban of the detrimental effect Israeli nuclearization would have on its relations with the United States. Also, in the early 1960s the United States asked for and received permission to inspect the Dimona reactor. These inspections were conducted on an annual basis.[144]

At the same time, the United States also distributed some carrots. In the framework of its Atoms for Peace program, the United States itself aided Israel's nuclear program in the 1950s. The Nachal Soreq Research Center was provided with an American-made small "swimming pool" type reactor producing five megawatts of thermal energy.[145] Later, in an effort to reduce Israeli security incentives for developing nuclear weapons, Israel was supplied with conventional weapons. Meyer Feldman, a former Assistant to President Kennedy, has confirmed that Kennedy offered Hawk surface-to-air missiles in return for an Israeli undertaking not to develop nuclear weapons.[146] During the Johnson administration "it was feared that excessive pressure on Israel, such as withholding conventional arms, might accelerate Israel's search for a nuclear option."[147] The Johnson administration therefore attempted to use a conventional arms bargain to extract an Israeli commitment not to produce nuclear arms. The attempt was made when the United States negotiated with Israel the supply of F-4 Phantom aircraft. Paul C. Warnke, then Assistant Secretary of Defense for International Security Affairs, forcefully voiced the demand that Israel provide such a commitment. The administration's effort failed but America's opposition to Israel's nuclear development was made quite clear.[148]

Beyond her general nonproliferation policy, there are some particular reasons why a harsh American response to Israeli nuclearization can be expected. The first reason is that America views Israel as occupying a strategic position in the efforts to curb proliferation. The premise is that if Israel, a small state with severe security problems, goes nuclear, many other states would be motivated to follow. Boskey and Willrich report that "Americans have expressed the fear that should Israel 'go nuclear' the entire structure of the N.P.T. would collapse."[149] Secondly, the United States sees Israel's possible nuclearization as particularly troublesome because of the intense involvement of both superpowers in the area. The concern is that the Middle East is more vulnerable than elsewhere to the danger that a local nuclear confrontation would escalate to a superpower nuclear exchange. The nightmare of an American–Soviet nuclear war causes much of the opposition to Mideast nuclearization. Thirdly, the United States is particularly concerned that Israeli nuclearization will accelerate the deterioration of America's ability to influence her allies. It would contribute to America's "loss of control" in a very sensitive and critical region. Finally, a highly negative American reaction to Israeli nuclearization can be expected on the basis of existing antiproliferation legislation. The Glenn amendment to the International Security Assistance Act of 1977 specifically prohibits providing economic assistance, military or security-supporting assistance, or military credits to any country that is not a nuclear weapons state (as defined in article IX(3) of the Treaty on the Nonproliferation of Nuclear Weapons) and that detonates a nuclear device. It also stipulates cutting off assistance to states that import or export a uranium enrichment facility or a plutonium reprocessing plant.[150] The Nuclear Nonproliferation Act of 1978 stipulates "that United States [nuclear] cooperation with a non-nuclear weapons state would cease if that state detonates a nuclear device, terminates or abrogates an agreement providing for IAEA safeguards, or materially violates an IAEA safeguards agreement or any guarantee it has given the United States under agreement for cooperation."[151] If Israel were to violate the provisions of these laws, a sharp American response would follow through the implementation of the sanctions contained therein.

There are, however, good reasons for the prediction that America's response to Israeli disclosure would also reflect her generally equivocal practice of antiproliferation policies. In Israel's case, as in others, the implementation of the policy will reflect both a low estimate of the chances of success and the presence of competing U.S. national interests. A number of considerations will greatly affect America's response. The first is that once disclosure occurs, it is a fait accompli. The genie cannot be put back in the bottle. American thinking would immediately be directed to the purpose of cutting losses. An immediate effort would be made to assess the situation and adjust to the new reality. Punishment at that point would appear to be quite senseless.

A second consideration in favor of continuing aid to Israel evolves from America's desire to prevent nuclear war. Once disclosure takes place and Israel moves to a nuclear deterrent posture, the United States would have an interest in increasing the nuclear threshold. A termination of the military aid program would undermine Israel's conventional capabilities and might require nuclear retaliation in response to intermediate level threats. A continuation of the aid program would enhance Israel's conventional "leg" and would increase the likelihood that only high-level threats would trigger the threat of nuclear retaliation. In fact, U.S. officials have already recognized this to be in America's interest. Testifying on March 16, 1977, before a subcommittee of the Senate Committee on Appropriations, Deputy Secretary of Defense Charles Duncan stated: "By improving the strength of conventional forces in certain countries we believe we have discouraged the pursuit of nuclear options and, where such an option already exists, stronger conventional forces increase the nuclear threshold."[152] The rationale for continuing the supply of conventional arms following small states' nuclearization has been elaborated by Richard Burt. Burt has pointed out that "arms transfers may have a more important role to play *after* proliferation has occurred than *before*. While the availability of specific items of conventional equipment is unlikely to satisfy many of the desires that might tempt a state to go nuclear, their existence could have an important impact on the decision whether nuclear weapons would actually be used in the event of conflict. Thus the transfer of conventional arms may have more utility in managing the process of proliferation than in halting it."[153] This would certainly provide some logic to a continuation of arms transfers to Israel following nuclearization.

A third consideration likely to moderate the American response is that for many Washingtonians disclosure would not come as a total surprise. To many in America's defense and arms control communities disclosure would merely confirm existing suspicions. Most members of these communities believe that Israel already has nuclear weapons and the absence of shock could smooth somewhat the character of the negative American reaction.

US special commitment to IS

A fourth moderating influence on America's negative reaction evolves from her interest in preventing further nuclear proliferation. Following Israeli disclosure, the dictates of nonproliferation would require that Israel sign and ratify the N.P.T. as a nuclear weapons state, to insure that she would not contribute to further proliferation. Obtaining Israeli ratification would require that she not be antagonized, thus helping to moderate the negative American reaction. This demonstrates the inherent conflict between the American desire to see that Israel does not develop nuclear weapons and the American desire to reduce the impact of such a nuclear policy if it is adopted. This problem, of course, is a familiar one with the tactics of commitment. Once the other side has taken the forbidden action, the state often does not want to carry out its threats. In this case, the United States not only would be concerned about the costs of carrying out any threats it has made to punish Israel, but also would want to reduce the degree to which Israel's going nuclear would lead to further proliferation. Thus, before the fact, the United States might want to argue that if Israel adopted an overt nuclear policy, such adoption would totally break the nonproliferation regime; but after the fact, the United States would want to make very different arguments in order to avert the very consequences that it had said Israel's nuclear posture would bring about.

The final and most important consideration to influence America's reaction is her long-standing commitment to Israel's security and survival. This unique commitment, based on a moral and ideological affinity, is likely to set the outer limits to America's negative reaction to Israeli nuclearization. It is likely to make Israel a "special case" with respect to nuclear nonproliferation. In fact, some evidence suggests that Israel is already considered a special case in this respect. One set of evidence revolves around the fact that in Israel's case the United States did not exert very strong pressure against nuclear development. The Johnson administration was not very forceful in its attempt to extract an Israeli promise not to produce nuclear weapons. In fact, after some delay,

President Johnson ordered the bureaucracy to withdraw its efforts to link such a promise to the supply of conventional arms.[154] The special attitude was even more apparent during the Nixon and Ford administrations. Shlomo Aronson reports that the former "never raised the nuclear issue with Israel during its term, and the American inspections at [the] Dimona [nuclear reactor] stopped in 1969."[155] In 1974, after Israel's President Ephraim Katzir stated that Israel had created a potential for making nuclear arms, Secretary of State Henry Kissinger—after repeated attempts to evade the issue—merely remarked that he would have used a different formulation.[156]

A second set of evidence regarding Israel's "special case" involves the fact that the United States did not react dramatically when she "found out" that Israel "had" nuclear weapons. If anything, the United States took steps that had the effect of contributing to the disclosure of the deterrent at the time: A briefing to the Senate Foreign Relations Committee by C.I.A. Director Richard Helms, on July 7, 1970, was the first official word that Israel had nuclear weapons.[157] This statement by the director of the C.I.A. was not followed by any reduction of American support of Israel. Actually, for other reasons, the United States dramatically increased conventional arms sales to Israel a few months later.

By the mid 1970s there seems to have emerged a trend in Washington to further the disclosure of Israeli nuclear weapons. On March 11, 1976, a senior C.I.A. official said at a private briefing that Israel was estimated to have 10 to 20 nuclear weapons ready for use. The briefing was given to 150 members of the American Institute of Aeronautics and Astronautics. Arthur Kranish published the briefing's content in the *Washington Post*, claiming he had been given permission to do so. When approached about this, C.I.A. Director George Bush took full responsibility but said there had been an understanding that it would not be published.[158] This was not the last C.I.A. report about Israeli nuclear weapons to be leaked. In early January 1978, a C.I.A. report dated September 4, 1974, stating its assessment that Israel had acquired nuclear weapons, found its way to the news media. In some ways it was even more startling than the not-so-off-the-record briefing of a year and a half earlier. For the first time, a U.S. government document defining Israel as a nuclear state was made available. The report cited Israeli purchases of large quantities of uranium, partly through subversive methods, and "the peculiar nature of Israeli efforts in the field of uranium enrichment as well as large investments in the development of a missile system capable of delivering nuclear warheads."[159] The C.I.A. announced the following day that it was sorry about the publication of the top-secret report. The agency claimed it was all a mistake of one of its officials who inadvertently declassified the document along with others that the agency had transmitted to the Department of Energy. Yet one wonders if this was really a mistake. The agents who declassified the document were John Despers, the intelligence officer in charge of nuclear proliferation, and John Wilson, the agency's spokesman.[160] The former must have understood the content of the report and its implications, and the latter must have been aware of the sensitivity of the issue. That two such experienced agents would so blunder is difficult to believe.

A month later another story came out. On March 1, 1978, an interdepartmental coordinating committee on nuclear issues published a 252-page document containing the minutes of meetings held in February 1976. It included the testimony of Carl Duckett, then C.I.A.'s Deputy Director of the Department of Science and Technology, to the effect that by 1968 the C.I.A. had already reported to President Johnson the existence of Israeli nuclear weapons. Duckett also testified that President Johnson ordered the Agency's director, Richard Helms, not to pass on the report on Israeli weapons to anyone, including Secretary of State Dean Rusk and Secretary of Defense Robert S. McNamara. Once again the story of how the report found its way to the press is almost as interesting as the report itself. The document included many blank spaces, of paragraphs which were deleted for security reasons. Some fifty copies were distributed. In only one of these copies the page telling of the Johnson–Helms conversation was "by mistake" not deleted. For some peculiar reason this particular copy found its way into the hands of John Fialka of the *Washington Star*. Needless to say, Fialka published the story immediately.[161]

These accounts have three things in common that may be helpful in predicting America's reaction to a disclosure of Israeli nuclear weapons. In all three cases the report, document, or briefing found its way to the mass media in a contrived manner. This suggests that elements of the U.S. government developed an interest in the disclosure of Israeli nuclear weapons. Second, all three cases do in fact constitute elements of disclosure, which was carried out despite the fact that any measure of disclosure involves sacrificing some nonproliferation interests. This may be taken as evidence that in Washington's view there are competing interests that justify the disclosure of Israeli nuclear weapons despite the sacrifice of some nonproliferation interests. The identity of the competing interests is beside the point. Some of the leaks may have come from officials interested in limiting conventional arms sales to Israel. Others might have been prompted by the wish to expose Israel as powerful and hence as capable of being more flexible in Mideast peace negotiations. Whatever the competing interests may be, as a result of their existence the American reaction to disclosure is likely to be less disastrous than some analysts expect.

A third common feature is the fact that in none of the instances when the United States "found out" about Israeli nuclear weapons—in 1968, 1974, or 1976, was the "finding" followed by a negative American reaction. Neither were the acts of disclosure in 1976 and 1978 followed by any such reaction. Actually, the contrary is the case. With the possible exception of 1978 all the dates mentioned constitute peak years of U.S. conventional arms supply to Israel. The same conclusion is reached on the basis of studying the White House reaction to these disclosures. For example, the 1978 leak of the 1974 report on Israeli acquisition of nuclear weapons elicited the following comment by Carter's White House

Press Secretary Jody Powell: "The Israeli government has declared that Israel is not a nuclear power and will not be the first to introduce nuclear weapons into the area. We accept this as the official position of the government of Israel."[162] Equally evasive was a subsequent statement by President Carter. Speaking to newspaper editors, Carter said the United States accepted Israeli statements with respect to her nuclear capability and added: "I don't have any independent sources of information beyond that."[163] Both statements involve fairly transparent efforts to avoid a negative reaction to elements of disclosure of Israeli nuclear weapons. These attitudes lead us to assume, if the circumstances are right and competing interests continue to exist, that the American reaction to Israeli disclosure will be less harsh than some have predicted.

Closer reading of the documents will also support a less pessimistic prediction regarding the likely U.S. response to Israeli disclosure. As mentioned earlier, the Glenn amendment to the International Security Assistance Act of 1977 requires a cutoff of all military and economic aid to states that violate the law's provisions. However, the sanctions stipulated by the 1978 Nuclear Nonproliferation Act are all limited to the realm of nuclear relations. States violating the law will suffer no more than the termination of U.S. nuclear cooperation agreements with them. To states that are dependent on U.S. military and economic aid but not dependent on U.S. nuclear exports, the stipulations of the Security Assistance Act are the only source of serious concern. Israel at present does not have a nuclear cooperation agreement with the United States, and the provisions of the Nuclear Nonproliferation Act cannot be applied to her. As for the Glenn amendment, as noted earlier, the law requires the cutoff of all economic and military assistance to states that either import or export a nuclear enrichment plant, import or export a nuclear reprocessing plant, or detonate a nuclear device.[164] Announcing that a nuclear deterrent capability exists does not per se constitute a violation of the law's provisions. A violation will occur only if disclosure is followed by a nuclear detonation or if it can be shown that an enrichment facility or a separation plant has been imported. Second, even with respect to the importation of enrichment or reprocessing facilities there are limitations to the application of the law. A state would have had to import a reprocessing plant or an enrichment facility *after* the date of the law's enactment— August 4, 1977—in order to be in violation of the law. This provision may exempt Israel from the law's application. Indeed, when the State Department spokesman was asked why the Glenn amendment was applied against Pakistan but not against India or Israel, he responded: "The Symington–Glenn amendments apply only to the transfer of equipment, materials and technology for the enrichment and reprocessing of uranium after the dates these amendments were enacted, August 4, 1977. We are not aware of any such transfers to Israel or India since the effective date of the Symington and Glenn amendments, and therefore, they do not apply."[165] Third, it should be noted that the Glenn amendment to the International Security Assistance Act contains a presidential escape clause. It gives the President the right to grant states a waiver from the law's sanctions. The clause stipulates that

> Notwithstanding [the law's provisions] . . . the President may furnish assistance which would otherwise be prohibited under such subsection if he determines and certifies in writing to the Speaker of the House of Representatives and the Committee on Foreign Relations of the Senate that the termination of such assistance would be seriously prejudicial to the achievement of United States non-proliferation objectives or otherwise jeopardize the common defense and security. The President shall transmit with such certification a statement setting forth the specific reasons therefor."[166]

The escape clause was requested by the Carter administration to allow competing national interests to be taken into account before punishment is applied.[167] As long as the President and Congress define the survival and security of Israel as a U.S. national interest, the escape clause could apply to the Israeli case. This could be important only if Israel were to be found in technical violation of these laws or if she were ever actually required to detonate a device. Furthermore, having utilized the escape clause in the case of Pakistan in 1981, its application to the Israeli case would not constitute a precedent.

~ It also deserves notice that the possibility of applying the Act's escape clause to Israel's case was indirectly and directly mentioned by both the law's principal author and the Carter administration's spokesmen who testified about it. In hearings on his proposed amendment, Senator John Glenn sketched a possible situation that might justify the use of the escape clause:

> I am thinking of a situation, perhaps, when there might be, for instance, some nations under attack. I don't think we need to put particular nations' names to this necessarily, although I don't object if anyone cares to, but let's say a nation is under attack. They have an unknown atomic weapons capability. They do in fact have a bomb. It has been secret all of this time. It would be quite a different thing if they set that thing off in the middle of the desert some place, as an example of their capability. No one would be hurt or killed, but they would do it to show what power they had in trying to stop a war that was under way, as opposed, say, to setting if off in the middle of an intensely populated city and maybe killing two million people, to pick a figure out of the air, to make their example."[168]

Senator Glenn thus agrees to the utilization of the escape clause in a situation far more extreme than mere disclosure. Indirectly, the actual use of a nuclear weapon is endorsed under specified conditions. A similar attitude is expressed by the Carter administration spokeswoman, Lucy Wilson Benson, Undersecretary of State for coordinating Security Assistance programs. The exchange between her and Senator Glenn about the presidential waiver is extremely revealing:

> *Mrs. Benson:* Without going into names of countries, I think that this is where it gets a little bit of a sticky wicket. If there was a Presidential waiver, then I think this would remove that problem, at least to a great degree.
>
> There could easily be times when, regardless of what a country did, we might want to go ahead with military assistance for other quite separate reasons.

Senator Glenn: Do you mean even if it set off a nuclear explosion?
Mrs. Benson: Yes, I could see how that might happen. The President, I believe, would need the flexibility to declare that even if they did set off an explosion—you used an example yourself earlier in the hearing of supposing that a country which was at war set off a nuclear explosion in the middle of the desert to show its capability. That would be quite different from setting off an explosion in the middle of a city.
Senator Glenn: I am not against giving the President some flexibility in this, as I indicated earlier. I think that that might make this more acceptable to a lot of people in the Mideast situation, of course, which is the one that always comes up in any discussion as to what happens if Israel is being overrun. Senator Javits addressed it the other day when Mr. Warnke was here, I believe.

I think in a situation like that the President should have some flexibility, and I certainly would not object to it.[169]

Another document supporting the proposition that Israel, at least to this date, constitutes a special case in Washington's general position on nuclear proliferation is a U.S. Senate report issued in 1977. As noted earlier, the 1978 Nuclear Non-Proliferation Act requires, as a condition of continued United States nuclear supply to a nonnuclear weapon state, that all its civil nuclear activities be under IAEA safeguards. A few months before the introduction of the bill, a Senate delegation visited the Middle East to investigate American foreign policy and nonproliferation interests in the region, with particular emphasis on the possible effects of the Nixon administration's proposal to sell nuclear power reactors to both Israel and Egypt. The delegation included Senators Ribicoff, Baker, Cannon, Eagleton, Glenn, Ford, Culver, Bumpers, Pearson, Griffin, Bellman, and Laxalt. Their report, dated June 1977, or two months after the administration bill had already been introduced, included, with only two dissenting votes, the following recommendation: "Notwithstanding the adequacy of assurances against diversion in the proposed agreements for Egypt and Israel, the delegation believes that ratification of the N.P.T. by Israel and Egypt, and the placement by Israel of its Dimona facility under IAEA safeguards, would provide added reassurance. Nonetheless, the delegation believes it would be counterproductive to require such measures as a pre-condition to the pending sales."[170] The recommendation amounts to an exemption of Israel from the spirit of existing antiproliferation legislation as well as from the precise provisions of an antiproliferation bill already introduced by President Carter. The importance of this report in attempting to predict the American response to Israeli disclosure is particularly great in view of the fact that at least some of the senators took a less-than-naive view of the nature of the activities at Dimona. Senator Pearson, for example, declared on his return from the trip that he was "convinced that the Israelis have nuclear bombs and would use them against the Arabs if their survival were profoundly threatened."[171] The administrations of Nixon and Ford took a similar position and refused to condition the possible sale on Israel's prior ratification of the N.P.T. This was reflected in Congressional testimony given by Undersecretary of State Joseph Sisco in 1974:

> [W]hy don't we insist on adherence to the Non-Proliferation Treaty as a condition for supplying the reactors? . . . The United States is committed to seeking the widest possible adherence to the Non-Proliferation Treaty. We hope that both Israel and Egypt will eventually join us and all other nations in subscribing to it. The agreements we propose to sign with them will reflect faithfully their support for the Treaty's objectives. However, it is clear that neither Israel nor Egypt sees its national interests presently served by becoming a party to the N.P.T. Over the short run virtually nothing is likely to alter these perceptions. Our efforts must be bent to helping build the conditions in which those perceptions can change. It is our hope that provision of peaceful nuclear facilities under strict controls against military use can create in time a momentum toward a climate consistent with the goal of nonproliferation within the region and between both nations and the United States.[172]

Similar sentiments were reflected a year later in the following exchange between Congressman Dupont and Assistant Secretary of State Alfred L. Atherton during hearings on the International Security Assistance Act of 1976.

> *Mr. Dupont:* Would you have any objection, Mr. Secretary, to an amendment similar to last year's amendment that prohibits the transfer of atomic reactors to either Israel or Egypt?

Mr. Atherton: Perhaps I could answer that, Mr. Dupont, since I was involved in the recent discussion on this.

I think we would indeed object to that. We feel this is an area where it is in our interest to be able to enter into cooperation with Egypt and with Israel on the assumption that we can conclude satisfactorily grant agreements of cooperation with both countries which were ——

Mr. Dupont: Would you object if the amendment were worded somewhat differently to say no delivery to countries who have not signed the Nuclear Non-Proliferation Treaty?

Mr. Atherton: I think we would also have problems with that, Mr. Dupont.

Mr. Dupont: Surely it is the policy of the State Department that everybody ought to sign the treaty.

Mr. Atherton: Indeed it is. We would like to see it signed and ratified but the realities are that a number of countries for reasons of their own have not yet done so and this is not going to keep them from getting nuclear reactors.

Our feeling is that it is highly preferable if they want to come to us and we can negotiate safeguards that I think you will see when this agreement is submitted, as it will be, to the Congress it will be very far-reaching in what has been accomplished in previous safeguard agreements.[173]

Surely Atherton's responses reflect the ambivalence surrounding the nonproliferation policy. One more example of what happens when U.S. nonproliferation policy must compete with other American interests in the Middle East can be found in a 1979 U.S. Senate debate about an amendment offered by Senator Jesse Helms, aimed at conditioning U.S. assistance to Israel and Egypt, following the 1979 peace treaty between them, on their prior ratification of the N.P.T. Senator Frank Church, Chairman of the Senate Committee on Foreign Relations, demanded that the amendment be dropped. His words reflect the basic dilemma involved in implementing U.S. nonproliferation policy:

If the amendment offered by the able Senator from North Carolina [Helms] were adopted, the effect of it would be to kill the bill. If the Senate wishes to kill the bill and give no further support to a peace initiative in the Middle East, this is the way to do it. . . . It is the declared statutory policy of the United States to do what it can to prevent the proliferation of nuclear weapons by attempting to discourage other governments from developing this capability. . . . [However] we cannot do it by the way suggested by this amendment. The least effective way I can conceive of is to say we are selecting out two countries that are attempting to make peace, that have signed a peace treaty after 30 years of war, and we are saying to them, "we will give you no help unless you two countries sign the non-proliferation pact." That is known as linkage, Mr. President. We are here today supporting this bill because we believe it serves the interests of this country. And we are to sacrifice the interests of this country in attempting to promote peace in the Middle East by linking our support to a demand that the principles that made peace must sign the non-proliferation pact? We know it will not work. We know it will defeat our own interests. We know that the adoption of the amendment will effectively kill the bill. For all these reasons, I strongly urge the Senate to reject the amendment.[174]

The Helms amendment was defeated on the Senate floor by a vote of 76 to 7. The vote reflected the Senate's priorities.

Finally, a 1979 vote at the United Nations General Assembly is also instructive. On December 11 of that year the General Assembly adopted by a vote of 97 to 10 with 38 abstentions an Iraqi-sponsored resolution calling on Israel to open all of her nuclear facilities to IAEA inspections. It further called on all nations to take all the necessary steps to prevent the transfer to Israel of such technology and fissile material as may be used for the production of nuclear weapons. The Iraqi resolution was consistent with the spirit of U.S. nonproliferation policy as articulated by the 1978 Nonproliferation Act, yet the United States chose to vote against the resolution.[175] As another reflection of the inconsistent way in which she pursues her nonproliferation policies, the vote against the resolution clearly involved sacrificing some nonproliferation interests. One can only speculate on what led the United States to vote that way. Most probably, the Carter administration did not want to raise a new issue of contention with Israel at the time that delicate negotiations on the Palestinian autonomy were being conducted. However, the precise nature of the competing interests is beside the point. For our purposes the instructive point is that when competing U.S. interests in the Middle East require that some nonproliferation interests be sacrificed, sacrificed they be.

If competing interests and considerations were likely to moderate a negative U.S. response to Israeli disclosure under the strongly antiproliferation Carter administration, there is all the more reason to expect such moderation under the more ambivalent Reagan presidency. True, the director of the U.S. Arms Control and Disarmament Agency, Eugene Rostow, began in August 1981 "preliminary diplomatic talks" regarding the possibility of establishing a Nuclear Weapons Free Zone in the Middle East. The idea was that a Mideast agreement be tailored according to the 1967 Treaty of Tlateloco, establishing such a zone in Latin America.[176] Also, President Reagan promised to seek a wider adherence to the N.P.T. in his July 1981 nonproliferation policy guidelines. However, when asked by a reporter whether Israel should sign the 1968 Treaty, his response was more than ambiguous. A transcript of the exchange reads as follows:

> Q.: Mr. President, how appropriate do you believe is Israel's decision not to sign the Nuclear Non-Proliferation Treaty and not to submit to inspection by the International Atomic Energy Agency? And I have a follow-up.
>
> The President: Well, I haven't given very much thought to that particular question there, the subject about them not signing that Treaty or, on the other hand, how many countries do we know that have signed it that very possibly are going ahead with nuclear weapons? It's, again, something that doesn't lend itself to verification.
>
> It is difficult for me to envision Israel as being a threat to its neighbors. It is a Nation that from the very beginning has lived under the threat from neighbors that they did not recognize its right to exist as a Nation.
>
> I'll have to think about that question you asked.[177]

In addition to this ambivalence, the Reagan administration continued the pattern of treating Israel as a "special case" in her nonproliferation efforts. Thus, no action against Israel was taken although the C.I.A. reportedly told the House Foreign Affairs Committee that Israel "was now believed to possess 10 to 20 nuclear weapons that could be delivered either by fighter-bombers or [by] Israel's domestically designed and built Jericho missile."[178]

The Reagan administration's assessment of Israel's nuclear status as well as its effort to avoid confronting her with the nuclear issue was also apparent in the formulation of anti-proliferation legislation. In December 1981 two members of the House Foreign Affairs Committee, Stephen J. Solarz and Jonathan B. Bingham, withdrew their proposed amendment to cut off aid to any nation that manufactures a nuclear weapon. They agreed to drop the provision after they were told, at a meeting with Undersecretary of State James L. Buckley, "that such a requirement might well trigger a finding by the Administration that Israel has manufactured a bomb."[179]

The fact that various factors are likely to moderate America's negative reaction to Israel's overt nuclearization in no way implies that a sharp negative reaction by the United States is not to be expected. On the contrary, such reaction is more likely than not. For a number of reasons disclosure would put Israel in a very difficult position. First, it would be awkward for the United States to exempt Israel from its general nonproliferation policy without jeopardizing the credibility of the entire endeavor. The President of the United States could not apply the legislation's escape clauses to Israel without further undermining the rationale of his nonproliferation policy. Second, on the issue of nuclear weapons Israel might not even enjoy the support of its traditional friends in the United States, who belong predominantly to the liberal wing of American politics. Some of Israel's most ardent supporters in the House and the Senate— such as Senator Alan Cranston and Congressman Jonathan Bingham—have also been in the forefront of America's nuclear nonproliferation policy. Israel would have to be extremely persuasive to secure their support on this issue. Israel's fewer friends on the conservative end of America's political spectrum are not likely to be of much help either, because they would be reacting principally to the general issue of American preparedness. Israel's nuclearization would be viewed as an example of the consequences of America's increasing inability to provide for the security of her allies. At the same time the conservatives would voice their concern about the long-term effect of the nuclearization of small states on America's ability to influence events abroad. Furthermore, the nuclear issue is one on which Israel probably will not even enjoy the strong support of the American Jewish community. Although less so now than before, the American Jewish community still identifies its values predominantly with the values of the Eastern liberal establishment. There will not be automatic support on the nuclear issue; indeed Israel will have a lot of explaining to do before this obstacle is overcome. Another source of condemnation will be the Eastern liberal press. The *New York Times, Washington Post, Christian Science Monitor, Boston Globe,* and others are sure to express their sharp disapproval. Israel would have to put forth an excellent case in order to avoid a fiasco in the American mass media. Finally, Israel may be sharply attacked by parts of the American arms control community. Many who for years have developed a deep personal interest in arms control within the administration, in Congressional staffs, and in Washington's "think tanks," are bound to react negatively. Some will schedule hearings and investigations; others will testify. In addition, those who have traditionally held a less sympathetic view of Israel are likely to take a vocal "we told you so" position. Israeli nuclearization will provide its adversaries in the American political system with effective ammunition. Odds are that the debate will get a bit nasty.

What can one make of the arguments and counterarguments about the expected American response to Israeli nuclearization? What can one predict on the basis of these numerous considerations and countervailing considerations? Two conclusions stand out: that the American response to disclosure is likely to be negative, and that the intensity of the negative response will depend very much on the precise context and manner in which disclosure is made. The intensity of the response may range from a mild pro-forma disapproval to a sharp termination of assistance and relations. It is also clear that the response to disclosure would depend much on the political character of the person occupying the White House. A highly popular president, dedicated to liberal causes, in-

territorial concessions + US → reaction to Is nuclear

fluential in the Congress and well on top of his job, could give a prohibitive American response to Israeli nuclearization. A less popular and able president, member of a minority party, lacking strong convictions about proliferation, and facing a hostile Congress, might well produce a "passable" reaction. Between these extremes there are many possible combinations and outcomes.

Some generalizations about circumstances that might moderate the negative American response may be in order. First, America's reaction will probably be less intense if Israel's adoption of overt nuclear deterrence takes place after some future proliferation of nuclear weapons has occurred. If Israeli disclosure is made after Taiwan, South Korea, or South Africa has gone nuclear, the American reaction to the Israeli case may be relatively moderate. Further proliferation will affect the basic premises of U.S. nonproliferation policy. Also, under such circumstances Israel could not be made a test case for that policy. Both considerations would directly influence the American response to Israeli nuclearization. Second, America's reaction is likely to be much moderated if Israel adopts nuclear deterrence after at least one Arab or, to a somewhat lesser degree, Moslem state has acquired a nuclear capability and can be demonstrated to have done so convincingly. Iraq and Pakistan are the most suitable condidates for this role in the intermediate future. Arab acquisition of nuclear weapons will make it far easier to explain why Israel must do the same. It would be difficult for the liberal wing of American politics to condemn Israel for going nuclear after that. Israeli nuclearization would then no longer be entirely immoral. Third, America's reaction may be less negative if disclosure is made on the eve of a total Arab attack aimed at Israel's destruction. If disclosure is conducted in an attempt to deter Arab forces massed on Israel's frontiers, odds are that the reaction would be more sympathetic. Fourth, some Washingtonians predict that America's negative reaction will be much more moderated if disclosure occurs within the framework of a "package" that includes Israeli willingness to implement drastic concessions on all the outstanding

[handwritten margin note: extra security]

territorial issues. The most effective way the Israeli government could moderate a prohibitively negative American reaction would be to structure the context of disclosure in a way that maximized attainment of U.S. national interests other than its antiproliferation interests. The willingness to forego U.S. antiproliferation interests may be expected to increase as the chances of attaining competing U.S. national interests appear to improve. Thus, if together with disclosure Israel takes dramatic steps that increase the likelihood of a regional political settlement, the odds in favor of a negative American reaction are apt to decrease. This would be particularly effective if the more "flexible" political posture could be tied to the extra security provided by a nuclear deterrent posture. Competing U.S. interests, such as the interest in stabilizing the Middle East subsystem, which results from the need to stabilize the supply of energy resources, would predominate and work to mitigate a possibly negative American reaction.

Israeli nuclearization should, therefore, appear in the framework of a peace program. The central theme should be the attainment of peace. Toward that end, Israel should be willing to undertake a dramatic effort to meet Arab demands on the West Bank and the Gaza Strip as well as to conduct a politically significant withdrawal on the Golan Heights. The strategic change from conventional defense to nuclear deterrence will appear as the key that enabled Israel to make such far-reaching concessions. Nuclearization will be promoted as the key to a comprehensive peace in the Middle East. In such an instance, America's negative reaction would be much moderated. That is, such moderation can be expected if the adoption of overt nuclear deterrence is made in the framework of a new political–military package. The package must include both an effort to meet Arab territorial demands and the adoption of an overall national security policy allowing Israel to make such a sacrifice.[180] If both parts of the package are initiated concurrently, America's specific response to nuclearization can be expected to soften considerably.

[handwritten margin notes: peace program is IS best way to introduce overt]

Nuclearization may also elicit an acceptable American response if it is adopted in the framework of meeting other states' political initiatives. One example is the Saudi peace plan, announced by Crown Prince Fahd in August 1981. Israel might accept the plan as a valid preliminary negotiating position and invite the Arabs to negotiate its specific components directly. If the concessions demanded of Israel are moderated in the framework of such negotiations and the adoption of overt nuclear deterrence is presented as Israel's prerequisite for making these concessions, America's response might not be entirely negative. Washington is finding it increasingly difficult to sustain simultaneously its commitment to Israel and its interests in Saudi Arabia and the Gulf states. The Reagan administration is particularly sensitive to this problem; many of its members are strongly committed to Israel and see it as a potential strategic asset to the United States, while many others are extremely attentive to U.S. interests in Saudi Arabia and the Gulf states. Seen from this perspective, America must adopt an approach that would make its support of Israel not detrimental to its close ties with Saudi Arabia. The way to go about this would be to boost Israel's security, thereby allowing her to dispense with those elements of her present policy that the Saudis find most objectionable. By accepting Israeli nuclearization while facilitating her ability to meet most demands of the Saudi peace plan, the United States could approach the answer to her present dilemma. Should overt nuclear deterrence be adopted in such a context, America's sensibilities would moderate her negative response.

Conversely, if Israel's adoption of a disclosed nuclear posture is coupled with an intransigent, inflexible, and belligerent political posture, the likelihood of a sharply negative American reaction, of the kind that Dowty and Evron have predicted, will increase almost to the point of certainty. If the context of disclosure is such that nuclearization appears to increase dramatically the costs of war while the conflict has reached an even higher level, the odds of a prohibitive American reaction will be very high. Under such circumstances, costs involved in Israel's nuclearization would not be offset by competing interests. America would still be tempted to try to cut her losses by adjusting to the fait accompli; it might still wish to continue aiding Israel so as to increase the nuclear threshold and reduce the odds of nuclear war; and it might want to continue befriending Israel in order to elicit her cooperation in preventing further proliferation. But these considerations are unlikely to endure the weight of factors compelling a sharply negative American response. The absence of an American response would threaten whatever remains of U.S. nonproliferation policy. The United States would come under tremendous pressure to cut off its aid to Israel even if the latter's nuclearization occurs without violating the stipulation of the International Security Assistance Act. In the absence of powerful competing considerations, the legislation's "spirit" would provide sufficient cause for extreme sanctions. U.S. government officials will claim that inaction would make the United States vulnerable to criticism that her nonproliferation efforts follow a double standard. Also, if Israeli nuclearization seems aimed at fortifying her hold on the West Bank, the Gaza Strip, and the Golan Heights, America's acquiescence will lead to expressions of extreme disappointment and anger among her friends in the Arab world. Whatever emerges of the "strategic consensus" America is currently attempting to forge among her friends in the Middle East would not survive such acquiescence. Arab–U.S. bilateral relations are also likely to deteriorate. Furthermore, if the adoption of overt nuclear deterrence is not coupled with a large measure of Israeli flexibility on the outstanding issues of its conflict with the Arabs, Israel's diplomatic isolation will grow. Its image as a "pariah" state, a term applied to nations that become increasingly estranged in the world community, would then be enhanced. Continuing to support Israel under such circumstances would increase dissension between America and her allies in Europe and the Pacific. Fear of such consequences would compel the United States to react forcefully to Israel's adoption of a disclosed nuclear posture.

Thus, in one political context—characterized by Israeli political and territorial generosity—America's reaction to Israeli nuclearization may well be acceptable. Under a different set of circumstances, when overt deterrence is accompanied by political inflexibility and intransigence, the United States can be expected to produce a sharply negative response. Structuring correctly the context in which disclosure takes place is probably the most important variable that Israel can manipulate to influence the intensity of the expected negative American reaction.

Much of the above discussion points to the critical importance of the manner of disclosure. To begin with, it would be helpful if disclosure could be made gradually. As Rosen has pointed out, the likelihood of a negative American reaction could be substantially reduced if "continued published rumors of Israeli nuclear weapons leads to a situation in which the world becomes inured to the idea, so that official disclosure is reduced to a fairly minor step."[181] To a large extent, however, gradual disclosure has meanwhile already occurred, partly due to the various "leaks" in Washington. Nevertheless, in the final stages of disclosure a superb information campaign will have to be launched to explain both Israel's needs for a nuclear deterrent posture and the likely effects of its adoption. Israel would have to be able to present a strong case in support of the proposition that the adoption of such a posture reduces the odds of war and is not detrimental to regional or global stability. Israel will also have to elaborate what positive steps the United States could take to reduce even further the likelihood that Israeli nuclearization might have a destabilizing effect on both the regional and the global level. The White House and the bureaucracy will have to be courted and Congress will have to be lobbied; the Jewish community will have to be mobilized and the concerns of the arms control community will have to be addressed; the mass media's inquiries will have to be answered and the American public will have to be made privy to the full range of considerations that have gone into Israel's decision. The difference between an efficient and an inefficient campaign may be critical.

The Chances of a Joint Soviet–American Response

A final question with regard to the superpowers' reaction to Israel's overt nuclearization involves the chances of a joint Soviet–American response, which might assume the form of a joint intervention aimed at disarming Israel's nuclear capability. Alternatively, a more comprehensive Soviet–American agreement to ban nuclear weapons from the entire Middle East may be considered. The agreement may be aimed at forcing the region's states to join the N.P.T. and to place their nuclear installations under IAEA inspections and safeguards. Finally, the United States and the Soviet Union might instead arrive at a common position expressed in the form of a joint declaration stating that they would act in concert against any of the states in the region that dared to use nuclear weapons first. Any of the above arguments could be achieved within the framework of a SALT III and SALT IV agreement covering the Middle East. The high sensitivity they attach to the region, their previous experience—notably in 1973—in confrontations over Mideast issues, and the common fear that a regional nuclear war might escalate to a superpower nuclear confrontation, may lead the United States and the USSR to such a joint venture.

Most elements that have been shown to constrain both superpowers' negative reaction to Israel's overt nuclearization are also likely to prevent them from adopting extreme responses in concert. Having dwelled on these considerations in previous sections, I need not repeat them here. There are additional reasons why the odds of a joint Soviet–American response can be assessed as relatively low. The basic interests of the two superpowers in the region are very different; their past behavior has been characterized by more conflict than cooperation. As Shelton Williams has noted, "The assumption of coordinated action would have to be based on the possibility that the mutual interests of the superpowers in nonproliferation outweighed other elements of political competition between them."[182] Williams regards this prospect as highly unlikely to occur. Both he and Michael Nacht view the interests that have traditionally tied the superpowers to their respective regional allies as much more important predictors of their behavior following nuclearization than the act of nuclearization itself. In Michael Nacht's words, "bilateral relations between the United States and the new nuclear state prior to weapons acquisition, which were in turn based upon a complex set of political, economic, military and historical considerations, have proven to be far more accurate indicators of future trends in U.S. policy than the acquisition by the state of nuclear weapons per se."[183] The persistence of differing and often conflicting interests stands in the way of a joint superpower interventionist action. Moreover, the current general atmosphere of Soviet–American relations would seem to preclude an effective nonproliferation joint venture. The entrance into the 1980s finds the United States increasingly frustrated with the Soviet Union's enormous buildup in both conventional and theater-nuclear capabilities. The Soviet invasion of Afghanistan in December 1979 struck a sharply negative note in Washington. Soviet unwillingness to allow the United States a free hand in the Iranian crisis of 1979 merely added to American suspicions. All this has occurred against the background of growing American dissatisfaction with Soviet-sponsored activities in Angola, Ethiopia, and South Yemen. Finally, with the advent of the more assertively anti-Soviet Reagan presidency in January 1981, and the imposition of martial law in Poland in December of that year, American–Soviet relations have returned to the Cold War atmosphere of the 1950s. Such Soviet–American relations make a forceful joint nonproliferation venture highly implausible.

Obviously, the Soviet Union would have to be made a full partner to a concerted superpower nonproliferation effort in the Middle East. Thus the United States—having invested much in reducing Soviet influence in the Arab–Israeli core conflict area—would have to accept renewed Soviet presence. This would entail severe political costs to the United States.

More specific problems are associated with the types of concerted Soviet–American actions considered above. A joint "no-first-use" declaration—stating that the United States and the Soviet Union would act in concert against any of the states in the region that dared to use nuclear weapons first—would seem implausible unless the superpowers also agree on a common policy regarding circumstances that might elicit nuclear threats. Important elements of the American political elite would object to having the United States curtail Israel's ability to threaten nuclear punishment without an equivalent Soviet commitment to curtail Syrian and Iraqi threats to Israel's security. The foreign and military policies of Syria and Iraq would thus have to be placed under tight Soviet control. As the superpowers find the control of regional allies increasingly difficult, it is highly doubtful that a Soviet commitment of this sort could be implemented in the 1980s. Moreover, such a commitment is likely to be regarded as undesirable by both Moscow and Washington even if its implementation were possible. Moscow will regard the overcoming of Syrian and Iraqi resistance to such control as involving excessive costs. Curtailing small states' freedom of action will jeopardize the Soviet Union's position throughout the Third World, particularly with movements of national liberation. From Washington's perspective Soviet control of Syrian and Iraqi foreign policies would mean that attempts to gain Western influence in the two countries would have to be written off.

With respect to the other types of joint Soviet–American action—Israel's nuclear disarmament and regional nuclear demilitarization—the first seems impossible without the second. Again, important elements of the American political elite will object to disarming Israel's nuclear capability without demilitarizing the entire region in the same way. Israel could not be disarmed without putting a lid on the nuclear activities of Iraq and Pakistan. Egyptian, Syrian, and Libyan activities would also have to be placed under tight control. This would involve policing activities of unprecedented dimensions. And again, it would encounter fierce opposition on the part of all states in the region. Resistance to colonialism would revive in a new form. It would involve extremely high costs to both superpowers. There are no indications that the United States and the Soviet Union would be willing to assume such costs.

David Gompert believes, however, that the superpowers' cost–gain calculations will change drastically after the first use or serious threat to use nuclear weapons is made. In his view, the outbreak of nuclear conflict "would generate a political shock wave affecting nearly every facet of international order and security." Gompert believes that "while neither superpower would consider proliferation itself so insufferable that it need accept or share responsibility for maintaining nuclear *peace*, nuclear *war* would not be similarly tolerated. Indeed, in the event of a regional nuclear war—or a serious scare—international consensus might shift from support of superpower noninvolvement in regional security matters to a demand for superpower peace-keeping." Under such circumstances Gompert does conceive the possibility of superpower collaboration to disarm a local nuclear power that initiates a nuclear exchange.[184] Although Gompert's hypothetical situation is not impossible, it is also not very likely. Since big-power rivalry did not cease following the first use of nuclear weapons, it is hard to see why it would after the second. The international system has adapted itself to the existence of nuclear weapons within its general competitive character. Doubtless more accommodation will have to be made once nuclear weapons are used again, this time in a regional affair. However, the expectation that big-power competition would end at that instant seems unwarranted.

Epilogue

Making the decision whether or not to alter Israel's strategy from conventional defense/offense to overt nuclear deterrence promises to be an extremely agonizing process. It is very difficult to weigh the advantages of the adoption of an overt nuclear deterrent against its inherent risks. The costs and benefits do not lend themselves to common measurement.

In reviewing the advantages of such a change, I must return to a central assertion advanced in this book—that nuclear weapons are able to provide their owners with effective deterrence. This conclusion is based on the following considerations. First, nuclear weapons can inflict enormous punishment and the enormity of the punishment is well known. The high levels of punishment involved and the greater likelihood that the dimensions of possible punishment will be perceived correctly both insure that a potential attacker will develop a sensitivity to these costs. Furthermore, nuclear deterrence allows the delivery of open threats, which can be unmistakable and clear enough to prevent misperception. Finally, nuclear deterrence promises to be stable because potential attackers are likely to refrain from attempting a disarming first strike. They will lack the requisite confidence in their ability to execute such a strike with perfect success and are bound to fear that their attempt may leave them exposed to extremely costly nuclear retaliation.

By providing effective deterrence, nuclear weapons have the capacity to reduce the likelihood of war, both conven-

Nuclear & conventional deter in Nuclear Realm

tional and nuclear. Nuclear attacks will be deterred by the prospect of nuclear retaliation; conventional attacks will be deterred by the fear that they may escalate into a nuclear exchange.

Stability
Nuclear weapons may also enhance stability. Such weapons favor states trying to defend their sovereignty and survival. This is due to the fact that deterrent confrontations are determined by the relative ability to inflict punishment and the relative willingness to absorb punishment in order to win the issue under dispute. States possessing more than a minimal arsenal of nuclear weapons will be able to inflict enormous punishment on each other. In confrontations between such states, the winner will therefore be the one who has the most at stake. The state more willing to absorb punishment will run higher risks. The state less willing to run risks will have to back down. The state defending its sovereignty and survival is likely to manifest far more willpower than a potential offender. Its survival is likely to be much more important to it than its destruction would be to a possible intruder. The offender will then face an opponent willing to undertake enormous risks; the balance of deterrence will tilt against him. Deterrent confrontations, given nuclear weapons, will be won by the state defending its essentials. This will favor the status quo and promises to enhance stability.

willpower

Will nuclear weapons actually have these beneficial effects in the Middle East? Could their introduction stabilize the Arab–Israeli conflict area? Will they provide Israel with the ability to deter ultimate threats to her survival? Will nuclear weapons also provide deterrence of lower-magnitude threats?

open enhances deter threats
Whether or not nuclear weapons will actually have the beneficial effects portrayed above depends largely on how they are introduced into the Middle East. If they are introduced openly with the adoption of overt, explicit, and disclosed nuclear deterrent postures, the benefits portrayed are indeed likely to follow. Open introduction enhances the credibility of threats and facilitates the elaboration of doctrines for the use of nuclear weapons, thus reducing the likelihood of their misuse. It also allows the development of strategic

dialogues between adversaries, thus leading to mutually shared definitions of what is likely to lead to nuclear retaliation and minimizing the possibility that war might erupt through misunderstanding. Moreover, a disclosed deterrent promotes mass and elite awareness of the constraints imposed by nuclear weapons. A widely shared appreciation of these constraints is a prerequisite to the beneficial consequences we predict would result from the introduction of nuclear weapons into the region.

If, on the contrary, nuclear weapons are introduced in an undisclosed, covert, and implicit fashion, the consequences are likely to be minimally negative at best and disastrous at worst. For decision makers, members of important elites, and the population at large, this manner of introduction provides no opportunity for socialization to the effects of nuclear weapons. As a consequence, consideration of these effects may not enter into the making of policy choices. At best this will not have detrimental consequences. The presence of nuclear weapons will be inconsequential if their existence is not known. The likelihood of conventional wars will remain unaffected, as will their course. However, disastrous consequences may also occur. A war launched against an undisclosed nuclear state may initially remain unaffected by the unknown presence of nuclear weapons. Yet once the nuclear state begins to lose the conventional battle, it may choose to utilize its nuclear capability. The absence of previous socialization and conceptualization about the uses and effects of nuclear weapons may lead to the unjustified use of nuclear devices as "war-fighting" weapons. Alternatively, if used as a deterrent, lack of prior socialization may lead an opponent to disregard the deterrent threat, either from ignorance or from assuming a bluff. If the threat is ignored, a demonstrative use will be inevitable. This is how undisclosed nuclear postures may lead to nuclear war.

These general considerations lead to a number of conclusions about the relations between nuclear weapons and Israel's security. First, should Israel wish to maximize her deterrent capacity, she should acquire the capability and adopt a doctrine of overt, disclosed, and explicit strategic nuclear deterrence. Second, once Israel adopts such a posture, she stands an excellent chance of deterring Arab efforts to challenge her basic survival. Thus effective general deterrence will have been gained. This gain will be retained even if the Arab states react by adopting nuclear deterrence postures of their own. The issue of Israel's survival will be more important to her than Israel's destruction will be to her neighbors. Once her survival is threatened, she will demonstrate greater willingness to run risks. The balance of deterrence will tilt in her favor. Finally, Israel's nuclear posture may also deter her neighbors from opting for lower levels of violence, such as limited mobile war, wars of attrition, and guerrilla warfare. Israel's ability to benefit from effective specific deterrence, however, would depend on the nature of the issue under dispute. Israel is unlikely to deter Arab efforts to regain some of the territories she has occupied since the June 1967 war. Her neighbors see these territories as their own, while Israel lacks a national consensus on the question of Israeli sovereignty over these territories. Thus the Arabs are likely to care more about these territories and will demonstrate greater willingness to run risks. In any effort to regain them, the balance of deterrence will tilt in the Arabs' favor. However, once Israel withdraws to borders that more nearly approximate the lines she held prior to the 1967 war, the balance of deterrence will turn to her advantage. She would be determined to resist Arab efforts to go beyond these lines or to harass her within them. Israel would care more and be bound to deter such efforts successfully. Under such a policy, the adoption of a nuclear deterrent strategy can be expected to yield important benefits.

At the same time, the adoption of strategic nuclear deterrence clearly involves a measure of risk. Irrational decision making may negate our benign expectations; lack of proper conceptualization about the uses of nuclear weapons may lead to their misuse; inability to maintain control over weaponry may lead to unauthorized delivery; vulnerability of command and control facilities may lead to the loss of control;

RISKS — Negative

the inherent difficulties of making calculations and controlling escalation in a multinuclear environment may lead to a breakdown of limitations; the horrifying specter of nuclear terror may bring us into a world very different from our own. In addition, a measure of risk is involved in possible U.S. and Soviet responses to regional nuclearization. If both superpowers decide to make the Middle East a test case of their nonproliferation efforts, this may well threaten whatever benefits could be derived from altering Israel's political–military strategy.

Throughout this study it has been asserted that although some of these risks are more worrisome than others, generally they are all of very low probability. Since the potential costs involved in these low-probability threats are so high, however, ignoring them would be highly irresponsible. Yet how does one weigh low-probability high-cost risks? How does one compare them with the enormous possible benefits of effective nuclear deterrence? Although effective nuclear deterrence promises peace and stability, a major breakdown of deterrence may bring catastrophic results. Hence, should we not prefer our present environment, which is less peaceful, less stable, and yet less risky?

An Israeli preference for maximizing benefits at the expense of higher risks would not be odd. Given the choice, Americans and Russians would probably elect to do the same. This can be demonstrated by considering the probable respective response of the two superpowers if they suddenly had the choice of eliminating their nuclear arsenals. Assuming for a moment that nuclear disarmament could be perfectly conducted and perfectly verified, would the citizens of the United States prefer the hazards and uncertainties of the prenuclear era? Would they choose a world liberated from the fear of nuclear catastrophe and yet one that requires mobilizing the enormous resources needed to match Warsaw Pact conventional forces? Would Americans prefer the less risky nonnuclear world even if it involved a greater probability that conventional world war would recur? On numerous occasions the French, British, and West German publics have shown a preference for strategic nuclear deterrence despite their awareness that each of their major cities is targeted for destruction by Soviet nuclear-tipped intermediate-range ballistic missiles. They prefer to live with the threat of total annihilation if this is the price they must pay to insure lower odds that they will experience the agonies of the two world wars again.

The central conclusion of this essay is that to maximize the odds of security and peace, Israel must adopt a doctrine of explicit strategic nuclear deterrence. The conclusion rests on the assessment made here of the benefits and risks of overt nuclear deterrence. Again, it should be emphasized that no part of this analysis assumes that Israel already possesses nuclear weapons. Since I do not know whether or not it has already produced such weapons, all that is implied here is that if Israel already possesses nuclear weapons, it should introduce them overtly in the framework of an explicit nuclear deterrence posture. And if Israel does not already possess such weapons, it should develop them and introduce them overtly later on.

Finally, a number of specific recommendations as to what Israel should avoid doing can also be distilled from this analysis. First, Israel should refrain from developing a doctrine and capability for counter-Soviet nuclear deterrence. In order to avoid extreme Soviet responses resulting from unnecessary anxieties about Israel's nuclear capability, Israel should try to convince Moscow that its nuclear deterrent posture does not constitute a threat to Soviet security. Second, to avert the political costs involved in being a test case for the superpowers' antiproliferation efforts, Israel should attempt to postpone the adoption of overt nuclear deterrence until a few more states have gone nuclear. Even better would be for Israeli disclosure to follow the acquisition of a nuclear capability by at least one Arab or Moslem state. However, a deterioration of the conventional balance may make it unwise to await such a development. Third, both to avert enormous political costs and to enhance the credibility of her deterrence, Israel should not go nuclear unless she concomitantly

IS should omit only when flexible w/ territories

adopts a flexible political posture with respect to the territories it has held since the 1967 war. The adoption of a nuclear deterrent posture that seems to be aimed at maintaining Israel's present hold over the West Bank, the Gaza Strip, and the Golan Heights would result in prohibitive political costs. If nuclear deterrence is not coupled with political flexibility, not only would the Soviet, American, and West European reactions be extremely negative, but a dramatic deterioration of relations between Egypt and Israel may also be expected. To avoid such costs, disclosure should accompany dramatic steps that increase the prospects of a regional political settlement.

Notes

1. The Logic of Going Nuclear

1. Harkabi, *Milchama Garinit*, p. 132 (in Hebrew).
2. Interview in *Der Spiegel*, according to UPI, March 27, 1976, and *Ha'aretz* (Israel), March 28, 1976. Also cited by *The Jerusalem Post* (Israel), March 28, 1976, and released by MENA, March 26, 1976. See FBIS, March 31, 1976, p. D7.
3. Interview in the *Washington Post*, according to *Yediot Ahronot* (Israel), March 28, 1976.
4. Interview in *Aktuelt* (Denmark), April 25, 1976; see FBIS, April 29, 1976, p. D1.
5. Beirut Radio, December 16, 1976; also *Al-Ahrām* (Egypt), August 7, 1975, according to A'ah, "Egypt, Israel and the Nuclear Bomb."
6. Interview in a Lebanese paper, according to UPI, July 2, 1977.
7. Interview in *Al-Anwār* (Lebanon), January 8, 1975, according to FBIS, January 9, 1975, pp. D1, D4. The interview was granted to *Al-Anwār*'s managing director, Bassam Furrayhah, in Cairo, January 7, 1975.
8. Interview in *Al-Ahrām*, April 30, 1976, according to AP, April 29, 1976.
9. Interview in *Al-Akhbār* (Egypt); see FBIS, June 18, 1974, p. D2. Also *Ha'aretz* (Israel), June 17, 1974.
10. According to AP, April 25, 1976.
11. *Akhbār al-Usbū* (Jordan), October 14, 1976.
12. Interview in *Al-Ahrām* (Egypt) quoted by *Yediot Ahronot* (Israel), October 5, 1976. Quoted also in FBIS, October 6, 1976, p. D1; see also interview in *Al-Hawādith* (Lebanon) according to UPI, January 23, 1975; interview in *Al-Madīna* (Saudi Arabia), December 7, 1975.
13. *Al-Akhbār* (Egypt), March 16, 1977.
14. *Al-Ahili* (Egypt), July 26, 1978.
15. *Cairo Domestic Service*, October 5, 1980.
16. *Cairo Domestic Service*, December 23, 1980.

17. *Al-Ahrām* (Egypt), February 17, 1981; MENA, February 16, 1981.
18. Interview by Cairo Radio, February 18, 1976.
19. *The Guardian*, April 28, 1977. According to FBIS (April 28, 1977, p. H1), President Asad was interviewed by a number of journalists from the United Kingdom. At the interview the following questions and answers were exchanged: "Question: Does the President have any comment on whether Israel possesses nuclear weapons? The President: We cannot say this is impossible. But if Israel possesses this weapon then we will possess it. . . ."
20. Interview in *Al-Nahār* (Lebanon) and Tashrīn (Syria), according to MENA, October 7, 1977.
21. See Haykal, "Frankly Speaking." For additional statements in the Arab press that treat the subject of Israeli nuclear weapons in future tense, see Radio Damascus, April 6, 1976, and January 17, 1977; *Al-Akhbār* (Egypt), December 4, 1975; *Al-Ahrām* (Egypt), October 27, 1975; *Al-Yamāma* (Saudi Arabia), August 15, 1975.
22. *Ha'aretz* (Israel), June 23, 1974; MENA, June 23, 1974; FBIS, June 24, 1974, p. D6.
23. According to UPI, from Rome, April 8, 1976.
24. See *Ma'ariv* (Israel), November 12, 1976.
25. AP, from Beirut, April 25, 1978.
26. *Al-Ahrām* (Egypt), November 23, 1973; FBIS, November 26, 1973, p. G2.
27. Already in 1974 President Sadat said in an interview with Iranian publisher Farhad Pas'udi that he believed Israel has a nuclear weapon. See FBIS, December 18, 1974, p. D1; also *New York Times*, December 17, 1974. In a television interview in 1975 Sadat said he was sure "that Israel has manufactured nuclear weapons," *Ha'aretz* (Israel), January 28, 1975. Later Sadat said, "We have received reports that Israel has succeeded in producing nuclear weapons in the Dimona reactor," interview in *Al-Usbū' al-'Arabī* (Lebanon), July 2, 1976. In a 1977 interview he was slightly more reserved and said that "Israel's possession of atomic bombs is a large possibility and we are studying it," interview with *Survival* transmitted by MENA, March 29, 1977, according to FBIS, March 30, 1977, p. D1. In a 1974 interview, former Egyptian Chief of Staff Gen. Shazly (Ret.) said: "Egypt has to believe that Israel has the atomic weapons at hand because of the announcement by Israel's Head of State Katzir that it could convert its nuclear capabilities to weapons-making in a few days. I don't think the capabilities could be converted in a few days unless they have the atomic weapons at hand" (UPI from London, December 3, 1974). In April 1981, Egypt's Minister of Foreign Affairs is reported to have told an ABC documentary on nuclear proliferation that Egypt believes that "Israel now possesses 27 Hiroshima-type nuclear bombs," *Ma'ariv* (Israel), April 26, 1981. Following Israel's June 1981 raid on Iraq's nuclear reactor, Egypt's Minister of Defense Abdel Halim Abu-Ghazala asked: "Do the indications

that Israel has acquired a nuclear bomb provide an Arab state with the right to strike against her in order to destroy this bomb?" (MENA, June 25, 1981).

Jordan's King Hussein has often expressed the view that Israel already possesses nuclear weapons. In a 1975 interview to a Swiss weekly, Hussein said: "The next war . . . although I cannot say whether nuclear arms will be used, this time the possibility exists" (Amman Domestic Service, January 10, 1975; see FBIS, January 10, 1975, p. F1). In a June 1977 interview Hussein said that "Israel has nuclear weapons and it had nuclear weapons during the October [1973] War, and that it has developed these weapons and continues to do so at present," interview with *Al-Qabas* (Kuwait); see FBIS, June 23, 1977, p. F1. According to MENA, June 23, 1977, Hussein also said in the same interview: "I have been confident for some time that Israel has nuclear weapons." Later in 1977 Hussein said with less certainty: "They have the capability and I believe they probably have the weaponry as well." Interview with *Chief Executive*, October–December 1977. By 1981, however, Hussein sounded confident once again. In a speech following Israel's bombing of the Iraqi research reactor, he accused Israel of being "the one who had introduced nuclear weapons into the Middle East," *Yediot Ahronot* (Israel), June 15, 1981. Saudi Arabia's Minister of Foreign Affairs was more cautious: "we have reason to believe [that Israel] possesses an 'atomic arsenal,'" interview with *Le Monde* (Paris) according to Reuters from Paris, January 20, 1977. Libya's Col. Muammar Qaddhafi, in a June 1981 speech, was quite certain that Israel possesses nuclear weapons: "In that reactor [Dimona], the Israelis are producing atomic bombs," *Yediot Ahronot* (Israel), June 12, 1981. The government of Iraq, however, is the most ardent proponent of the view that Israel has acquired nuclear weapons. In a 1977 memo to the Arab League, Iraq stated that "despite the fact that Israel did not officially declare that she possesses nuclear weapons, there is not a shadow of doubt that she in fact possesses such weapons," *Al-Usbū' al-'Arabī* (Lebanon), October 17, 1977; see also *Roz-al-Yussuf* (Egypt), October 10, 1977. A year later, in a speech to the United Nations General Assembly Political Commission, Iraq's delegate Salah 'Umar al-Ali said that "the Zionist enemy is storing [nuclear] weapons" (Baghdad INA, October 25, 1978; see FBIS, October 25, 1978). On July 13, 1979, Iraq's delegate to the U.N. submitted a memo stating "clear evidence that the Zionist entity has nuclear weapons" (Baghdad INA, July 14, 1979). Iraq issued a similar statement a year later in a letter to U.N. Secretary General Kurt Waldheim (Baghdad INA, July 31, 1980; see FBIS, August 4, 1980, p. E2). Thus, in a January 1981 interview, Iraq's President Sadam Hussein demanded that "Israel must announce its readiness to destroy its nuclear weapons," *Al-Anbā* (Kuwait), January 19, 1981. In June 1981, Iraq's Minister of Foreign Affairs, Sa'adun Hamadi, said that "the enemy [Israel] possesses nuclear weapons and this is known internationally" (*Washington Post*, June 10, 1981).

28. United Nations General Assembly, "Israeli Nuclear Armament," Report of the Secretary General, A/36/431, September 18, 1981 (Pursuant to U.N. General Assembly Resolution 34/89 of December 11, 1979).

29. Chari, "The Israeli Nuclear Option," pp. 347, 349, 350. Chari further elaborates: "Evaluating the nuclear capabilities of Israel, the important aspects to note are that it has an unsafeguarded reactor producing plutonium, the scientific and technological know-how needed to fabricate weapons, and an adequate delivery system. It is unlikely that it has the processing facilities, at present, to produce enough weapons-grade plutonium for a weapons programme."

30. Unfortunately, I am bound by the author's request not to identify the study or its author.

31. Mandelbaum, "International Stability and Nuclear Order," p. 68.

32. Dowty, "Israel and Nuclear Weapons," pp. 6–7.

33. Stone, "The Strategic Role of the United States Bombers," p. 341.

34. Gallois, Balance of Terror, p. 108.

35. Brodie, Strategy in the Missile Age, pp. 291–92.

36. U.S. Congressional Budget Office, Counterforce Issues, p. 3.

37. Freedman, "Israel's Nuclear Policy," p. 119.

38. Leonard Harris, The Massada Plan.

39. Allison, The Essence of Decision; Morgan, Deterrence, pp. 60–73.

40. Morgan, Deterrence, p. 68.

41. Brodie, Strategy in the Missile Age, p. 292.

42. Michael Brenner, "Decision Making in a Nuclear Armed World," p. 153.

43. Garwin, "Reducing Dependency," p. 113.

44. Brennan, ed., The Implications of Precision Weapons, pp. 18–19, 21; Warner, "Tactical Nuclear Weapons," pp. 24–30; Colin Gray (discussion) in Wellnitz, ed., LASL Panel on Tactical Nuclear Warfare, p. 36.

45. Robert Jervis, "Deterrence Theory Revisited," ACIS Working Paper No. 14, p. 21.

46. Gompert et al., Nuclear Weapons and World Politics, p. 274.

47. Aron warns: "The method best suited to counter the risk of war through misunderstanding is . . . communication between the enemies must be maintained at all times" (The Great Debate, p. 58).

48. Gallois, Balance of Terror, p. 121.

49. Snyder, "Deterrence and Defense," pp. 56–57; see also Morgan, Deterrence.

50. Schelling, Arms and Influence, p. 2.

51. The term "passive" is here used for activities short of the actual employment of violence. The British use this term to suggest something quite different—namely that retaliation is automatic. See Waltz, Foreign Policy and Democratic Politics, pp. 145–48.

52. Brodie, Strategy in the Missile Age, pp. 291–93. It should be stressed that these distinctions are made for purely heuristic and analytical pur-

poses. In reality the distinctions are not that sharp. Since "forces" comprise both men and equipment, they also constitute "value." Thus "forces" can also be the target of deterrent strategies. Nevertheless, whereas in defense and offense the aim is to destroy the war-fighting capability of these forces, in deterrence and compellence, the emphasis is placed on the costs involved in the destruction of these forces.

53. Schelling, *Arms and Influence*, p. 4.

54. Schelling, *Arms and Influence*, pp. 1–18. U.S. Secretary of Defense Robert S. McNamara spoke in June 1962 of the idea that deterrence may operate in wartime (*ibid.*, p. 24). See also Snyder, "Deterrence and Defense," pp. 63–64; Morgan discusses "deterrence in war time" and believes it should be distinguished from "deterrence" aimed at preventing an attack (*Deterrence*, p. 27).

55. Schelling chose not to distinguish between active and passive compellence (*Arms and Influence*, p. 70).

56. *Ibid.*, p. 3.

57. U.S. Congressional Budget Office, *U.S. Strategic Nuclear Forces*, p. xi.

58. Marvin Kalb and Bernard Kalb, *Kissinger*, p. 236; Morgan discusses the possibility of nonmilitary deterrent threats (*Deterrence*, p. 27).

59. Haykal, "The Strategy of the War of Attrition," p. 418.

60. Maj. Gen. (Res.) Avraham Adan, "Milchemet Hahatasha" (On the War of Attrition), *Yediot Ahronot* (Tel Aviv), Friday Supplement, May 4, 1979, p. 9.

61. For the view that guerrilla warfare does *not* constitute a form of deterrence or compellence, see Dougherty and Pfaltzgraff, *Contending Theories of International Relations* p. 254.

62. Schelling, *Arms and Influence*, p. 6.

63. Hughes, "Cutting the Gordian Knot."

64. Yair Evron, "The Demilitarization of Sinai," pp. 18–23. See also Snyder, "Deterrence and Defense," pp. 65–66, and his "Deterrence by Denial and Punishment."

65. Thus Steven Canby asserts that "deterrence works in two ways: by a threat of punishment if a hostile act is initiated, or by denying the initiator the objective of his act" (*The Alliance and Europe*, p. 2). The assertion that one can deter effectively by promising to deny the adversary the attainment of his objectives is quite common in the strategic literature. Robert Shreffler states that the aim of his favorite "new nuclear force" based on the employment of mininukes is "to structure a defensive force of such high quality and responsiveness that it serves as the overriding deterrent." See "The New Nuclear Force," p. 301. Richard L. Garwin seems to accept the notion of deterrence by denial in stating that "strengthened defensive capabilities for NATO's nonnuclear forces would provide a sufficient deterrent to conventional attack by Warsaw Pact forces" ("Reducing Dependency on Nuclear Weapons," p. 110). He returns later to the same notion

by noting that "during periods in which NATO's nonnuclear capabilities and readiness were not clearly adequate to repel and, therefore, deter, a Warsaw Pact invasion, NATO has relied on American-supplied tactical nuclear weapons" (*ibid.*, p. 134).

66. Ross, "Rethinking Soviet Strategic Policy," p. 143.

67. That the "costs" element in deterrence by denial implies merely the destruction of the attacking forces is made clear in a recent Congressional Budget Office study, which explained that "it is not apparent how [theater] nuclear forces [in Europe] are intended to deter a Soviet attack. It could be by the threat of inflicting or triggering unacceptably high damage to Warsaw Pact territory, or it could be by their capability to deny the Soviet Union its military objectives by destroying the attacking forces." U.S. Congressional Budget Office, *Planning U.S. General Purpose Forces*, p. 29.

68. Brodie prefers the term "basic deterrence" to "general deterrence" (*Strategy in the Missile Age*, p. 273); Morgan uses the term "immediate deterrence" but in a somewhat different fashion (*Deterrence*, pp. 31–43).

69. For a more complete exposé of the ingredients of national power see Hans J. Morgenthau, *Politics Among Nations*, pp. 106–44.

70. A number of scholars have pointed to the "intentions" and "will" of the parties involved as important determinants of outcomes in deterrent confrontations. Henry Kissinger notes "the will to employ force" (see *Nuclear Weapons and Foreign Policy*, p. 132), and Pierre Gallois discusses "the threatened nation's desire to resort to force rather than appeasement" (see *Balance of Terror: Strategy for the Nuclear Age*). Oran R. Young notes the importance of "intensity of feeling" (*The Politics of Force*, pp. 33–216, 387, 391), and Alexander George found that the "strength of U.S. motivation" and the "asymmetry of motivation favoring the U.S." contribute to successful deterrence (Alexander George et al., *The Limits of Coercive Diplomacy*).

Robert Jervis ("Deterrence Theory Revisited," *World Politics*) notes that scholars of deterrence have only recently realized the importance of the intrinsic interests of the parties involved in determining the outcomes of deterrent confrontations between them (p. 314). Thus Snyder and Diesing discuss "the relative intensity of interests at stake" as one of the two main determinants of bargaining power: see Snyder and Diesing, *Conflict Among Nations*. The relationship between intrinsic interests and the willingness to absorb costs has been emphasized by Steven Rosen. He uses the term "willingness to suffer," and regards the latter as an important source of national power (see his "War Power and Willingness to Suffer").

71. As Stephen Maxwell has noted, "In most disputes between nuclear powers, both share an interest in avoiding at least all-out nuclear war. At the same time, both wish to gain the objective at issue between them so far as this is compatible with the avoidance of all-out war. The price each

will be prepared to pay to gain the disputed objective will depend on the value each puts on the objective. Other things being equal, the power that puts the higher value on the objective will win the contest, though not necessarily without bloodshed" (*Rationality in Deterrence*, p. 1).

72. Snyder calls it the "balance of intentions" ("Deterrence and Defense," p. 75).

73. As Bernard Brodie put it, "President Kennedy had the psychological advantage, not only in superiority of power, but in the fact, too, that the disturbance to security was taking place in his back-yard rather than in Khrushchev's. . . . The fact that Cuba was only ninety miles from the tip of Florida but many thousands of miles from the Soviet Union was seen by both sides to be decisively important in determining the attitudes that both could accept" (*War and Politics*, pp. 426–28).

74. Raymond Aron concurs with Brodie: "All circumstances in this instance combined to favor the Americans. . . . The average Soviet citizen knew nothing about the Cuban People's Republic and might have found it rather difficult to understand why he should expose himself to terrifying danger for the sake of so trifling an objective. . . . The psychological factor, therefore, was weighted heavily in favor of the United States, since it was superior locally in conventional arms and its stakes in the encounter were infinitely greater than what the Russians could expect to gain" (*The Great Debate*, pp. 160–61).

75. Morgan stresses that "the leaders of an opposing state will value national survival above almost everything else" (*Deterrence*, p. 58).

76. "The Problems of Limited War," p. 100. This view is seconded by Brodie: "deterrence of direct, strategic, nuclear attack upon targets within the house territory of the United States. In that instance there is little or no problem of credibility as concerns our reactions, for the enemy has little reason to doubt that if he strikes us we will try to hit back" (*Strategy in the Missile Age*, p. 273).

77. Gallois, *Balance of Terror*, p. 199.

78. To cite just one example of the advantages of defense, Gallois points out that "if, for instance, in November 1956, the Hungarian government had possessed the means to inflict only three 'Hiroshimas' on the U.S.S.R., it is probable that the fear of such retaliation would have imposed negotiation and a new modus vivendi between Budapest and Moscow, and that neither repression nor occupation would have occurred" (*Balance of Terror*, p. 149).

79. Both the Soviets and the Chinese were, at different times, mistakenly thought to be insensitive to costs. See Brodie, *Strategy in the Missile Age*, p. 280, and Alice Langley Hsieh, "Communist China and Nuclear Force," pp. 159, 166–69.

80. Schelling, *Arms and Influence*, p. 35; Brodie, *Strategy in the Missile Age*, pp. 300–01.

81. Prior to the invention of aircraft, victory was a prerequisite to punishment. See Schelling, *Arms and Influence*, pp. 12, 16, 21, 22; Morgan, *Deterrence*, p. 31.

82. Aron states that nuclear weapons make it "no longer necessary to disarm a country in order to annihilate it" (*The Great Debate*, p. 198).

83. Stephen Van Evera, "The Effects of Nuclear Proliferation," p. 4.

84. Aron, *The Great Debate*, p. 197.

85. For the role of the horrors of Hiroshima and Nagasaki in enhancing the future effectiveness of nuclear deterrence, see Brodie, *War and Politics*, p. 56.

86. Morgan, *Deterrence*, p. 59. In the prenuclear world, estimating the degree of punishment by conventional weaponry in advance of hostilities was extremely difficult, such as, for example, predicting the effects of strategic conventional bombing. See Osgood, "The Expansion of Force"; Morgan, *Deterrence*, p. 58.

87. Snyder, "Deterrence and Defense," p. 61.

88. Blainey, *The Causes of War*; see also Brodie, *Strategy in the Missile Age*, p. 224.

89. Alain C. Enthoven, "American Deterrent Policy," p. 123.

90. Schelling, *Arms and Influence*, p. 20.

91. Objections to this proposition may be formulated to the effect that considering punishment in its entirety can be avoided in the nuclear era as well. Nuclear weapons can be delivered against a single enemy city in order to signal resolve. In addition, limited nuclear war options raise the specter of more measured uses of nuclear weapons, thus allowing decisionmakers the option of thinking incrementally about punishment in the nuclear era. The strength of such objections rests, however, on the likelihood attributed to scenarios of limited nuclear use. I tend to view them as highly unlikely, as I shall argue later in discussing the problems of limiting nuclear war.

92. Snyder, "Deterrence and Defense," p. 75.

93. Aron, *The Great Debate*, p. 58.

94. Aron, *The Great Debate*, p. 34.

95. Gallois, *Balance of Terror*, p. 128.

96. "The Effects of Nuclear Proliferation," p. 5; Brodie, *Strategy in the Missile Age*, pp. 191–92.

97. Jervis, "Why Nuclear Superiority Doesn't Matter," p. 618. See also Hans J. Morgenthau, "The Four Paradoxes of Nuclear Strategy," pp. 30–31.

98. U.S. Congressional Budget Office, *Counterforce Issues*, p. 9.

99. *Ibid.*; see also Paul H. Nitze, "Assuring Strategic Stability," p. 215.

100. U.S. Congressional Budget Office, *Counterforce Issues*, pp. 27–29; see also Gray, "The M-X Debate," p. 106.

101. Conover, "U.S. Strategic Nuclear Weapons and Deterrence," p. 11.

102. U.S. Congressional Budget Office, *U.S. Strategic Nuclear Forces*, pp. 16–17.

103. Brodie, "The Development of Nuclear Strategy," p. 9.

104. Mandelbaum, "International Stability and Nuclear Order," pp. 37–39.

105. Garwin, "Reducing Dependency on Nuclear Weapons," p. 91.

106. *Flight International*, June 17, 1978. See also Drew Middleton, "Cruise Missiles to be Effective but Expensive," *New York Times*, June 14, 1978; George Wilson, "Cruise Missiles 'Letter Perfect' in Test," *Washington Post*, June 22, 1978; "Soviets Held Defenseless against Cruise Missiles," *Washington Post*, June 2, 1978; and "Cruise Missiles Called Costly to Counter," *Aviation Week and Space Technology*, June 12, 1978.

107. Metzger, "Cruise Missiles," p. 4.

108. U.S. Congressional Budget Office, *U.S. Strategic Nuclear Forces*, pp. 33–34.

109. U.S. Congressional Budget Office, *Counterforce Issues*, p. 10.

110. Metzger, "Cruise Missiles," p. 4; Conover, "U.S. Strategic Nuclear Weapons," p. 5; Pechman et al., *Setting National Priorities*, p. 261.

111. U.S. Congressional Budget Office, *Counterforce Issues*, p. 13.

112. Gompert, *Nuclear Weapons and World Politics*, p. 257; see also Brodie, *War and Politics*, pp. 391–92. The Minuteman 3 is reported to carry three 0.2-megaton MIRVs while the Poseidon is to deliver about ten MIRV warheads of some tens of kilotons each (or fourteen warheads, according to another estimate). See Edward Luttwak, *A Dictionary of Modern War*, p. 131. The more recent U.S. MX missile is designed to carry nine to eleven reentry vehicles, each containing a warhead in the 400-kiloton range; see "USAF Plans Test of MX Trench Concept," in *Aviation Week and Space Technology* (October 17, 1977), p. 18. The U.S. Trident SLBM will have six to ten reentry vehicles, each warhead in the 200–300 kiloton range (see *Newsweek*, July 17, 1978). For comparison, Hiroshima was destroyed by a 14-kiloton weapon (see Brodie, "The Development of Nuclear Strategy," p. 15).

113. U.S. Congressional Budget Office, *Counterforce Issues*, pp. 27–29.

114. Hiroshima and Nagasaki were destroyed by a total of 40 kiloton equivalents.

115. Brodie refers to Albert Wohlstetter's "The Delicate Balance of Terror" (*War and Politics*, p. 380). In a more recent forum Brodie states: "I must add before leaving the Wohlstetter article that I could never accept the implications of his title—that the balance of terror between the Soviet Union and the United States ever has been or ever could be delicate. My reasons have to do mostly with human inhibitions against taking monumental risks. . . . The point is more relevant today than ever before because of the numbers and variety of American forces that an enemy would need to have a high certitude of destroying in one fell swoop" ("The Development of Nuclear Strategy," pp. 6–7).

116. Waltz, *Man, the State, and War*.

117. Robert Jervis, "Cooperation Under the Security Dilemma"; Ste-

phen Van Evera, "Nuclear Weapons, Nuclear Proliferation and the Causes of War."

118. Waltz, *Man, the State, and War*, p. 159.

119. *Ibid.* See also Jervis, "Cooperation Under the Security Dilemma," p. 167.

120. Waltz, *Man, the State, and War*, pp. 159–60, 182, 184–85.

121. Jean Jacques Rousseau, *A Lasting Peace*, trans. Vaughan; quoted in Waltz, *Man, the State, and War*, p. 180.

122. Jervis, "Cooperation," pp. 187–88.

123. As Raymond Aron put it, "If a nation's deterrent forces are invulnerable, it will not fear the enemy's first strike, will not panic in a crisis, and hence will not be tempted to strike the first blow since there is no risk of being suddenly disarmed" (*The Great Debate*, p. 81).

124. *Ibid.*, p. 208.

125. Brodie, *Strategy in the Missile Age*, p. 301.

126. Jervis, "Cooperation," pp. 169–70.

127. Herz, "Idealist Internationalism and the Security Dilemma."

128. Kissinger, *A World Restored*, p. 2.

129. Aron, *The Great Debate*, p. 212.

130. Brodie, *Strategy in the Missile Age*, p. 224.

131. Jervis, "Cooperation," p. 169.

132. Geoffrey Blainey, *The Causes of War*, p. 113.

133. Aron, *The Great Debate*, p. 211.

134. Brodie, *Strategy in the Missile Age*, pp. 224–25.

2. Israeli Security and Nuclear Weapons

1. Data on Israel, Egypt, Syria, Iraq, Saudi Arabia, and Jordan taken from *Demographic Year Book 1977* (New York: United Nations Publishing Service, 1978). Data on Libya taken from *Who's Who in the Arab World 1974/1975* (Beirut: Publitee Publications).

2. Burt, *New Weapons Technologies*, p. 19.

3. According to the late President Sadat, the Aswan Dam itself is immune to atomic weapons because it is built on a huge granite rock foundation: see his interview in the Saudi paper *Ukaz*, published by *Al-Jumhūrīyya* (Egypt), February 21, 1976; see FBIS, February 22, 1976, p. D1.

Theoretically there are two ways to contaminate the dam water. The first is by creating a water-burst on the dam waters. Under particular conditions of dam depth the effects of the water-burst will be similar to those of a ground-burst; namely, gravel will be picked up from the bottom and will later descend in the form of radioactive fallout.

The second alternative is to ground-burst *near* the Aswan Dam. The result will be that radioactive debris will fall into its waters. In both cases if one could stop the flow of water out of the dam for a whole month, the radioactivity would probably decay. Some elements, however, would continue to contain serious potential long-term hazards (delayed fallout) that are likely to have biological effects throughout the food cycle (plants, cows' milk, etc.). See Glasstone and Dolan, *The Effects of Nuclear Weapons*, pp. 410, 583, 604.

4. Harkavy, *Israel's Nuclear Weapons*, pp. 33–35.

5. Interview in *Al-Ahrām* (Egypt), July 20, 1975.

6. Interview in *Al-Hawādith* (Lebanon), according to MENA from Cairo, January 23, 1975. Gamassy used a similar expression in an interview to *Al-Ahrām*, October 5, 1976: see FBIS, October 5, 1976, p. D1.

7. Interview in *Al-Akhbār* (Egypt), June 18, 1974: see FBIS, June 18, 1974, p. D2.

8. Interview in *Al-Ahrām* (Egypt), April 30, 1976.

9. Interview with journalists who accompanied Sadat on his flight back from Gabbon, July 1976; interview to *Al-Usbū' al-'Arabī* (Lebanon), July 2, 1977.

10. Interview with *Al-Qabas* (Kuwait), September 11, 1980.

11. Amman Domestic Service, January 10, 1975: see FBIS January 10, 1975, p. F1.

12. Interview on NBC's *Meet the Press*, according to *Yediot Ahronot* (Israel), June 15, 1981.

13. Muhammad Jabber al-Nasr, "The Arab Nuclear Program . . . When and Where?" *Al-Anwār* (Lebanon), June 26, 1974. Hebrew translation.

14. Commentary, Saut Al-Arab radio station, December 12, 1974.

15. al-Ayubi, "The Truth about the Nuclear Challenge between Egypt and Israel."

16. Hassan A'ah, "Egypt, Israel and the Nuclear Bomb," *Al-Tali'a* (Egypt), September 1975. Hebrew translation.

17. *Al-Sha'b* (Algeria), "Israel's Nuclear Threat," March 16, 1976.

18. *Al-Ard* (Syria), "The Israeli Nuclear Threat after the October War," September 21, 1977.

19. See also *Tashrīn* (Syria), "Nuclear Weapons, Israel and Peace," May 1, 1975; *Al-Ard* (Syria), "Stability and Nuclear Deterrence," August 21, 1976; Haykal, "Frankly Speaking"; and *idem*, "Israeli Nuclear Weapons."

20. *Ma'ariv* (Israel), November 12, 1976.

21. *Al-Sayyad* (Lebanon), "An Interview with an Egyptian Statesman Well Informed in the Conflict's Process," February 26, 1976.

22. *Al-Ahrām al-Iqtisādī* (Egypt), "Israel and Nuclear Weapons," September 1, 1976.

23. Digby, "New Weapons and the Dispersal of Military Power," p. 40. Richard Burt concurs that the proliferation of precision strike systems would threaten "soft and even hard targets of an adversary without resort to nuclear blackmail." "Nuclear Proliferation and Conventional Arms Transfer: The Missing Link," p. 17.

24. U.S. Congressional Budget Office, *Planning U.S. General Purpose Forces*, p. 26.

25. Kennedy, *Thirteen Days*, pp. 37, 51.

26. Hasanayn Haykal, in *Al-Ahrām* (Egypt), October 15, 1965; cited by Evron, "The Arab Position," pp. 22–23.

27. Nasser stated that if Israel was indeed constructing a bomb, it would mean "the beginning of war between us and Israel, because we cannot permit Israel to manufacture an atomic bomb. It is inevitable that we should attack the base of aggression, even if we have to mobilize four million men to destroy it"; quoted in the *Jewish Observer and Middle East Review*, December 23, 1960, pp. 3–4; cited by Bader, *The United States and the Spread of Nuclear Weapons*, p. 69.

28. Broadcast by Baghdad Radio, February 20, 1966. See BBC Summary of World Reports, February 22, 1966; cited by Evron, "The Arab Position," p. 24.

29. *Al-Ahrām* (Egypt), October 15, 1965; cited by Evron, "The Arab Position," pp. 22–23.

30. Ahmad Khalifa, in *Al-Huria* (Lebanon), October 20, 1965. See also Saleh Sibel's lecture presented to the Arab Cultural Club in Beirut on November 5, 1965, as published in *Al-Anwār* (Lebanon), November 6, 1965, and *Al-Hayat* (Lebanon), November 13, 1965; all cited by Evron, "The Arab Position," pp. 20, 30, 31.

31. In an interview to *Al-Akhbār* (Egypt), according to *Ha'aretz* (Israel), June 19, 1974.

32. According to AP from Cairo, April 26, 1976; see also "Egypt to Get A-Bomb if Israel Explodes One," *Washington Post*, May 1, 1976. Fahmy issued similar statements to Cairo Radio on October 12, 1975; see FBIS, October 16, 1975, p. D1; see also his statement to Cairo Radio on January 28, 1976; FBIS, January 27, 1976, p. D1.

33. Bernard Gwertzman, "Egypt Said to Urge Arms Curb in Pact," *New York Times*, November 8, 1978.

34. *Ma'ariv* (Israel), May 17, 1979.

35. See speech by Iraq's delegate to the U.N., Salah Umar al-Ali, Baghdad INA, October 25, 1978; FBIS, October 25, 1978.

36. Interview to *Al-Anbā* (Kuwait), January 19, 1981.

37. *Al-Sha'ab* (Egypt), February 17, 1981.

38. Ibrahim Nafi, "Egypt's Nuclear Disarmament: How?" *Al-Ahrām*, February 20, 1981; FBIS, February 26, 1981, p. D4.

39. Radio Monte Carlo, August 1, 1980; repeated in interview to *Tashrin* (Syria), August 5, 1980.

40. *Al-Qabas* (Kuwait), October 6, 1980; see also *Al-Hamishmar* (Israel), October 7, 1980.

41. *International Herald Tribune*, November 10, 1980.

42. *The Nation*, June 8, 1976, quotes *The Boston Globe*.

43. Louise Lief, "Egypt Reviews Its Stance as Mideast Nuclear Arms Swell," *Christian Science Monitor*, August 18, 1980.

44. In an interview in the Kuwait newspaper *Al-Kuwaiti al-Yaum*, according to *Akhbār al-Usbū'* (Jordan), October 14, 1976.

45. In 1975, before the national conference of the Party of Socialist Unity, Gamassy said: "In the field of nuclear research Israel is far ahead of us . . . if Israel should decide to use a nuclear weapon in the battlefield, we shall use the weapons of mass destruction which are at our disposal." See *Al-Ahrām* and *Al-Akhbār* (Egypt), July 25, 1975; and FBIS, July 31, 1975, pp. D2, D3. In an interview to *Al-Ahrām* a year later Gamassy restated his position: "The introduction of nuclear weapons and their use in the Middle East will create a new and serious situation, and Israel will be held responsible. Israel must not forget that there are also other types of weapons of mass destruction"; according to *Yediot Ahronot* (Israel), October 5, 1976; see also FBIS, October 6, 1976, p. D3.

46. Interview in *Al-Usbū' al-'Arabī* (Lebanon), July 2, 1977.

47. Interview with Farhad Pas'udi, proprietor and chairman of the Iranian Ittela'at publishing enterprise; see FBIS, December 18, 1974, pp. D1, D3.

48. Interview in *Al-Anwār* (Lebanon), January 8, 1975; see FBIS, January 9, 1975, p. D1. Interview to French Television, see FBIS January 27, 1975, p. D2. *Al-Ahrām* (Egypt), January 25, 1975; see FBIS, January 28, 1975, p. D6. Press conference in Rome; see *Ha'aretz* (Israel), April 9, 1976. Interview with Bassam Furrayhah, general director of the Lebanese Al-Sayyad publishing house; see FBIS, January 4, 1976, p. D2.

49. *Al-Madīna* (Saudi Arabia), December 7, 1975, according to Riyadh SNA, December 6, 1976; see FBIS, December 8, 1976, and *Ha'aretz* (Israel), December 8, 1976; interview to *Al-Hawādith* (Lebanon), according to MENA from Cairo, January 23, 1975.

50. MENA from Cairo, August 16, 1974. In an interview to *Al-Akhbār* (Egypt), June 18, 1974, Fahmy said that "Egypt is capable of exploding an atomic device if Israel introduces this horrible weapon into the area"; see FBIS, June 18, 1974, p. D2. Two years later, Fahmy told *Al-Ahrām*: "If Israel explodes an atomic device, Egypt will obtain a similar weapon or manufacture it. We have scientists capable enough to mount a reaction in this field, and there are no scientific or technological barriers in our way." *Washington Post*, May 1, 1976.

51. Interview to Cairo Radio, December 17, 1976. Similarly, Bassam al-Asaly argued that "there is a final point in constructing the independent force: nuclear weapons. . . . Ownership of this weapon is not something to take pride in, but is rather a 'must' that the war has imposed upon the Arabs, . . . particularly when all evidence indicates that Israel has 10 nuclear weapons of the 20 kiloton type" ("Reviewing the Components of Arab Strategy").

52. Damascus Domestic Service, April 27, 1977; see FBIS April 28, 1977, p. H2.

53. "Rumors of Libyan Atomic Bomb Quest Raise Fears," *Washington Post*, July 30, 1979.

54. Adrian Berry, "Soviet deal could give Libyans 20 A-bombs a year," *Daily Telegraph*, December 7, 1978.

55. "Iraq's Nuclear Arms Option," *Washington Post*, August 8, 1978.

56. "Iraq Seeks Aid Getting Atomic Weapons for Arabs," *Washington Post*, June 24, 1981.

57. *Al-Ahrām*, according to MENA, November 23, 1973. See also *Washington Post*, November 24, 1973; FBIS, November 26, 1973, pp. G1, G2; also Haykal, "Frankly Speaking" and "Israeli Nuclear Weapons."

58. See interview with Dr. Kamal Affat, Chairman of the Egyptian Atomic Energy Commission, *Al-Sharak al-Awsat* (Saudi Arabia), March 15, 1979, p. 3.

59. Paul Jabber, "A Nuclear Middle East," p. 11; see also *Akhir Sā'a* (Egypt), April 18, 1979.

60. John K. Cooley, "Egypt Assessing Nuclear Strength," *Christian Science Monitor*, January 2, 1975.

61. John K. Cooley, "Cairo Steers Clear of A-race," *Christian Science Monitor*, June 9, 1969.

62. See Yiftah, *Hayidan Hagarini Bamizrach Hatichon*, p. 7; *Akhir Sā'a* (Egypt), April 18, 1979. For the Al-Quatarah depression canal, see MENA, July 13, 1974. See FBIS, July 16, 1974.

63. Cooley, "Egypt Assessing Nuclear Strength."

64. "Egypt to Buy French Reactors," *Christian Science Monitor*, June 20, 1977.

65. MENA, September 25, 1978. See BBC, October 3, 1978.

66. Bernard Gwertzman, "U.S. Aide Lauds Safeguards in Israel–Egypt Reactor Deal," *International Herald Tribune*, August 4, 1976.

67. MENA, May 20, 1980. See BBC, June 2, 1980, and *Ma'ariv* (Israel), May 22, 1980.

68. *Al-Assar* (Lebanon and Cypress), October 10, 1980.

69. MENA, December 24, 1980; see FBIS, December 30, 1980.

70. Ronald Koven, "France, Egypt Sign Deal for Atomic Power Plants," *Washington Post*, February 13, 1981.

71. "Egypt Ratifies Nuclear Nonproliferation Pact," *International Herald Tribune*, February 17, 1981.

72. Roger Matthews, "Egypt Wants to Buy U.K. Nuclear Power Stations," *Financial Times*, February 18, 1981; "Cairo Asks U.S. for 2 Atomic Plants," *Jerusalem Post*, February 27, 1981.

73. Judith Miller, "U.S. Pact Allows Egyptians to Buy 2 Atom Reactors," *New York Times*, June 30, 1981.

74. MENA, April 28, 1981. See BBC, May 12, 1981; *Ma'ariv*, July 29, 1981.

75. *Ma'ariv* (Israel), April 12, 1981.

76. Yiftah, *Hayidan Hagarini Bamizrach Hatichon*, p. 8; Paul Jabber, "A Nuclear Middle East," pp. 11–12, 42.

77. Paul Jabber, "A Nuclear Middle East," p. 12.

78. Freddy Eitan, "Delayed Reaction," *Jerusalem Post*, August 22, 1980.

79. William Branigan, "Iraqi Buildup Stirs Concern," *Washington Post*, February 27, 1978; "Iraq's Nuclear Arms Option," *Washington Post*, August 8, 1978; "How Iraq Lost Its Nuclear Option," *Foreign Report*, April 11, 1979, p. 2.

80. *Shield* (Switzerland), July 14, 1978; *Davar* (Israel), June 29, 1978; "How Iraq Lost Its Nuclear Option," *Foreign Report*, April 11, 1979, p. 2.

81. Ronald Koven, "Saboteurs Bomb French Plant Building Two Reactors for Iraq," *Washington Post*, April 7, 1979.

82. *Ibid.*; see also Michael Field, "Reactor for Iraq 'Sabotaged by Israeli agents,'" *Daily Telegraph*, April 14, 1979.

83. *Yediot Ahronot* (Israel), May 6, 1979; Flora Lewis, "France Said to Pledge to Replace Iraq-Bound Reactor," *New York Times*, May 9, 1979.

84. Milton R. Benjamin, "France Plans to Sell Iraq Weapons-Grade Uranium," *Washington Post*, February 28, 1980.

85. *Ha'aretz* (Israel), September 18, 1980.

86. *Ma'ariv* (Israel), September 28, 1980.

87. "Iran Bombs Nuclear Site in Baghdad," *International Herald Tribune*, October 1, 1980; Ronald Koven, "Iraq Blocks Inspection of its Nuclear Reactors," *Washington Post*, November 7, 1980.

88. *Ha'aretz* (Israel), February 20, 1981.

89. "Murder in Paris," *Foreign Report*, June 25, 1980.

90. *Ha'aretz*, July 18, 1980.

91. "France Delivers Iraqi Uranium, Sources Disclose," *International Herald Tribune*, July 16, 1980.

92. Ronald Koven, "Iraq Said to Block Nuclear Inspections," *International Herald Tribune*, November 7, 1981.

93. Richard Burt, "Iraq Said to Get A-Bomb Ability with Italy's Aid," *New York Times*, March 18, 1980.

94. (Brazil): "Brazil Will Sell Uranium to Iraq," *International Herald Tribune*, January 9, 1980. (Portugal): *New Scientist* (Britain), August 28, 1980; *Ma'ariv* (Israel), March 4, 1980; and *Ha'aretz* (Israel), April 7, 1981. (Niger): *Ma'ariv* (Israel), April 4, 1980; *Ha'aretz* (Israel), April 13, 1981; and Ned Temko, "Mideast Nuclear Threat—Tale of Murder, Intrigue," *Christian Science Monitor*, April 8, 1980. (West Germany): Paul Lewis, "Iraq was Reportedly Stockpiling Uranium," *International Herald Tribune*, June 19, 1981.

95. In a recent statement, President François Mitterrand disclosed a secret French–Iraqi agreement providing for the presence of French engineers on site at Osiraq until 1989. See Ronald Koven and Jim Hoagland,

"Mitterrand Says France Will Hold Iraq to Strict Conditions on Any New Reactor," *Washington Post*, June 18, 1981. The intensity of French involvement in the reactor's operation after 1983 remains unclear, however. Hence, the extent to which these Frenchmen might have become an obstacle to clandestine irradiation of natural uranium at Osiraq also cannot be ascertained.

96. *Ibid.*; and "Cheysson Says Atomic Aid to Iraq is Cut Off," *International Herald Tribune*, June 26, 1981.

97. David Treadwell, "Iraq Foreign Minister Vows Nuclear Effort Will Go On," *International Herald Tribune*, June 16, 1981; "Iraqi Leader Says Raid Will Not Stop Program," *Washington Post*, July 13, 1981; David B. Ottaway, "Saudis Offer Financing for Iraqi Reactor," *Washington Post*, July 17, 1981.

98. *Le Monde* (France), August 22, 1981; see FBIS, August 28, 1981, p. E3.

99. In interview with *Le Matin* (France), according to MENA, August 26, 1981.

100. "Iraq Was Reportedly Stockpiling Uranium."

101. *Al-Hamishmar* (Israel), June 11, 1981, quotes Israel's Chief of Staff, General Rafael Eitan.

102. *Ha'aretz* (Israel), June 14, 1981.

103. "Portugal to Sell Iraq Unenriched Uranium," *Washington Post*, July 17, 1981.

104. *Ha'aretz* (Israel), April 4, 1980; Radio Bandeirantes—São Paulo (Brazil), January 25, 1980. See BBC, February 5, 1980.

105. Hirsh Goodman, "Iraq's Nuclear Plans Set Back by Three Years," *Jerusalem Post*, June 9, 1981.

106. Paul Jabber, "A Nuclear Middle East," p. 14.

107. *Nucleonics Week*, February 23, 1978; *Nuclear Canada*, April 4, 1978.

108. *Al-Sayyād* (Lebanon), July 24, 1978.

109. See *Newsweek*, April 3, 1978, p. 4; *Al-Ba'th* (Syria), April 23, 1978; *Al-Manar* (Arabic newspaper published in London), May 6, 1978; *Al-Watan al-'Arabī* (Lebanese paper published in Paris), May 13, 1978; *Al-difā'a al-'Arabī* (Lebanon), August 1978; *Foreign Report*, January 31, 1979.

110. *Al-Difā'a al-Arabī* (Lebanon), August 1978.

111. *Al-Thawra* (Syria), November 17, 1979.

112. See *Business Week*, April 14, 1980; *Ha'aretz* (Israel), June 16, 1981 and July 8, 1981; *International Herald Tribune*, June 17, 1981; *8-Days* (London), July 25, 1981.

113. *Ma'ariv* (Israel), September 24, 1980, cites Britain's *New Scientist*.

114. Paul Jabber, "A Nuclear Middle East," p. 12.

115. See Hasanayn Haykal, *Al-Ahrām*, November 23, 1973: FBIS, November 26, 1973, p. G2; see also Charles Holley, "Nuclear Proliferation and the Middle East," *The Middle East*, July 1975, p. 19; *Yediot Ahronot*

(Israel), April 15, 1979, cites *Washington Star; Foreign Report*, August 9, 1978, p. 4.

116. *Yediot Ahronot* (Israel), February 2, 1979, cites the *Financial Times*.

117. "France Is to Build Libyan Atomic Plant," *New York Times*, March 23, 1976.

118. "Rumors of Libyan Atomic Bomb Quest Raise Fears," *Washington Post*, July 30, 1979.

119. *Foreign Report*, August 9, 1978, p. 3.

120. *Foreign Report*, June 18, 1980, p. 2.

121. R. R. Subramanian, "Pakistan's Nuclear Posture," *Hindustan Times*, May 29, 1979.

122. Milton R. Benjamin, "Pakistan Building Secret Nuclear Plant," *Washington Post*, September 23, 1980; "Pakistan Nears Test of A-Bomb, Magazine Says," *International Herald Tribune*, July 24, 1981.

123. Judith Miller, "U.S Aides Studying Pakistani Reactor," *New York Times*, September 30, 1981; "Pakistan Going Nuclear?" (Editorial), *International Herald Tribune*, October 2, 1981.

124. "Pakistan Making Its Own Nuclear Fuel," *Jerusalem Post*, September 1, 1980; Benjamin, "Pakistan Building Secret Nuclear Plant."

125. "The Bomb Behind the Wall," *The Economist*, September 15, 1979; Don Oberdorfer, "Pakistan: The Quest for Atomic Bomb," *Washington Post*, August 27, 1979.

126. *Foreign Report*, June 18, 1980.

127. Marwah, "India and Pakistan: Nuclear Armed Rivals in South Asia."

128. Edward Girardet, "Is Qaddafi Financing Pakistan's Nuclear Bomb?" *Christian Science Monitor*, December 19, 1979; *Al-Hamishmar* (Israel), December 12, 1979.

129. John M. Geddes, "Bonn Says Firm Illegally Sent Pakistan Gear that Can Be Used for Atomic Bombs," *Wall Street Journal*, July 16, 1981.

130. *Ha'aretz* (Israel), April 15, 1979, cites Cord Meyer's article in *Washington Star*. Mr. Meyer was CIA station chief in London; see also Girardet, "Is Qaddafi Financing Pakistan's Nuclear Bomb?"; "Libya's Arms Depot," *Newsweek*, July 9, 1979; Leonard Downie, Jr., "U.S. Says Evidence Shows Pakistan Planning A-Bomb," *Washington Post*, September 21, 1981.

131. *Foreign Report*, August 9, 1978; *Arabia and the Gulf*, September 4, 1979; *Al-Qabas* (Kuwait), August 30, 1978.

132. *Ha'aretz* (Israel), February 18, 1979, cites *Paris Match*; see also *Al-Nahda* (Kuwait), January 20, 1979.

133. John K. Cooley and Lisa Kaufman, "Deterring a Qaddafi Bomb," *Washington Post*, December 23, 1980; *Foreign Report*, July 9, 1981.

134. David Buchan, "Gate Shuts on Pakistan's Nuclear Path," *Financial Times*, April 11, 1979.

135. See *Ma'ariv* (Israel), August 29, 1979, cites the *Times of India; Financial Times*, September 1, 1979; *The Economist*, November 17, 1979.

136. Paul Jabber, "A Nuclear Middle East," p. 13; Thomas O'Toole, "Moscow Building Libya's Second Nuclear Reactor," *Jerusalem Post*, December 18, 1977; *Ma'ariv* (Israel), October 4, 1978; "Soviets Supply Nuclear Plants, Labs, to Libya," *International Herald Tribune*, October 4, 1978; "Russia Signs Accord with Libya to Build Nuclear Power Plant," *Wall Street Journal*, October 4, 1978; *Yediot Ahronot* (Israel), February 7, 1979; "Rumors of Libyan Atomic Bomb Quest Raise Fears," *Washington Post*, July 30, 1979.

137. "The Middle East's Nuclear Bomb Ambitions," *Middle East Newsletter*, April 23–May 6, 1979. The American Federation of Scientists nevertheless asserts that the Soviet deal would allow the Libyans to develop about twenty atomic bombs a year. See Adrian Berry, "Soviet Deal 'Could Give Libyans 20 A-Bombs a Year,'"*Daily Telegraph*, December 7, 1978.

138. Paul Jabber, "A Nuclear Middle East," p. 13; a large number of Libyans are also reported to be undergoing training in nuclear engineering in Finland and Sweden in connection with the construction of the new power reactor. See *Ha'aretz* (Israel), October 26, 1980; *Le Matin* (France), November 11, 1980. Reagan Administration officials confirmed that in 1981 some two hundred Libyans were studying nuclear physics in the United States. See *Ma'ariv* (Israel), July 9, 1981.

139. "Islamic Bomb for Sale," *Time*, December 24, 1979; see also "France Explains Sales of Niger Uranium Ore," *Washington Star*, January 4, 1980; Robert Kaylord, "Niger Tells of Uranium Sale to Libya," *International Herald Tribune*, April 13, 1981.

140. Alan Dowty adheres to this view in almost all his writings; see "Nuclear Proliferation: The Israeli Case," 99; see also Bader, *The United States and the Spread of Nuclear Weapons*, p. 90; Haselkorn, "Israel: From an Option to a Bomb in the Basement?" p. 150.

141. Peculiar as it may seem today, the argument about an asymmetry in vulnerability of populations was advanced more than twenty years ago to support the proposition that the United States suffers strategic inferiority. In *Le Monde*, on December 6, 1957, the French delegate to the United Nations disarmament committee wrote: "Only just achieved, strategic equality means America's greater vulnerability. As a matter of fact, the American population is much denser than Russia's: 170 million inhabitants living in less than ten million square kilometres, as opposed to 200 million in an area twice as large" (quoted by Gallois, *Balance of Terror*, p. 50).

142. Interview in *Al-Ahrām*, according to *Yediot Ahronot* (Israel), October 5, 1976; see also FBIS, October 6, 1976, p. D3.

143. To the journalists accompanying him on his flight back from Gabbon in July 1977, Sadat said (my italics): "Should Israel use nuclear weap-

ons against us *we will lose a million men, but this will still have left us with 39 million*. According to my plans I shall act to take the life of a million Israelis in exchange for the life of a million Egyptians and this will end Israel's existence. As you know, there is a triangle in Israel whose vertex is in Jerusalem and whose base is Tel-Aviv and Haifa. In this small triangle a third of Israel's population resides and according to our planning we will be able to exterminate a third of this number."

144. *The Guardian* (London), April 28, 1977.

145. UPI from Cairo, July 2, 1977.

146. In interview with *Tashrīn* (Syria), August 5, 1980. Talas repeated this statement to *Al-difā'a al-Arabī* (Lebanon), September 17, 1980, and in *Al-Qabas* (Kuwait), October 6, 1980. See also *Al-Hamishmar* (Israel), October 7, 1980.

147. This view is repeated by the Lebanese pro-Palestinian *Al-Muharrir*, according to Saut al-Arab Radio Station, December 12, 1974; also by Tawfiq Hassan, Damascus Home Radio, April 6, 1976.

148. A'ah, "Egypt, Israel, and the Nuclear Bomb."

149. U.S. Congressional Budget Office, *U.S. Strategic Nuclear Forces*, p. x.

150. Freedman, "Israel's Nuclear Policy," p. 119.

151. A'ah, "Egypt, Israel, and the Nuclear Bomb." The full quotation is as follows (my italics):

"*The use of atomic energy for military purposes* is developing in a direction that favours the Arabs' traditional enemy [Israel], but *does not favour the Arabs*. This is so not only from the point of view of production, but also *from the point of view of deterrence* and the tactical and strategic use of these weapons.

"This weapon was invented for the purpose of deterrence and the bombing of the large cities and concentrations of innocent civilians. . . . In light of this *we see that the Arab states, and particularly Egypt, stand out in their spaciousness, and in the distance of their important cultural centres from Israel. They suffer from the existence of densely populated centres. Cairo, for example, during daytime, has a population of 8 million people. This fact naturally has no equivalent in Israel.*

"We must also take into account the fact that the *Arab cities lack Jewish inhabitants which might have otherwise constituted some constraint upon Israel's freedom of action*"

152. al-Anfuri, "Signs of Armed Conflict with Israel."

153. al-Ayubi, "The Truth about the Nuclear Challenge between Egypt and Israel." The full quotation is as follows (my italics):

"A few Arab theoreticians have developed the theory that counter-city strategy is better suited for the Arabs than for the Israelis. This is so in light of the narrow area of the Zionist state and the density of her population, as compared to the wide Arab lands which enjoy the dispersion of targets. This theory is based on a superficial study of the problem. *The density of the Israeli population in lands conquered in 1948 is no greater than Egyptian density in the Delta and the narrow strip of land of the Nile Valley. A nuclear explosion will have a similar effect in both cases.* In addition, Egypt has three weak points:

"1. The Aswan Dam, whose atomic destruction will cause great floods which will flood the Nile Valley and destroy the cities and villages. Radioactive dust carried by the flood waters will pollute the land.

"2. The narrow strip of the Nile Valley causes the blast effect of a nuclear explosion to be greater than usual. This will result from the fact that the blast will be imprisoned by the two walls of the Valley.

"3. The existence of the Sinai desert as a buffer zone between Egypt and Israel results in Israel's ability to bomb Egyptian targets in the Delta and the Nile Valley without fear that Israel will be contaminated in the process.

"Israel, on the other hand, benefits from the inability of Egypt to bomb the Israeli cities for fear of causing radioactive pollution in the cities of Syria, Lebanon, West Bank and Jordan due to their proximity to . . . [Israel]."

154. It must be remembered that a policy of strategic surrender, such as was pursued by Denmark during World War II, was adopted only when a state was at a radical disadvantage in the ability both to defend and to inflict costs.

155. Hasanayn Haykal interview on Kuwait television, February 17, 1975.

156. Haykal, "The Bomb."

157. UPI from London, December 3, 1973.

158. *Chief Executive*, October–December 1977.

159. al-Ayubi, "The Truth About the Nuclear Challenge Between Egypt and Israel."

160. Ahmad Samih Khalidi, "An Appraisal of the Arab–Israeli Military Balance," *Middle East Forum* (1966), 42, no. 3; cited by Steven Rosen, "A Stable System of Nuclear Deterrence in the Arab–Israeli Conflict," p. 1372.

161. Mahar 'Abd al-Fattah, "A Little Diplomacy, Fatah, the Time of Decision has Come," *Al-Akhbār*, December 4, 1975; see FBIS, December 12, 1975, p. D2.

162. Ahmad, "The Future of the Arab–Israeli Conflict."

163. Raymond Aron stated that "Israel is a small country in close proximity to Egypt, whose cities in turn are of major importance; this would make for a highly unstable situation in that the advantages of a preemptive strike would be enormous and quite possibly decisive" (*The Great Debate*, pp. 238–39).

164. Dowty, "Nuclear Proliferation," p. 99, and "Israel and Nuclear Weapons," p. 20.

165. Hoffmann, "Letter to the Editor," p. 14.

166. Yair Evron, "Letter to the Editor," p. 6.

167. Leonard Beaton, "Capabilities of Non-Nuclear Powers," in Buchan, ed., *A World of Nuclear Powers?* p. 25; Buchan, *ibid.*, p. 8.

168. "The central hypothesis is that apocalyptic visions and doomsday

images have been accepted too readily and out of proportion to the arguments that are given. A stable system of mutual deterrence may be viable in the Middle East and may be a positive contribution to the political de-escalation of the Arab–Israeli conflict" (Rosen, "A Stable System of Mutual Nuclear Deterrence," p. 1370); also pp. 1374–77.

169. For an analysis of the vulnerabilities of nuclear forces of medium powers see Kemp, *Nuclear Forces for Medium Powers.*

170. Pranger and Tahtinen, *Nuclear Threat in the Middle East,* pp. 25, 29, 31; Harkavy, *Israel's Nuclear Weapons,* p. 33.

171. Brodie, *Strategy in the Missile Age,* p. 218.

172. Rosen, "A Stable System of Mutual Nuclear Deterrence," p. 1375.

173. Following the U.S.–Saudi 1981 arms deal, five Boeing E-3A Sentry aircraft are to be delivered to Saudi Arabia in the mid 1980s.

174. Brodie, *Strategy in the Missile Age,* p. 184.

175. U.S. Congressional Budget Office, *Counterforce Issues,* p. 10.

176. Luttwak, *A Dictionary of Modern War,* p. 143.

177. Rosen, "A Stable System of Mutual Nuclear Deterrence," p. 1375.

178. Drell and Von Hippel, "Limited Nuclear War," p. 30.

179. al-Ayubi, "The Truth About the Nuclear Challenge Between Egypt and Israel."

180. Three 60-kiloton weapons, if ground-burst, given 30-mph winds, would create fallout (1,100 rads) causing 100 percent deaths extending to some 58 miles. The width of such a contaminated area would be some four miles. Given a general direction of northwest to such winds, an Arab counterforce attack of this sort might well annihilate Damascus. Calculations are based on Glasstone and Dolan, *The Effects of Nuclear Weapons,* pp. 401, 430; see also Drell and Von Hippel, "Limited Nuclear War," pp. 27–37; Enthoven, "American Deterrent Policy," p. 130.

181. See Wellnitz, *LASL Panel on Tactical Nuclear Warfare,* p. 71.

182. In excerpts from Sadat's memoirs, published in *Time,* March 20, 1978, Sadat states: "We received nothing at all from the Soviet satellite which followed up the fighting. I would like to put this on record as a point of historical significance insofar as the Soviet Union claims to champion the Arab cause" (p. 47).

183. Concern about such a situation has been communicated to me by a number of scholars who read various drafts of this work.

184. This calculation is based on U.S. Congress, Office of Technology Assessment, *The Effects of Nuclear War,* pp. 39–45.

3. Israel, Nuclear Weapons, and Peace

1. Dowty, "Nuclear Proliferation," p. 91.

2. Dowty, "Israel and Nuclear Weapons," pp. 19–20; see also Evron, "Israel and the Atom," pp. 1332–33.

3. Haykal, "Frankly Speaking."

4. Tucker, "Israel and the United States," p. 40.

5. See Ahmad, "The Future of the Arab–Israeli Conflict"; *Rūz al-Yūsuf* (Egypt) May 2, 1976; *Al-Qabas* (Kuwait), May 11, 1976; *Al-Akhbār* (Egypt), December 4, 1975; *Al-Sayyād* (Lebanon), February 26, 1976; *Al-Usbū' al-'Arabī* (Lebanon), April 26, 1976.

6. Morgan, *Deterrence*, p. 109.

7. Jervis, "Deterrence Theory Revisited," ACIS Working Paper no. 14, p. 11.

8. For the updated version of the 1973 war see Rosen, "What a Fifth Arab-Israeli War Might Look Like."

9. *Al-Madīna* (Saudi Arabia), December 6, 1976, according to Riyadh SNA, December 6, 1976; see FBIS, December 8, 1976.

10. *Al-Anwār* (Lebanon), January 8, 1975, in interview granted to managing editor Bassam Furrayhah; see FBIS, January 9, 1975, p. D4. On another occasion Sadat stated in response to a question about Israel's nuclear threat: "My feeling about this is that they are continuing the same old policy which they pursued before the October War, that is, trying to intimidate and terrorize the Arabs. We will not be frightened or intimidated. Even if the Israelis use a nuclear bomb against us we will not surrender and we will not submit to Israel's conditions even if Israel asks us to do this for a hundred years" (interview to French television; see FBIS, January 27, 1975, p. D2).

11. Ibrahim Nafi, "Israel's Nuclear Disarmament: How?" *Al-Ahrām*, February 20, 1981; see FBIS, February 26, 1981, p. D5.

12. Press conference in Vienna, according to AP from Cairo, April 13, 1976.

13. In Rome, according to UPI from Rome, April 8, 1976. See also *Ha'aretz* (Israel), April 9, 1976.

14. Interview to *Ittelā'āt* (Iran), June 14, 1976.

15. Schelling, *Arms and Influence*, pp. 159, 160.

16. al-Nasr, "The Arab Nuclear Program . . . When and Where?"

17. In *Al-Ahrām*, November 23, 1973; see FBIS, November 26, 1973, p. G1.

18. Ahmad Baha' al-Din, "Declaration of Israel as a Nuclear State Eliminates Its Excuse About Secure Borders," *Al-Ahrām* (Egypt), November 28, 1978; see JPRS, November 28, 1978, pp. 51–53.

19. On December 14, 1981, the Israeli Knesset voted to extend its "law, jurisdiction, and administration" to the Golan Heights. The step was widely interpreted to imply the permanent annexation of the territory and may indeed propel the extension of Israel's national consensus to include the defense of the Heights. This outcome is by no means self-evident, however. If anything, the circumstances surrounding the decision proposed by Prime Minister Menachem Begin may have diminished the odds that such a consensus would emerge. The Knesset vote of 63 to 21 in favor

of the decision was achieved after most of the opposition Labor Party boycotted the session to protest the haste with which the Prime Minister arranged to have the Knesset adopt the new legislation. Instead of forging a new national consensus, the Knesset decision may polarize the Israeli public with respect to the nation's foreign and defense policies. Had the area been annexed by Israel immediately after the 1967 war, and had it been accompanied by a corresponding socialization process, a national consensus engulfing the Golan Heights might well have emerged.

20. Wohlstetter, "NATO and the Nth + 1 Country," p. 215.

21. Ibid.

22. See Brig. Gen. Aryeh Shalev, "Security Arrangements in Sinai," p. 24.

23. See Philip Karber, in Wellnitz, LASL Panel on Tactical Nuclear Warfare, p. 27.

24. U.S. Congressional Budget Office, U.S. Strategic Nuclear Forces, p. 5.

25. Record, "The Defense of Europe," p. 23.

26. Cited by Shreffler, "The New Nuclear Force," pp. 297–98.

27. The figure is hypothetical and somewhat arbitrary. It assumes 50 percent casualties for a fighting force roughly equivalent in size to what Israel had in the Sinai during the October 1973 war.

28. Brodie, Strategy in the Missile Age, p. 332.

29. See Wellnitz, LASL Panel on Tactical Nuclear Weapons, p. 46.

30. Martin, "Flexibility in Tactical Nuclear Response," p. 256.

31. See Wellnitz, LASL Panel on Tactical Nuclear Weapons, p. 26.

32. Ibid., pp. 26 and 35.

33. Ibid., p. 38.

34. U.S. Congressional Budget Office, Planning U.S. General Purpose Forces, p. 23.

35. Shreffler, "The New Nuclear Force," p. 296; Sandoval, "Consider the Porcupine"; see also Osborn and Bowen, "How to Defend Western Europe."

36. Kenneth N. Waltz, "What Will the Spread of Nuclear Weapons Do To the World?" p. 177.

37. Shreffler, "The New Nuclear Force," p. 296.

38. Ibid., p. 310.

39. See Karber statement in Wellnitz, LASL Panel on Tactical Nuclear Weapons, p. 27.

40. Canby, The Alliance and Europe, p. 5.

41. See Martin, "Flexibility in Tactical Nuclear Response," pp. 258–59. Martin argues that "it seems highly improbable that the hope of denying all penetrations and thereby achieving a barrier defense would be vindicated. In that case, nuclear action would not be contained to a narrow strip of devastation and the problem of restoring the front and recovering lost territory would not be solved."

42. In the European front the adoption of early use of small-yield nuclear forces would encounter two additional problems. First, the inter-NATO political problems involved in adopting an early-use doctrine would be considerable. An automatic early-use doctrine is unlikely to be adopted because its adoption would require the different governments to surrender all flexibility on a question of major importance: the decision when to use nuclear weapons. An early—but not automatic—use would be impractical because by the time the consent of all governments involved is obtained, it would be anything but early. Each government would take its time making the decision, fearing that escalation would be inevitable. The second problem is that the adoption of the proposed doctrine would be meaningless if the Soviets refused to follow suit. They are likely to adhere to the use of large-yield theater nuclear weapons, hence canceling whatever discriminatory power NATO's small-yield nuclear weapons would have. See Digby, "Precision Weapons," p. 171; Canby, *The Alliance and Europe*, p. 4; Martin, "Flexibility in Tactical Nuclear Response," pp. 260–61.

43. See, for example, Dowty, "Israel and Nuclear Weapons," p. 19.

44. Reuters, from Tokyo, April 26, 1976. See also *Al-'Amal* (Tunisia), April 24, 1976.

45. Paris, AFP, January 5, 1975; see FBIS, January 6, 1975, p. A18.

46. Voice of Palestine (clandestine), December 4, 1974; see FBIS, December 5, 1974, pp. A3, A4.

47. Fuad Jabber, *Israel and Nuclear Weapons*, pp. 204–6.

48. *Ibid.*, pp. 205–7.

49. *Ibid.*

50. Haykal, "Frankly Speaking."

51. *Ha'aretz* (Israel), January 1, 1979.

52. Reported by U.S. Congressman Paul Findley (R–Ill.) at a press conference in Washington, according to UPI, December 1, 1978. Arafat gave a similar statement in public when interviewed on CBS's *60 Minutes* on March 26, 1977.

53. *Yediot Ahronot* (Israel), September 10, 1979, p. 3.

4. The Risks of a Nuclear Middle East

1. Most prominent among them have been Yair Evron and Alan Dowty. See especially the former's "Israel and the Atom: The Uses and Misuses of Ambiguity," "Letter to the Editor," and "Some Effects of the Introduction of Nuclear Weapons in the Middle East"; and also the latter's "Nuclear Proliferation: The Israeli Case."

2. Marwah, "India's Nuclear and Space Programs," pp. 113–14.

3. Mandelbaum, "International Stability and Nuclear Order," p. 66.

4. Aron, *The Great Debate*, pp. 61–62; Hoffmann, "Nuclear Proliferation and World Politics," pp. 89–90.

5. Morgan, *Deterrence*, p. 13.

6. See David Krieger, "What Happens If . . .?" p. 52.

7. Dowty, "Israel and Nuclear Weapons," p. 20.

8. Evron, "Letter to the Editor," p. 6.

9. Gupta, "The Indian Dilemma," p. 59; see also Rikhi Jaipal, "The Indian Nuclear Explosion," p. 47.

10. Dowty, "Nuclear Proliferation," p. 102.

11. Rosen, "A Stable System," p. 1374.

12. Brodie, *Strategy in the Missile Age*, p. 280.

13. Gupta, "The Indian Dilemma," p. 59; Hsieh, "Communist China and Nuclear Force," pp. 159, 166–69.

14. Brodie, *Strategy in the Missile Age*, p. 280.

15. With respect to this issue I concur with one of Israel's foremost civilian strategists, the late Saadia Amiel, who stated in an interview he granted in 1974 as follows: "I do not adhere to the 'crazy states' thesis. Look at Qaddafi. When we had downed his plane he had some 100 [French] Mirage [jet fighters] and yet he launched none of these against us" (reported by Uri Milstein, "Document: A National Strategy for the 1980's," *Ha'aretz*, Weekly Supplement, August 18, 1978, p. 27).

16. "Qaddafi Planning a Rapid Deployment Force," *New York Times*, November 20, 1981.

17. Jervis, "Deterrence Theory Revisited," *World Politics*, p. 299.

18. Morgan, *Deterrence*, p. 116.

19. Pranger and Tahtinen, *Nuclear Threat in the Middle East*, p. 3.

20. Evron, "Some Effects of the Introduction of Nuclear Weapons in the Middle East," p. 107.

21. See Brodie, *War and Politics*, pp. 64–66, 79, 179–80.

22. *Ibid.*, p. 179.

23. Statement by Brig. Gen. Lynwood Lennon, Deputy Director for Nuclear and Chemical Matters, Office of the Deputy Chief of Staff for Operations and Plans; see Wellnitz, *LASL Panel on Tactical Nuclear Warfare*, p. 35.

24. "Excerpts from a Soviet Booklet on Nuclear War," *New York Times*, November 21, 1981.

25. Schelling, *Arms and Influence*, p. 12.

26. Interview in *Al-Hawādith* (Lebanon); MENA from Cairo, January 23, 1975 (my italics).

27. Interview with CBS's Walter Cronkite, according to MENA, June 22, 1974; see FBIS, June 24, 1974.

28. Interview with ABC's "Issues and Answers," according to MENA, October 27, 1975; see FBIS, November 5, 1975, pp. D40, D41.

19. Interview in *Al-Ahrām*, according to MENA from Cairo, February 22, 1975.

30. Interview to *Ma'ariv* (Israel), November 7, 1980.

31. Evron, "Some Effects of the Introduction of Nuclear Weapons in the Middle East," pp. 116–120.

32. Garwin, "Reducing Dependence on Nuclear Weapons," p. 98; Admiral Noel Gayler concurs: "if we use the most important measure . . . the number of deaths . . . the consequence of a strategic nuclear exchange is quite insensitive to the force levels involved. The calculations are perfectly straightforward; it results from the fact that saturation takes place very early. The way the wind is blowing on a particular day makes more difference than the force levels of the contenders." See Wellnitz, *LASL Panel on Tactical Nuclear Warfare*, p. 72.

33. Cited in Conover, "U.S. Strategic Nuclear Weapons and Deterrence," p. 22–24.

34. See Gallois, *Balance of Terror*, p. 20.

35. Cited in Conover, "U.S. Strategic Nuclear Weapons and Deterrence," p. 24. Mandelbaum demonstrated Kissinger's lament by pointing out that the United States gained very little from the superiority it enjoyed in strategic nuclear weapons up to the late 1950s. See his "International Stability and Nuclear Order," pp. 43–44. However, his argument is open to the criticism that as a status-quo power the United States didn't even try. Hence, his example is not very convincing.

36. Gallois, *Balance of Terror*, p. 197. Gallois describes the ineffectiveness of nuclear coalitions.

37. Cited by Aron, *The Great Debate*, p. 163.

38. Ciro E. Zoppo, "France as a Nuclear Power," pp. 149–50; Albert Wohlstetter, "NATO and the *N*th + 1 Country"; Hoffmann, "Nuclear Proliferation and World Politics," p. 121.

39. Aron, *The Great Debate*, p. 123.

40. Robert Rosenberg, "Iraq Nuclear Programme Worries Arabs," *Jerusalem Post*, November 3, 1980. See also *Ma'ariv* (Israel), August 10, 1979.

41. *Nucleonics Week*, February 23, 1978.

42. "Saudis Reported Aiding in Bomb," *Washington Star*, January 19, 1981.

43. Gen. Ahmad Badawi, interview in *Ma'ariv* (Israel), November 7, 1980. See also "Egypt Fearful Libya Might Get A-Weapons," *Washington Post*, November 8, 1980.

44. Hoffmann, "Nuclear Proliferation and World Politics," p. 107.

45. See Kenneth N. Waltz, "International Structure, National Force, and the Balance of World Power"; Deutch and Singer, "Multipolar Power Systems"; Rosecrance, "Bipolarity, Multipolarity and the Future."

46. Deutch and Singer argue that less attention would lead to less involvement and hence less conflict ("Multipolar Power Systems").

47. Kohl, *French Nuclear Diplomacy*, p. 154.

48. Van Evera, "Nuclear Weapons, Nuclear Proliferation and the Causes of War."

49. Enthoven, "American Deterrent Policy," p. 131.

50. See the entire issue of *The Defense Monitor* 7 (June 1978).

51. Brodie, *Strategy in the Missile Age*, p. 311.

52. Gallois, *Balance of Terror*, p. 62.

53. *Ibid.*, p. 18.

54. Brodie was pessimistic about the chances of controlling a nuclear war in Europe. See his *Strategy in the Missile Age*, p. 335. Some argue that an important cause for difficulties in controlling a Continental nuclear war is Soviet doctrine, which is said to discard the possibility of controlling nuclear war in Europe. See Record, "The Defense of Europe by Nuclear or Conventional Forces," p. 23; Conover, "U.S. Strategic Nuclear Weapons and Deterrence," p. 45; and Record in Wellnitz, *LASL Panel on Tactical Nuclear Warfare*, p. 37.

55. Brodie, *Strategy in the Missile Age*, pp. 310–11.

56. *Ibid.*, p. 334.

57. Gallois, *Balance of Terror*, p. 199.

58. Aron, *The Great Debate*, pp. 62–63; Lewis Dunn, "Nuclear Proliferation and World Politics," p. 101.

59. Evron, "Some Effects of the Introduction of Nuclear Weapons into the Middle East," p. 116.

60. Dunn, "Nuclear Proliferation and World Politics," p. 98.

61. See *The Defense Monitor*, June 1978, p. 2.

62. Rosen, "A Stable System of Nuclear Deterrence," p. 1380.

63. Schelling, "Who Will Have the Bomb?" pp. 89–90; Waltz, "What Will the Spread of Nuclear Weapons Do To the World?" p. 190.

64. Dunn, "Nuclear Proliferation and World Politics," p. 108.

65. Krieger, "What Happens If . . .?" p. 51.

66. Dunn, "Nuclear Proliferation and World Politics," p. 102.

67. Schelling, "Who Will Have the Bomb?" p. 88.

68. See Aron, *The Great Debate*, p. 117; Dunn, "Nuclear Proliferation and World Politics," p. 98.

69. Roberta Wohlstetter, "Terror on a Grand Scale," pp. 100–1.

70. Rosenbaum, "Nuclear Terror," pp. 153–54; Krieger, "What Happens If . . .?" pp. 51–53; R. Wohlstetter, "Terror on a Grand Scale," p. 99; Schelling, "Who Will Have the Bomb?" pp. 83–84; Jenkins, "The Potential for Nuclear Terrorism," p. 2, and "The Impact of Nuclear Terrorism" (unpublished paper), p. 8; Dunn, "Nuclear Proliferation and World Politics," p. 105; Kupperman, "Nuclear Terrorism: Armchair Pastime or Genuine Threat?" (unpublished paper), p. 2.

71. Rosenbaum, "Nuclear Terror," pp. 153–54; Krieger, "What Happens If . . .?" p. 51.

72. Rosenbaum, "Nuclear Terror"; Krieger, "What Happens If . . ."; R. Wohlstetter, "Terror on a Grand Scale," p. 100; Kupperman, "Nuclear Terrorism," p. 11.

73. "Arafat, Qadhafi Feuding; PLO Post in Libya Seized," *International Herald Tribune*, December 12, 1979.

74. Schelling, "Who Will Have the Bomb?" pp. 78, 83–84.

75. Kupperman, "Nuclear Terrorism," p. 8.

76. Jenkins, "The Potential for Nuclear Terrorism," p. 10; see also Gompert, *Nuclear Weapons and World Politics*, p. 251.

77. Kupperman, "Nuclear Terrorism," p. 8; see also Jenkins, "The Potential for Nuclear Terrorism," p. 2.

78. Schelling, "Who Will Have the Bomb?" pp. 83–84; Gompert, *Nuclear Weapons and World Politics*, p. 252.

79. Jenkins, "The Impact of Nuclear Terrorism," p. 14.

80. R. Wohlstetter, "Terror on a Grand Scale," p. 102. See also Jenkins, "The Potential for Nuclear Terrorism," p. 8.

81. Gompert, *Nuclear Weapons and World Politics*, p. 251.

82. Jenkins, "The Potential for Nuclear Terrorism," p. 8.

83. R. Wohlstetter, "Terror on a Grand Scale," p. 102.

84. Jenkins, "The Potential for Nuclear Terrorism," p. 3; Kupperman, "Nuclear Terrorism," p. 10.

85. "Who Will Have the Bomb?" pp. 84, 86.

86. Jenkins, "The Potential for Nuclear Terrorism," p. 9.

87. *Ibid.*, p. 10.

5. The Superpowers' Response to a Nuclear-Armed Israel

1. Dowty, "Nuclear Proliferation," p. 99, and "Israel's Nuclear Policy," p. 19.

2. Bader, *The United States and the Spread of Nuclear Weapons*, p. 93.

3. Boskey and Willrich, *Nuclear Weapons: Prospects for Control*, p. 70.

4. Bell, "Israel's Nuclear Option," pp. 384–85.

5. Peter Mangold, "The Soviet Record in the Middle East," p. 102.

6. Duffy, "Soviet Nuclear Exports," pp. 83–85.

7. Wettig, "Soviet Policy on the Nonproliferation of Nuclear Weapons," p. 1060.

8. Benjamin S. Lambeth, "Nuclear Proliferation and Soviet Arms Control Policy," pp. 312–13, 318.

9. Marwah, "India's Nuclear and Space Programs," p. 118.

10. Duffy, "Soviet Nuclear Exports," p. 97.

11. Cited by Shirin Tahir-Kheli, "Pakistan's Nuclear Option and U.S. Policy," pp. 363–64.

12. Cited by William W. Lowrance, "Nuclear Futures for Sale: To Brazil from West Germany, 1975," p. 147.

13. *Ma'ariv* (Israel), August 29, 1977.

14. Goldschmidt, "A Historical Survey of Nonproliferation Policies," p. 84; see also Wettig, "Soviet Policy," p. 1064.

15. Duffy, "Soviet Nuclear Exports," p. 98.

16. Paul Jabber, "A Nuclear Middle East," pp. 12–13.

17. See Schiff, *October Earthquake, Yom Kippur 1973*. Schiff, the military correspondent of Israel's daily *Ha'aretz*, claimed in the framework of his account of October 24, 1973: "American espionage satellites add details from the Middle East. Two Russian brigades, equipped with ground-to-ground Scud missiles, have deployed east of Cairo. When the missile brigades passed through the Bosphorus, sensitive recorders noted nuclear weapons aboard their ships. Now the Russians seem to want to display the Atomic weaponry they have brought to Egypt. Nuclear warheads can clearly be seen on the satellite photographs" (see pp. 289–90).

18. Quandt, *Decade of Decisions*, p. 198. Note that as opposed to Schiff's account, Quandt does not mention that the "nuclear ship's" cargo also included Scud missiles. Quandt also treats the existence of nuclear weapons on board as less certain.

19. *Ibid.*

20. Major Yishai Kordova and Lt. Col. Avi-Shai, "Haiyum Hagarini Hasovieti Beshalhay Milhemet Yom Hakipurim."

21. Freedman, "Israel's Nuclear Policy," p. 18.

22. In fact, even as the Soviets negotiated the supply of conventional weapons of a sophisticated nature, they sometimes demanded that their use would require prior clearance with Moscow. With respect to MIG-23's, Sadat notes that the Soviets demanded "that to operate these aircraft in particular, prior permission had to be granted by Moscow." *Time*, March 20, 1978, p. 45.

23. Bray and Moodie, "Nuclear Politics in India," p. 12.

24. See Yehoshua Tadmor, "After Asad's Visit to Moscow," *Davar* (Israel), March 2, 1978.

25. Lambeth, "Nuclear Proliferation," p. 319.

26. Tucker, "Israel and the United States," p. 40.

27. Dowty, "Nuclear Proliferation," p. 93.

28. Freedman, "Israel's Nuclear Policy," p. 18.

29. Haykal, "Frankly Speaking."

30. Aron, *The Great Debate*, p. 239.

31. Waltz, "What Will the Spread of Nuclear Weapons Do to the World?" p. 190.

32. Chari, "The Israeli Nuclear Option," p. 353.

33. Bell, "Israel's Nuclear Option," pp. 386; Haselkorn, "Israel: From an Option to a Bomb in the Basement?" p. 165.

34. Haselkorn, p. 166.

35. Bell, "Israel's Nuclear Option," p. 386.

36. Steven J. Rosen, "Nuclearization and Stability in the Middle East," p. 10.

37. Dowty, "Israel and Nuclear Weapons," pp. 15–16.

38. Rosen, "A Stable System," p. 1382.

39. On June 5, 1967, President Johnson used the Red Line to threaten intervention if the Soviets intervened on the Arab's behalf. On October 23, 1973, the United States put its forces in worldwide alert to deter a possible Soviet move to "police" a cease-fire.

40. Kennan, *A Cloud of Danger*, p. 85.

41. A. Wohlstetter, "NATO and the Nth + 1 Country," p. 198.

42. Gallois, *Balance of Terror*, p. 141.

43. Becker, "Nuclear Israel: Potential and Policy," p. 19.

44. Chari, "The Israeli Nuclear Option," p. 353.

45. Nacht, "The United States in a World of Nuclear Powers," p. 168.

46. Much of this section is based on dozens of interviews conducted by this writer in Washington, D.C., during February and March 1979. Interviewed were officials of the U.S. government, staff members of the Congress, journalists, fellows of academic institutions, and other distinguished members of the Washington community. Due to the sensitivity of the subject, all interviews were conducted on a "background" and "not for attribution" basis.

47. Dowty, "Nuclear Proliferation," p. 99; see also Dowty, "Israel and Nuclear Weapons," p. 19.

48. Evron, *The Role of Arms Control in the Middle East*, p. 9.

49. Haselkorn, "Israel: From an Option to a Bomb in the Basement?" p. 140; Dowty, "Israel and Nuclear Weapons," pp. 16–17; A. Wohlstetter, "NATO and the Nth + 1 Country," p. 200. Wohlstetter notes that with respect to the British involvement in the Suez affair, nuclear weapons "failed to make them more resolute against the possibility of economic sanctions by their principal ally."

50. Dowty, "Nuclear Proliferation," p. 95.

51. See Gelb, "The Atom is a Constant in U.S. Foreign Policy," *New York Times*, March 14, 1976; Williams, *The U.S., India, and the Bomb*, p. 7; Aron, *The Great Debate*, pp. 237–38.

52. Quoted by Rosecrance, *The Dispersion of Nuclear Weapons*, p. 310.

53. Foster, "New Directions in Arms Control and Disarmament."

54. Buchan, *A World of Nuclear Powers?* p. 3; Bader, *The United States and the Spread of Nuclear Weapons*, p. 2; Hoffmann, "Nuclear Proliferation and World Politics," p. 92.

55. See also Vital, *The Inequality of States*, p. 160.

56. Long, "Nuclear Proliferation," p. 52; see also Buchan, *A World of Nuclear Powers?* p. 3; Bader, *The United States and the Spread of Nuclear Weapons*, p. 12.

57. Hoag, "Nuclear Strategic Options and European Force Participation," p. 231.

58. Statement by Fred C. Iklé, Director of the Arms Control and Disarmament Agency, September 18, 1974. See "Special Report: The Export of Nuclear Technology," U.S. Department of State, Bureau of Public Affairs, Office of Media Services, no. 9, October 1974.

59. Bader, *The United States and the Spread of Nuclear Weapons*, p. 18.

60. *Ibid.*, pp. 22–23, 26, 40; see also Goldschmidt, "A Historical Survey of Non-Proliferation Policies," p. 72.

61. Statement by Fred C. Iklé, Director of the Arms Control and Disarmament Agency, September 18, 1974. See "Special Report: The Export of Nuclear Technology."

62. David Hoffman, "Aliens Gain U.S. Atomic Arms Lore," *Philadelphia Inquirer*, May 19, 1979. Cites a report by the U.S. Congress, General Accounting Office.

63. Statement by Fred C. Iklé, Director of the Arms Control and Disarmament Agency, September 18, 1974. See "Special Report: The Export of Nuclear Technology."

64. Mancur Olson, Jr., *The Logic of Collective Action*; see also Mancur Olson, Jr., and Richard Zeckhauser, "An Economic Theory of Alliances."

65. Long, "Nuclear Proliferation," p. 53.

66. Statement by Fred C. Iklé, Director of the Arms Control and Disarmament Agency, September 18, 1974. See "Special Report: The Export of Nuclear Technology."

67. Long, "Nuclear Proliferation," p. 53.

68. Gelb, "The Atom is a Constant in U.S. Foreign Policy," *New York Times*, March 14, 1976.

69. *Ibid.*

70. Bader, *The United States and the Spread of Nuclear Weapons*, pp. 15–16, 27. Bader notes that criticism of the discriminatory character of America's nuclear policy persisted despite this program.

71. *Ibid.*, p. 31.

72. Kohl, *French Nuclear Diplomacy*, p. 52.

73. *Ibid.*, pp. 50–51; Bader, *The United States and the Spread of Nuclear Weapons*, p. 35.

74. Bader, *ibid.*, p. 35.

75. Kohl, *French Nuclear Diplomacy*, p. 51.

76. Bader, *The United States and the Spread of Nuclear Weapons*, p. 38.

77. Kohl, *French Nuclear Diplomacy*, p. 51.

78. Bader, *The United States and the Spread of Nuclear Weapons*, p. 45.

79. Kohl, *French Nuclear Diplomacy*, p. 222.

80. *Ibid.*, p. 223.

81. Bader, *The United States and the Spread of Nuclear Weapons*, pp. 52, 58.

82. *Ibid.*, p. 59.

83. Goldschmidt, "A Historical Survey of Non-Proliferation Policies," p. 76.

84. Alan Cranston, "How Congress Can Shape Arms Control," p. 208.

85. Robert Gillette, "U.S. Squelched Apparent S. Korea A-Bomb Drive," *Los Angeles Times*, November 4, 1978.

86. Nacht, "The United States in a World of Nuclear Powers," p. 163; see also Marwah, "India's Nuclear and Space Programs," p. 118, and Ashok Kapur, "Nth Powers and the Future," p. 94.

87. Tahir-Kheli, "Pakistan's Nuclear Option and U.S. Policy," p. 367.

88. Karl Kaiser, "The Great Nuclear Debate," pp. 89–90; see also Lowrance, "Nuclear Futures for Sale," pp. 150, 162–63.

89. "Kissinger's Nuclear Remark Riles French," *San Francisco Chronicle*, August 12, 1976.

90. U.S. House, *Hearings on H.R. 11963*, p. 13.

91. Kapur, "Nth Power and the Future," p. 91.

92. Message from the President of the United States, James Earl Carter, to the United States Congress, April 27, 1977.

93. Michael Brenner, "Carter's Non-Proliferation Strategy," pp. 333–34. See also Edward Walsh and J. P. Smith, "U.S. Acts to Curb Plutonium, Asks Allies to Assist," *Washington Post*, April 8, 1977.

94. U.S. Congress, Public Law 95-242, *The Nuclear Non-Proliferation Act of 1978*.

95. Smith and Rathjens, "Reassessing Nuclear Nonproliferation Policy," pp. 878–79.

96. Statement by State Department spokesman Hodding Carter, reported by Reuter's from Washington, April 6, 1979.

97. Smith and Rathjens, "Reassessing Nuclear Nonproliferation Policy," pp. 879–80. See also Richard Burt, "U.S. Shifting Policy on Limiting Spread of A-Arms," *New York Times*, October 19, 1977.

98. Jonathan Kandell, "France Cancels Contract on A-Plant for Pakistan," *International Herald Tribune*, August 24, 1978.

99. "A Step Backward on Proliferation," *Washington Post* (Editorial), April 11, 1977.

100. See Kaiser, "The Great Nuclear Debate," p. 101.

101. To avoid an earlier clash the administration approved the export of 1,000 pounds of enriched uranium to three European nations just twenty-four hours before the Act was to go into effect. See Thomas O'Toole and Jim Hoagland, "Uranium Exports Quietly Approved Just Before Ban," *Washington Post*, April 16, 1978.

102. See testimony by Undersecretary of State Lucy Benson, in U.S. Senate, Committee on Foreign Relations, *Hearings on S-1160*, p. 234.

103. *Ibid.*

104. Robert G. Kaiser, "Carter Switch to Allow N-Reactor Study," *International Herald Tribune*, August 25, 1978.

105. Milton R. Benjamin, "U.S. Fails in Effort to Halt Global Nuclear Expansion," *International Herald Tribune*, December 4, 1979.

106. The letter was designed to elicit support in the state of Idaho, where much breeder-reactor research was to be conducted. See Robert D.

Hershey, Jr., "Breeder Support by Carter Questioned," *New York Times*, October 31, 1980.

107. Hobart Rowen, "U.S. Shifted on Bonn–Brazil Nuclear Deal," *Washington Post*, May 10, 1977; "Brazil, Germany Reaffirm A-Pact Opposed by U.S.," *International Herald Tribune*, March 11–12, 1978.

108. See the editorial of *Washington Post*, May 13, 1977.

109. See Bradley Graham, "Europeans Rebuff U.S. Bid on Nuclear Sales to Argentina," *Washington Post*, February 10, 1981.

110. Brenner, "Carter's Non-Proliferation Strategy," p. 340.

111. Tahir-Kheli, "Pakistan's Nuclear Option and U.S. Policy," pp. 366–67.

112. Henry L. Trewhitt, "U.S., Europe at Odds over Nuclear Fuel," *Baltimore Sun*, May 9, 1978; David Burnham, "Export of Uranium to India Approved," *New York Times*, March 24, 1979.

113. Richard Burt, "Carter to Approve India's Atom Fuel," *New York Times*, June 16, 1980.

114. Martin Tolchin, "House, Rebuffing Carter, Votes to Block Uranium for India," *New York Times*, September 19, 1980; Judith Miller, "Senate Votes, 48–46, to Approve Selling Atom Fuel to India," *New York Times*, September 25, 1980.

115. Richard Burt, "U.S. Panel Rejects Atom Fuel for India," *New York Times*, May 17, 1980.

116. *International Herald Tribune*, April 18, 1979.

117. Associated Press, from Karachi (Pakistan), April 11, 1979.

118. *International Herald Tribune*, December 31, 1979; *Ma'ariv* (Israel), December 31, 1979; *Ha'aretz* (Israel), January 1, 1980; William Borders, "U.S.–Pakistan Relations at Crucial Point," *International Herald Tribune*, January 3, 1980; "A Tilt to Pakistan," *Newsweek*, January 14, 1980, pp. 12, 15.

119. Bernard Gwertzman, "A Serious Rebuff in Pakistan," *New York Times*, March 8, 1980.

120. "Zia Calls $400 Million 'Peanuts,'" *International Herald Tribune*, January 18, 1980; "U.S. Aides Say Drive on Arming Pakistan Has Been Suspended," *New York Times*, March 7, 1980.

121. Smith and Rathjens, "Reassessing Nuclear Nonproliferation Policy," pp. 889–90.

122. Don Cook, "Superpowers Are Warned on Defections From Nuclear Nonproliferation Treaty," *International Herald Tribune*, August 13, 1980; Paul Lewis, "Short Fuses at the Nuclear Treaty Review," *New York Times*, August 18, 1980.

123. Richard Burt, "Lack of Plutonium for Warheads Stirs Debate on Increasing Output," *New York Times*, September 16, 1980.

124. Tahir-Kheli, "Pakistan's Nuclear Option and U.S. Policy," p. 361.

125. *Ha'aretz* (Israel), December 12, 1978.

126. Duffy and Adams, *Power Politics*, pp. 1, 46.

127. Duffy, "Soviet Nuclear Exports," p. 104; see also Brenner, "Carter's Non-Proliferation Strategy," p. 341. By 1980 the United States for the first time imported enriched uranium from the Soviet Union. See Thomas O'Toole, "U.S. Agency Allows Import of Russian Uranium Fuel," *International Herald Tribune*, March 7, 1980.

128. Robert Lindsey, "Reagan Says America Should Not Bar Others From A-Bomb Output," *New York Times*, February 1, 1980.

129. According to Senator John Glenn. See "Nuclear Arms Proliferation: Searching for Safeguards," *New York Times*, April 26, 1981.

130. Judith Miller, "Attack Complicates New Reagan Policy," *New York Times*, June 10, 1981.

131. See Edward A. Gargan, "U.S. Aide Defends Sale of F-16's to Pakistan," *New York Times*, November 3, 1981; Barbara Crossette, "Pakistan Jet Deal Backed by Panel," *New York Times*, November 20, 1981.

132. See Judith Miller, "U.S. Aide Reports Pakistani Assurance of No Plans to Produce Nuclear Arms," *International Herald Tribune*, June 26, 1981; "Accounting Lapses Cited for Pakistani Plutonium," *International Herald Tribune*, October 1, 1981; Stuart Auerbach, "Potential Seen for Pakistan A-Bomb by '83," *Washington Post*, December 8, 1981.

133. Michael J. Berlin, "U.S., Iraqis Agree On U.N. Resolution Condemning Israel," *Washington Post*, June 19, 1981; see also Shai Feldman, "The Raid on Osiraq: A Preliminary Assessment." CSS Memorandum no. 5 (Tel Aviv University, Center for Strategic Studies, August 1981).

134. Jessica Tuchman Mathews, "Letting Nuclear Danger Spread," *Washington Post*, December 2, 1981.

135. "Reagan Emphasizes Policy to Contain Nuclear Arms," *International Herald Tribune*, July 17, 1981.

136. Mathews, "Letting Nuclear Danger Spread."

137. Warren Hoge, "Brazil Is Given Exemption by U.S. From Ban on Purchase of A-Fuel," *International Herald Tribune*, October 18, 1981.

138. Walter Pincus, "U.S. to Raise Output of Arms-Grade Plutonium," *International Herald Tribune*, October 12, 1981.

139. Joanne Omang, "Nuclear Industry Finding Reagan Not the Good Friend It Had Hoped," *Washington Post*, June 30, 1981; Don Oberdorfer, "U.S. Said to Move Toward Easing of Nuclear Exports," *International Herald Tribune*, October 12, 1981.

140. "U.S. to Offer Atom Secrets to Australia," *New York Times*, November 20, 1981.

141. Michael Bar-Zohar, *Ben-Gurion*, p. 1389.

142. *Ibid.*, pp. 1391–92.

143. Bader reports that "President Kennedy ... pressed Ben Gurion very hard to place [the] Dimona [reactor] under safeguards" (*The United States and the Spread of Nuclear Weapons*, p. 89).

144. John W. Finney, "Israel Permits U.S. to Inspect Atom Reactor,"

New York Times, March 14, 1965; John W. Finney, "U.S. Again Assured on Negev Reactor," *New York Times*, June 28, 1966.

145. John K. Cooley, "Cairo Steers Clear of A-Race," *Christian Science Monitor*, June 9, 1969.

146. See *New York Times*, June 16, 1968; cited by Evron, "Israel and the Atom," p. 1338.

147. Quandt, *Decade of Decisions*, p. 80.

148. *Ibid.*, pp. 66–67. See also: Hedrick Smith, "U.S. Assumes the Israelis Have A-Bomb or Its Parts," *New York Times*, July 18, 1970.

149. Boskey and Willrich, *Nuclear Weapons*, pp. 34–35.

150. U.S. Congress, Public Law 95-92, *International Security Assistance Act of 1977*, pp. 620–21.

151. *The Congressional Record,* April 29, 1977, p. S-6789; see also U.S., Congress, Public Law 95-242, *The Nuclear Non-Proliferation Act of 1978*.

152. Statement issued to the Senate Committee on Appropriations by Deputy Secretary of Defense Charles Duncan, March 16, 1977. This writer was present at the hearing.

153. Burt, "Nuclear Proliferation and Conventional Arms Transfer," p. 26.

154. Quandt, *Decade of Decisions*, pp. 66–67. Quandt reports that during negotiations on the sale of F-4 Phantom jets to Israel,

the N.P.T. issue was discussed at length with Israeli representatives. The most the Israelis would say was that they would not be the first ones to 'introduce' nuclear weapons in the Middle East. In trying to clarify what this meant, U.S. officials discovered that it was understood by Israeli Ambassador Rabin to mean that Israel would not be the first to 'test' such weapons or to reveal their existence publicly. Paul Warnke, Assistant Secretary of Defense, then sent a letter to Rabin spelling out the American understanding of what nonintroduction of nuclear weapons meant: no production of a nuclear device. Before the issue was ever resolved, Johnson ordered the bureaucracy to end the search for a quid pro quo on the F-4s. Pressures were mounting for an affirmative United States response to the Israeli request; political candidates were all endorsing the Israeli position; in July the Senate passed a resolution calling for the sale of F-4s to Israel. Finally, on October 9, Johnson publicly announced that Israel would be allowed to purchase the phantoms.

155. Aronson, "Israel's Nuclear Options," p. 7.

156. *Ma'ariv* (Israel), December 12, 1974.

157. Hedrick Smith, "The U.S. Assumes the Israelis Have A-Bomb or Its Parts," *New York Times*, July 18, 1970.

158. See Arthur Kranish, "CIA: Israel Has 10–20 A-Weapons," *Washington Post*, March 15, 1976; David Binder, "C.I.A. Says Israel Has 10–20 A-Bombs," *New York Times*, March 16, 1976; *The Economist*, March 20, 1976.

159. *Yediot Ahronot*, January 27, 1978.

160. See *Ma'ariv*, January 29, 1978.

161. *Ma'ariv*, March 2, 1978.

162. *Ibid.*

163. *Ma'ariv*, April 9, 1978.

164. U.S. Congress, Public Law 95-92, *International Security Assistance Act of 1977*, pp. 620–21.

165. State Department spokesman's response to question taken at noon press briefing, April 6, 1979.

166. U.S. Congress, *International Security Assistance Act of 1977*, p. 621.

167. U.S. Senate Committee on Foreign Relations, *Hearings on S-1160*, p. 234.

168. *Ibid.*, p. 226.

169. *Ibid.*, pp. 234–35.

170. U.S. Senate, *Senate Delegation Report on American Foreign Policy and Non-Proliferation Interests in the Middle East*, p. 51.

171. *Miami Herald*, November 25, 1976, p. 28A.

172. Statement by Undersecretary of State Joseph Sisco to the Hamilton-Fraser Subcommittee of the House Foreign Affairs Committee on September 16, 1974. See "Special Report: The Export of Nuclear Technology," U.S. Department of State, Bureau of Public Affairs, Office of Media Services, no. 9, October 1974.

173. U.S. House, Committee on International Relations, *Hearings on H.R. 11963*, pp. 194–95.

174. *The Congressional Record*, May 14, 1979, pp. S-5748 and S-5751.

175. *Ha'aretz* (Israel), December 12, 1979.

176. Bernard Gwertzman, "U.S. Starts Seeking Mideast Atom Ban," *New York Times*, August 14, 1981.

177. President Ronald Reagan's press conference, June 17, 1981.

178. Judith Miller, "3 Nations Widening Nuclear Contacts," *New York Times*, June 28, 1981.

179. Judith Miller, "2 in House Withdraw Atom Curb," *New York Times*, December 9, 1981.

180. See Shai Feldman, "Peacemaking in the Middle East."

181. Rosen, "A Stable System," p. 1381.

182. Williams, *The U.S., India, and the Bomb*, p. 11.

183. Nacht, "The United States in a World of Nuclear Powers," p. 164.

184. Gompert, *Nuclear Weapons and World Politics*, pp. 234–35.

Bibliography

A'ah, Hassan. "Egypt, Israel, and the Nuclear Bomb." *Al-Tali'a* (Egypt), September 1975. Hebrew trans.

Abdallah, Hisham. "The Characteristics of the Fifth Arab–Israeli War." *Shu'ūn Filastīniyya* (Lebanon), November 10, 1975.

Abel, Eli. *The Missile Crisis.* Philadelphia: Lippincott, 1966.

Ahmad, Muhammad Sayid. "The Future of the Arab–Israeli Conflict After the October War." *Shu'ūn Filastīniyya* (Lebanon), March 1976. Hebrew trans.

Alexander, Yonah. "Terrorism and the Media in the Middle East." In Yonah Alexander and S. M. Finger, eds., *Terrorism: Interdisciplinary Perspectives*, pp. 167–99. New York: McGraw-Hill, John Jay Press, 1977.

Allison, Graham T. *Essence of Decision: Explaining the Cuban Missile Crisis.* Boston: Little, Brown, 1971.

Allison, Graham T., and Frederic Morris. "Precision Guidance for NATO: Justification and Constraints." In Johan J. Holst and Uwe Nerlich, eds., *Beyond Nuclear Deterrence*, pp. 207–22. New York: Crane, Russak, 1977.

Amiel, Saadia. "Deterrence by Conventional Forces." *Survival* (March–April 1978), 20:58–62.

al-Anfuri, Amin. "Signs of Armed Conflict with Israel." *Al-Majalla al-Askarīyya* (Syria), October 1975. Hebrew trans.

Aron, Raymond. *The Great Debate: Theories of Nuclear Strategy.* Garden City, N.Y.: Doubleday, 1965.

—— *On War.* Terence Kilmartin, tr. New York: Norton, 1968. First appeared in French as *De la Guerre* in 1957.

Aronson, Shlomo. "Israel's Nuclear Options." ACIS Working Paper no. 17. Los Angeles: Center for Arms Control and International Security, University of California, November 1977.

——— "Nuclearization of the Middle East: A Dovish View." *Jerusalem Quarterly* (Winter 1977), no. 2, pp. 27–44.

al-Asaly, Bassam. "Reviewing the Components of Arab Strategy." *Al-Majalla al-Askarīyya* (Syria), August–September 1975. Hebrew trans.

al-Ayubi, Lt. Col. (Ret.) Hitam. "The Truth About the Nuclear Challenge Between Egypt and Israel." *Al-Usbū' al-'Arabī* (Lebanon), July 1 and July 8, 1974. Hebrew trans.

Bader, William. *The United States and the Spread of Nuclear Weapons*. New York: Pegasus, 1968.

Barnaby, C. F., ed. *Preventing the Spread of Nuclear Weapons*. Pugwash Monograph 1. London: Souvenir Press, 1969.

Bar-Zohar, Michael. *Ben-Gurion: A Political Biography, Part III*. Tel Aviv: Am Oved, 1977. In Hebrew.

Beaton, Leonard. "Capabilities of Non-Nuclear Powers." In Alastair Buchan, ed., *A World of Nuclear Powers?*, pp. 13–38. Englewood Cliffs, N.J.: Prentice-Hall, 1966.

——— *Must the Bomb Spread?* London: Penguin, 1966.

——— "Why Israel Does Not Need the Bomb." *The New Middle East* (April 1969), no. 7.

Beaufré, André. *Stratégie pour demain*. Tel Aviv: Ma'archot, 1977. Hebrew trans.

Becker, Bonita I. "Nuclear Israel: Potential and Policy." M.A. thesis, George Washington University, Department of Political Science, 1976.

Bell, J. Bowyer. "Israel's Nuclear Option." *Middle East Journal* (Autumn 1972), 26.

Birnbaum, Karl. "The Swedish Experience." In Alastair Buchan, ed., *A World of Nuclear Powers?*, pp. 68–75. Englewood Cliffs, N.J.: Prentice-Hall, 1966.

Blainey, Geoffrey. *The Causes of War*. New York: Free Press, 1973.

Boskey, Bennett, and Mason Willrich. *Nuclear Weapons: Prospects for Control*. New York: Donellin, 1970.

Bray, Frank U. J., and Michael Moodie. "Nuclear Politics in India." *Survival* (May–June 1977), 19:111–16.

Breecher, Michael. *The Foreign Policy System of Israel*. London: Oxford University Press, 1972.

Brennan, Donald G., ed. *The Implications of Precision Weapons for American Strategic Interests*. Final Report HI-2204-RR. Croton-on-Hudson, N.Y.: Hudson Institute, January 31, 1975.

Brenner, Michael. "Carter's Non-Proliferation Strategy: Fuel Assurances and Energy Security." *ORBIS* (Summer 1978), 22:333–56.

—— "Decision Making in a Nuclear Armed World." In Joseph I. Coffey, ed., *Nuclear Proliferation: Prospects, Problems, Proposals*, pp. 147–61. Annals of the American Academy of Political Science, no. 430. Philadelphia, March 1977.

Brodie, Bernard. "The Development of Nuclear Strategy." ACIS Working Paper No. 11. Los Angeles: Center for Arms Control and International Security, University of California, February 1978.

—— *Strategy in the Missile Age*. Princeton: Princeton University Press, 1959.

—— *War and Politics*. New York: Macmillan, 1973.

—— "What Price Conventional Capabilities in Europe?" In Henry A. Kissinger, ed., *Problems of National Strategy*, pp. 313–28. New York: Praeger, 1965.

Buchan, Alastair, ed. *A World of Nuclear Powers?* Englewood Cliffs, N.J.: Prentice-Hall, 1966.

Bull, Hedly. *The Control of the Arms Race*. London and New York: Praeger, 1961.

Burnham, David. "The Case of the Missing Uranium." *The Atlantic* (April 1979), 243:78–82.

Burt, Richard. *New Weapons Technologies: Debate and Directions*. Adelphi Paper no. 126. London: International Institute for Strategic Studies, 1976.

—— "Nuclear Proliferation and Conventional Arms Transfer: The Missing Link." Discussion Paper no. 76. Santa Monica, Calif.: California Seminar on Arms Control and Foreign Policy, 1977.

Calder, Nigel, ed. *Unless Peace Comes: A Scientific Forecast of New Weapons*. New York: Viking, 1968.

Canby, Steven. *The Alliance and Europe: Part IV: Military Doctrine and Technology*. Adelphi Paper no. 109. London: International Institute for Strategic Studies, 1975.

Chari, P. R. "The Israeli Nuclear Option: Living Dangerously." *International Studies* (July–September 1977), 16:343–55.

Collins, John M. *American and Soviet Military Trends Since the Cuban Missile Crisis*. Washington, D.C.: Center for Strategic and International Studies, Georgetown University, 1978.

Conover, C. Johnston. "U.S. Strategic Nuclear Weapons and Deterrence." Rand Memo P-5967. Santa Monica, Calif.: Rand Corporation, August 1977.

Cranston, Alan. "How Congress Can Shape Arms Control." In Alan Platt and Lawrence D. Weiler, eds., *Congress and Arms Control*, pp. 205–13. Boulder, Colo.: Westview Press, 1978.

Dean, Harry. "Conventional Arms Transfers to Africa: Some Patterns and Problems." Paper presented at IISS/ACA Conference on Conventional Arms Transfers, Bellagio, Italy, May 1979.

Deshinkar, G. D. "Deterrence With or Without Weapons." *Alternatives* (Institute for World Order) (1978–79), 4:133–44.

Deutch, Karl W., and J. David Singer. "Multipolar Power Systems and International Stability." In James Rosenau, ed., *International Relations and Foreign Policy*, pp. 315–25. New York: Free Press, 1964. Reprinted from *World Politics* (1964), 16:390–406.

De Weerd, H. A. "The British Effort to Secure an Independent Deterrent, 1952–1962." In R. N. Rosecrance, ed., *The Dispersion of Nuclear Weapons*, pp. 87–100. New York: Columbia University Press, 1964.

Digby, James, "New Non-Nuclear Military Technology: Implications and Exploitable Opportunities." Rand Memo P-5836. Santa Monica, Calif.: Rand Corporation, March 1977.

—— "New Weapons and the Dispersal of Military Power." Santa Monica, Calif.: California Seminar on Arms Control and Foreign Policy, January 1978.

—— "Precision Guided Munitions: Capabilities and Consequences." Rand Memo P-5257. Santa Monica, Calif.: Rand Corporation, June 1974.

—— *Precision Guided Weapons.* Adelphi Paper no. 118. London: International Institute for Strategic Studies, 1975.

—— "Precision Weapons: Lowering the Risks with Aimed Shots and Aimed Tactics." In Johan J. Holst and Uwe Nerlich, eds., *Beyond Nuclear Deterrence*, pp. 155–76. New York: Crane, Russak, 1977.

Dougherty, James E., and Robert Pfaltzgraff. *Contending Theories of International Relations.* New York: J. B. Lippincott, 1971.

Douglas, Joseph D. "Soviet Nuclear Strategy in Europe Revisited." *Cyclon* (Tel Aviv) (September 1978), no. 3, pp. 43–55. In Hebrew.

Dowty, Alan. "Israel's Nuclear Policy." *Medina, Mimshal Vayahasim Benleumi'im* (State, Government, and International Relations) (Spring 1975), no. 7.

—— "Israel and Nuclear Weapons." *Midstream* (November 1976), 22:7–22.

—— "Nuclear Proliferation: The Israeli Case." *International Studies Quarterly* (March 1978), 22:79–120.

Drell, Sidney D., and Frank Von Hippel. "Limited Nuclear War." *Scientific American* (November 1976), 235:27–37.

Dudzinski, S. J., Jr., and James Digby. "The Strategic and Tactical Implications of New Weapons Technologies." Rand Memo P-5765. Santa Monica, Calif.: Rand Corporation, December 1976.

Duffy, Gloria C. "Soviet Nuclear Exports." *International Security* (Summer 1978), 3(1):83–110.

Duffy, Gloria C., and Gordon Adams. *Power Politics: Nuclear Industry and Nuclear Export.* New York: Council on Economic Priorities, 1978.

Dunn, Lewis A. "Military Politics, Nuclear Proliferation and the Nuclear Coup d'Etat." *Journal of Strategic Studies* (May 1979), 1:31–49.

—— "Nuclear Proliferation and World Politics." In Joseph I. Coffey, ed., *Nuclear Proliferation: Prospects, Problems, Proposals,* pp. 96–109. Annals of the American Academy of Political Science, no. 430. Philadelphia, March 1977.

Enthoven, Alain C. "American Deterrent Policy." In Henry A. Kissinger, ed., *Problems of National Strategy,* pp. 120–34. New York: Praeger, 1965.

Evron, Yair. "The Arab Position in the Nuclear Field: A Study of Policies up to 1967." *Cooperation and Conflict* (1973), no. 1, pp. 19–31.

—— "The Demilitarization of Sinai." *The Jerusalem Papers on Peace Problems.* Jerusalem: Leonard Davis Institute for International Relations, Hebrew University of Jerusalem, 1975.

—— "Deterrence in the Middle East." Forthcoming.

—— "Israel and the Atom: The Uses and Misuses of Ambiguity, 1957–1967." *ORBIS* (Winter 1974), 17:1326–43.

—— "Letter to the Editor." *Commentary* (February 1976), 62.

—— *The Role of Arms Control in the Middle East.* Adelphi Paper no. 138. London: International Institute for Strategic Studies, 1977.

—— "Some Effects of the Introduction of Nuclear Weapons in the Middle East." In Asher Arian, ed., *Israel: A Developing Society,* pp. 105–26. Tel Aviv: Pinhas Sapir Center for Develop-

ment, Tel Aviv University, and Van Gorom, Assem, Netherlands, 1980.

Falk, Richard A. "How a Nuclear War Can Start . . . in the Middle
East." *Bulletin of the Atomic Scientists* (April 1979), 35:23–24.

Feldman, Shai. "Peacemaking in the Middle East: The Next Step."
Foreign Affairs (Spring 1981) 59(4):756–80.

—— "The Raid on Osiraq: A Preliminary Assessment." CSS Memorandum no. 5. Tel Aviv: Tel Aviv University, Center for Strategic Studies, August 1981.

Foster, William C. "New Directions in Arms Control and Disarmament." *Foreign Affairs* (July 1965), 43:485–601.

Freedman, Lawrence. "Israel's Nuclear Policy." *Survival* (May–June
1975), 17:114–20.

Frye, Alton. "Slow Fuse on the Neutron Bomb." *Foreign Policy*
(Summer 1978), 31:95–102.

Gallois, Pierre M. *Balance of Terror: Strategy for the Nuclear Age.*
Boston: Houghton Mifflin, 1961.

—— "French Defense Planning—The Future in the Past." *International Security* (Fall 1976), 1(2):15–31.

—— "U.S. Strategy and the Defense of Europe." In Henry A. Kissinger, ed., *Problems of National Strategy*, pp. 288–312. New
York: Praeger, 1965.

Garwin, Richard L. "Reducing Dependency on Nuclear Weapons."
In David C. Gompert et al., *Nuclear Weapons and World Pol-
itics, Alternatives for the Future*, pp. 83–137. 1980s Project/
Council on Foreign Relations. New York: McGraw-Hill, 1977.

George, Alexander, David Hall, and William Simons. *The Limits
of Coercive Dipomacy.* Boston: Little, Brown, 1971.

George, Alexander and Richard Smoke. *Deterrence in American
Foreign Policy.* New York: Columbia University Press, 1974.

Glasstone, Samuel and Philip J. Dolan. *The Effects of Nuclear
Weapons.* Prepared and published by the U.S. Department of
Defense and U.S. Department of Energy. Washington, D.C.:
Government Printing Office, 1977.

Goldschmidt, Bertram. "A Historical Survey of Non-Proliferation
Policies." *International Security* (Summer 1978), 2:69–87.

Gompert, David C. et al. *Nuclear Weapons and World Politics,
Alternatives for the Future.* 1980s Project/Council on Foreign
Relations. New York: McGraw-Hill, 1977.

Gottlieb, Gidon. "Israel and the A-Bomb." *Commentary* (February
1961), no. 31.

Gray, Colin S. "The M-X Debate." *Survival* (May–June 1978), 20:105–12.

Greenwood, Ted, et al. *Nuclear Proliferation: Motives, Capabilities, and Strategies for Control.* 1980s Project/Council on Foreign Relations. New York: McGraw-Hill, 1977.

Gupta, Sisir. "The Indian Dilemma." In Alastair Buchan, ed., *A World of Nuclear Powers?* pp. 55–67. Englewood Cliffs, N.J.: Prentice-Hall, 1966.

Hanrieder, Wolfram F. and Larry V. Buel. *Words and Arms: A Dictionary of Security and Defense Terms.* Boulder Colo.: Westview Press, 1979.

Harkabi, Gen. (Res.) Yehoshafat. *Al-Haguerrilla* (On Guerrilla). Tel Aviv: Ma'archot, 1971. In Hebrew.

—— *Milchama Garinit Veshalom Garini* (Nuclear War and Nuclear Peace). Tel Aviv: Ma'archot, 1964. In Hebrew.

Harkavy, Robert. *Israel's Nuclear Weapons: Spectre of Holocaust in the Middle East.* Denver: Denver University Press, 1977.

Harris, Leonard. *The Massada Plan.* New York: Crown, 1976.

Haselkorn, Avigdor. "Israel: From an Option to a Bomb in the Basement?" In Robert M. Lawrence and Joel Larus, eds., *Nuclear Proliferation: Phase II,* pp. 149–81. Lawrence: University of Kansas Press, 1974.

Haykal, Muhammad Hasanayn. "The Bomb." *Al-Ahrām* (Egypt), November 23, 1973. Hebrew trans.

—— "Frankly Speaking: The Israeli Atomic Bombs . . . Why Was Israel Obliged to Make the Bomb?" *Al-Ra'y* (Jordan), January 20, 22, 24, 26, 1976. Trans. by Joint Publications Research Service, JPRS 66788, February 13, 1976.

—— "Israeli Nuclear Weapons, Supply of Arms from the West and the Question: Why Are the Arabs Silent?" *Al-Anwār* (Lebanon), June 12, 1977. Hebrew trans.

—— "The Strategy of the War of Attrition." In Walter Laqueur, ed., *The Israel–Arab Reader.* New York: Bantam, 1976.

Herz, John H. "Idealist Internationalism and the Security Dilemma." *World Politics* (January 1950), 2:157–80.

Hoag, Malcolm W. "Nuclear Strategic Options and European Force Participation." In R. N. Rosecrance, ed., *The Dispersion of Nuclear Weapons,* New York: Columbia University Press, 1964.

Hobbes, Thomas. *Leviathan.* New York: Washington Square Press, 1970. First edition published by A. Cooke, London, 1651.

Hoffmann, Stanley. "Letter to the Editor." *Commentary* (February 1976), no. 62.
—— "A New Policy for Israel." *Foreign Affairs* (April 1975), 53:405–31.
—— "Nuclear Proliferation and World Politics." In Alastair Buchan, ed., *A World of Nuclear Powers?* pp. 89–121. Englewood Cliffs, N.J.: Prentice-Hall, 1966.
Holst, Johan J. and Uwe Nerlich, eds. *Beyond Nuclear Deterrence.* New York: Crane, Russak, 1977.
Howard, Michael. "Haestrategim Haclassim." *Cyclon* (Tel Aviv) (September 1978), no. 3, pp. 4–48. Reprinted from Michael Howard, *Studies in War and Peace* (London: Temple Smith, 1970).
Hsieh, Alice Langley. "Communist China and Nuclear Force." In R. N. Rosecrance, ed., *The Dispersion of Nuclear Weapons.* New York: Columbia University Press, 1964.
Hughes, G. Philip. "Cutting the Gordian Knot: A Theater Nuclear Force for Deterrence in Europe." *ORBIS* (Summer 1978), 22:309–32.
Jabber, Fuad. "Israel's Nuclear Options." *Journal of Palestine Studies* (Autumn 1971).
—— "Israel's Nuclear Option and U.S. Arms Control Policies." California Seminar on Arms Control and Foreign Policy, Research Paper no. 9. Los Angeles: Crescent Publications, 1972.
—— *Israel and Nuclear Weapons: Present Options and Future Strategies.* Published for the International Institute for Stragegic Studies. Tel Aviv: Bustan, 1972. Hebrew edition.
Jabber, Paul. "A Nuclear Middle East Infrastructure, Likely Military Postures and Prospects for Strategic Stability." ACIS Working Paper no. 6. Los Angeles: Center for Arms Control and International Security, University of California, 1978.
Jaipal, Rikhi. "The Indian Nuclear Explosion." *International Security* (Spring 1977), 1:44–51.
Jenkins, Brian Michael. "The Impact of Nuclear Terrorism." Unpublished paper, September 1978.
—— "The Potential for Nuclear Terrorism." Rand Memo P-5876. Santa Monica, Calif.: Rand Corporation, May 1977.
Jervis, Robert. "Cooperation Under the Security Dilemma." *World Politics* (January 1978), 30:167–214.
—— "Deterrence Theory Revisited." ACIS Working Paper no. 14

(Los Angeles: Center for Arms Control and International Security, University of California, 1978).

—— "Deterrence Theory Revisited." *World Politics* (January 1979), 31(2):289–324.

—— "Why Nuclear Superiority Doesn't Matter." *Political Science Quarterly* (Winter 1979—80), 94(4):617–33.

Kahn, Herman. *On Escalation: Metaphors and Scenarios.* New York: Praeger, 1965.

—— *Thinking About the Unthinkable.* New York: Horizon, 1962.

Kaiser, Karl. "The Great Nuclear Debate: German–American Disagreements." *Foreign Policy* (Spring 1978), 30:83–110.

Kalb, Marvin and Bernard Kalb. *Kissinger.* New York: Dell, 1974.

Kapur, Ashok. "*N*th Powers and the Future." In Joseph I. Coffey, ed., *Nuclear Proliferation: Prospects, Problems, Proposals,* pp. 84–95. Annals of the American Academy of Political Science, no. 430. Philadelphia, March 1977.

Karber, Philip A. "Hamaahapecha Hatactit Badoctrina Hosovietit" (The Tactical Revolution in Soviet Doctrine). *Ma'archot* (Tel Aviv) (January 1974), no. 260, pp. 48–56. Hebrew trans.

Keeny, Spargeon M. et al. *Nuclear Power, Issues, and Choices.* Report of the Nuclear Energy Study Group, Ford Foundation. Cambridge, Mass.: Ballinger, 1977.

Kemp, Geoffrey. *Nuclear Forces for Medium Powers. Part I: Targets and Weapons Systems,* Adelphi Paper no. 106; *Part II: Strategic Requirements and Options,* Adelphi Paper no. 107. London: International Institute for Strategic Studies, 1974.

Kemp, Geoffrey, ed. *American Defense Policy since 1945: A Preliminary Bibliography.* Compiled by Ted Greenwood. Lawrence: Regents Press of Kansas, 1974.

Kennan, George F. *A Cloud of Danger.* Boston: Little, Brown, 1977.

Kennedy, Robert F. *Thirteen Days.* London: Pan Books, 1969.

Kissinger, Henry A. *The Necessity for Choice: Prospects of American Foreign Policy.* New York: Harper, 1961.

—— *Nuclear Weapons and Foreign Policy.* New York: Harper, 1957.

—— "The Problems of Limited War." In Robert J. Art and Kenneth N. Waltz, eds., *The Use of Force,* pp. 99–115. Boston: Little, Brown, 1971.

—— *A World Restored.* Boston: Houghton Mifflin, 1973.

Kissinger, Henry, ed. *Problems of National Strategy.* New York: Praeger, 1965.

Klippenberg, Erik. "New Technologies: Some Requirements." In
    John J. Holst and Uwe Nerlich, eds., *Beyond Nuclear Deterr-
    ence*, pp. 149–55. New York: Crane, Russak, 1977.
Kohl, Wilfrid L. *French Nuclear Diplomacy*. Princeton: Princeton
    University Press, 1971.
Kordova, Major Yishai and Lt. Col. Avi-Shai. "Haiyum Hagarini
    Hasovieti Beshalhay Milhemet Yom Hakipurim" (The Soviet
    Nuclear Threat Toward the End of the Yom Kippur War).
    Ma'archot (Tel Aviv) (November 1978), no. 266, pp. 37–42. In
    Hebrew.
Krieger, David. "What Happens If . . . ? Terrorists, Revolutionaries,
    and Nuclear Weapons." In Joseph I. Coffey, ed., *Nuclear Pro-
    liferation: Prospects, Problems, Proposals*, pp. 44–57. Annals
    of the American Academy of Political Science, no. 430. Phila-
    delphia, March 1977.
Kupperman, Robert H. "Nuclear Terrorism: Armchair Pastime or
    Genuine Threat?" Unpublished paper, July 1978.
Lambeth, Benjamin S. "Nuclear Proliferation and Soviet Arms Con-
    trol Policy." *ORBIS* (Summer 1970), 4:298–325.
Lawrence, Robert M. and Joel Larus, eds. *Nuclear Proliferation:
    Phase II*. Lawrence: University of Kansas Press, 1974.
Lebow, Richard Ned. *Between Peace and War: The Nature of In-
    ternational Crisis*. Baltimore and London: Johns Hopkins
    University Press, 1981.
Lieber, Robert J. "The French Nuclear Force." *International Af-
    fairs* (1966), 42:421–31.
Long, Clarence D. "Nuclear Proliferation: Can Congress Act in
    Time?" *International Security* (Spring 1977), 1:52–79.
Lowrance, William W. "Nuclear Futures for Sale: To Brazil from
    West Germany, 1975." *International Security* (Fall 1976),
    1:147–66.
Luttwak, Edward. *Coup d'Etat*. Greenwich Conn.: Fawcett Books,
    1968.
—— *A Dictionary of Modern War*. New York: Harper & Row, 1971.
—— "SALT and the Meaning of Strategy." *Washington Review*
    (April 1978), no. 1.
Mandelbaum, Michael. "International Stability and Nuclear Order."
    In David C. Gompert et al., *Nuclear Weapons and World Pol-
    itics: Alternatives for the Future*, pp. 15–80. 1980s Project/
    Council on Foreign Relations. New York: McGraw-Hill, 1977.

Mangold, Peter. "The Soviet Record in the Middle East." *Survival* (May–June 1978), 20:98–104.

Martin, Lawrence. "Flexibility in Tactical Nuclear Response." In Johan J. Holst and Uwe Nerlich, eds., *Beyond Nuclear Deterrence*, pp. 255–65. New York: Crane, Russak, 1977.

Marwah, Onkar. "India's Nuclear and Space Programs: Intent and Policy." *International Security* (Fall 1977), 2:96–121.

—— "India and Pakistan: Nuclear Armed Rivals in South Asia." Paper prepared for the World Peace Foundation Conference on Non-Proliferation, Cambridge, Mass., May 1–2, 1980.

Maxwell, Stephen. *Rationality In Deterrence*. Adelphi Paper no. 50. London: International Institute for Strategic Studies, 1969.

McPeak, Col. Merrill A. "Israel: Borders and Security." *Foreign Affairs* (April 1976), 54:426–43.

Metzger, Robert S. "Cruise Missiles: Different Missions, Different Arms Control Impact." *Arms Control Today* (January 1978), no. 8.

Morgan, Patrick. *Deterrence*. Beverly Hills and London: Sage Publications, 1977.

Morgenthau, Hans J. *Politics Among Nations*. New York: Knopf, 1968.

—— "The Four Paradoxes of Nuclear Strategy." *American Political Science Review* (March 1964), 58(1):23–35.

Morrison, Philip and Paul F. Walker. "A New Strategy for Military Spending." *Scientific American* (October 1978), no. 239.

Nacht, Michael. "The United States in a World of Nuclear Powers." In Joseph I. Coffey, ed., *Nuclear Proliferation: Prospects, Problems, Proposals*, pp. 162–74. Annals of the American Academy of Political Science, no. 430. Philadelphia, March 1977.

al-Nasr, Muhammad Jabber. "The Arab Nuclear Program . . . When and Where?" *Al-Anwār* (Lebanon), June 26, 1974. Hebrew trans.

Nitze, Paul H. "Assuring Strategic Stability in an Era of Detente." *Foreign Affairs* (January 1976), 54:207–32.

—— "The Relationship Between Strategic and Tactical Nuc'ear Forces." *International Security* (Fall 1977), 2:122–32.

Olson, Mancur, Jr. *The Logic of Collective Action: Public Goods and the Theory of Groups*. Cambridge: Harvard University Press, 1965.

Olson, Mancur, Jr., and Richard Zeckhauser. "An Economic Theory of Alliances." *Review of Economics and Statistics* (August 1966), 48:266–79.

Osborn, Palmer and William Bowen. "How to Defend Western Europe." *Fortune*, October 9, 1978, pp. 150–56.

Osgood, Robert E. "The Expansion of Force." In Robert J. Art and Kenneth N. Waltz, eds., *The Use of Force*, pp. 29–55. Boston: Little, Brown, 1971.

—— "Stabilizing the Military Environment." In Dale J. Hekhuis, Charles G. McClintock, and Arthur Burns, eds., *International Stability*, pp. 83–113. New York: Wiley, 1964.

Pechman, Joseph A., et al. *Setting National Priorities: The 1979 Budget*. Washington, D.C.: Brookings Institution, 1978.

Pranger, Robert J. "Nuclear War Comes to the Middle East." *Worldview* (July–August 1977), 20:41–44.

Pranger, Robert J., and Roger P. Lubrie, eds. *Nuclear Strategy and National Security Points of View*. Washington, D.C.: American Enterprise Institute, 1977.

Pranger, Robert J., and Dale R. Tahtinen. *Nuclear Threat in the Middle East*. Washington, D.C.: American Enterprise Institute, 1975.

Quandt, William B. *Decade of Decisions: American Policy Toward the Arab–Israeli Dispute, 1967–1976*. Berkeley: University of California Press, 1977.

Quester, George. "Israel and the Non-Proliferation Treaty." *Bulletin of the Atomc Scientists*, June 1969.

—— *The Politics of Nuclear Proliferation*. London and Baltimore: Johns Hopkins University Press, 1974.

—— "Strategic Bombing in the 1930's and 1940's." In Robert J. Art and Kenneth N. Waltz, eds., *The Use of Force*, pp. 184–202. Boston: Little, Brown, 1971.

Record, Jeffrey. "The Defense of Europe by Nuclear or Conventional Forces." *Cyclon* (Tel Aviv) (September 1978), no. 3, pp. 19–23. Reprinted from *Military Review* (October 1974).

Rogers, P. F. "The Neutron Bomb." *Army* (September 1977), pp. 30–35.

Rosecrance, R. N. "Bipolarity, Multipolarity and the Future." *Journal of Conflict Resolution* (1966), 10:314–27.

—— ed. *The Dispersion of Nuclear Weapons, Strategy and Politics*. New York: Columbia University Press, 1964.

Rosen, Steven J. "War Power and Willingness to Suffer." In Bruce

Russett, ed., *Peace, War, and Numbers*, pp. 165–83. Beverly Hills and London: Sage, 1972.

—— "Nuclearization and Stability in the Middle East." *Jerusalem Journal of International Relations* (Spring 1976), 1:1–32.

—— "The Proliferation of Land-Based Technologies: Implications for Local Military Balances." ACIS Working Paper no. 12. Los Angeles: Center for Arms Control and International Security, University of California, 1978.

—— "A Stable System of Mutual Nuclear Deterrence in the Arab–Israeli Conflict." *American Political Science Review* (December 1977), 71:1367–83.

—— "What a Fifth Arab–Israel War Might Look Like: An Exercise in Crisis Forecasting." ACIS Working Paper no. 8. Los Angeles: Center for Arms Control and International Security, University of California, 1977.

Rosenbaum, David M. "Nuclear Terror." *International Security* (Winter 1977), 1(3):140–61.

Ross, Dennis. "Rethinking Soviet Strategic Policy: Inputs and Implications." In Wolfram F. Hanrieder, ed., *Arms Control and Security: Current Issues*, pp. 137–67. Boulder, Colo.: Westview Press, 1979.

Sandoval, Robert R. "Consider the Porcupine: Another View of Nuclear Proliferation." *Bulletin of the Atomic Scientists* (May 1976).

Schelling, Thomas C. *Arms and Influence.* New Haven: Yale University Press, 1966.

—— *Strategy of Conflict.* Cambridge, Mass.: Harvard University Press, 1960.

—— "Who Will Have the Bomb?" *International Security* (Summer 1976), 1(1):77–91.

Schmidt, Helmut. *Defense or Retaliation.* Edinburgh and London: Oliver & Boyd, 1962.

Shalev, Brig. Gen. (Res.) Aryeh. "Security Arrangements in Sinai Within the Framework of a Peace Treaty with Egypt." CSS Paper no. 3. Tel Aviv: Center for Strategic Studies, Tel Aviv University, October 1978.

Shreffler, Robert. "The Neutron Bomb for NATO Defense: An Alternative." *ORBIS* (Winter 1978), 21:959–73.

—— "The New Nuclear Force." In Stockholm International Peace Research Institute, *Tactical Nuclear Weapons: European Perspectives*, pp. 296–341. London: Taylor & Francis, 1978.

Smith, Gerard and George Rathjens. "Reassessing Nuclear Non-proliferation Policy." *Foreign Affairs* (Spring 1981), vol. 59, no. 4.

Snyder, Glenn H. *Deterrence and Defense: Toward a Theory of National Security.* Princeton: Princeton University Press, 1961.

—— "Deterrence and Defense." In Robert J. Art and Kenneth N. Waltz, eds., *The Use of Force*, pp. 56–76. Boston: Little, Brown, 1971.

—— "Deterrence by Denial and Punishment." In David Bobrow, ed., *Components of Defense Policy*, pp. 209–37. Chicago: Rand McNally, 1965.

Snyder, Glenn and Paul Diesing. *Conflict Among Nations.* Princeton: Princeton University Press, 1977.

Sommer, Theo. "The Objectives of Germany." In Alastair Buchan, ed., *A World of Nuclear Powers?* pp. 39–54. Englewood Cliffs, N.J.: Prentice-Hall, 1966.

Stockholm International Peace Research Institute. *The Near-Nuclear Countries and the N.P.T.* New York: Humanities Press, 1972.

—— *Tactical Nuclear Weapons: European Perspectives.* London: Taylor & Francis, 1978.

Stone, Jeremy. "The Strategic Role of the United States Bombers." In Robert J. Art and Kenneth N. Waltz, eds., *The Use of Force*, pp. 339–46. Boston: Little, Brown, 1971.

Symington, Stuart. "The Washington Nuclear Mess." *International Security* (Winter 1977), 1(3):71–78.

Tahir-Kheli, Shirin. "Pakistan's Nuclear Option and U.S. Policy." *ORBIS* (Summer 1978), 22:357–74.

Tucker, Robert W. "Israel and the United States: From Dependence to Nuclear Weapons?" *Commentary* (November 1975), 60:29–43.

—— "Reply to the Letters to the Editor." *Commentary* (February 1976), no. 62.

Tzipis, Kosta. "Cruise Missiles." *Scientific American* (February 1977), pp. 20–29.

Ullman, Richard. "After Rabat: Middle East Risks and American Roles." *Foreign Affairs* (January 1975), 53(2):284–96.

U.S. Army. *A Primer on Nuclear Weapons Capabilities.* U.S. Army Nuclear Agency, Nuclear Notes no. 6. Virginia: Fort Belvoir, June 1977.

U.S. Congress. Public Law 95-92. *International Security Assistance*

Act of 1977. Washington, D.C.: Government Printing Office, August 5, 1977.

—— Public Law 95-242. *The Nuclear Non-Proliferation Act of 1978.* Washington, D.C.: Government Printing Office, March 10, 1978.

U.S. Congressional Budget Office. *Counterforce Issues for the U.S. Strategic Nuclear Forces.* Washington, D.C.: Government Printing Office, January 1978.

—— *Planning U.S. General Purpose Forces: The Theater Nuclear Forces.* Washington, D.C.: Government Printing Office, January 1977.

—— *U.S. Strategic Nuclear Forces: Deterrence Policies and Procurement Issues.* Washington, D.C.: Government Printing Office, April 1977.

U.S. House. Committee on International Relations. *Hearings on H.R. 11963, International Security Assistance Act of 1976.* Washington, D.C.: Government Printing Office, November 6–7, 10–13, 17–20, December 2–4, 9–12, 16–18, 1975; January 28, February 3–5, 10, 17–19, 1976.

U.S. Office of Technology Assessment. *Nuclear Proliferation and Safeguards.* New York and London: Praeger, 1977.

—— *The Effects of Nuclear War.* Washington, D.C., Government Printing Office, 1979.

U.S. Senate. Committee on Armed Services. *Military Implication of the Treaty on the Non-Proliferation of Nuclear Weapons: Hearings.* 91st Cong., 1st sess. Washington, D.C.: Government Printing Office, 1969.

—— Committee on Foreign Relations. Subcommittees on Africa; Foreign Assistance; and Arms Control, Oceans, and International Environment. *Hearings on S-1160.* Washington, D.C.: Government Printing Office, April 21–22, 28, May 2, 1977.

—— *Senate Delegation Report on American Foreign Policy and Non-Proliferation Interests in the Middle East.* 95th Cong., 1st sess. Washington, D.C.: Government Printing Office, 1977.

Van Evera, Stephen. "The Effects of Nuclear Proliferation." Berkeley, University of California, Department of Political Science. Unpublished paper, 1976.

—— "Nuclear Weapons, Nuclear Proliferation and the Causes of War." Berkeley, University of California, Department of Political Science. Unpublished paper, 1978.

Vital, David. "Double Talk or Double Think?" *International Affairs* (July 1968), 44:419–33.

—— *The Inequality of States.* Oxford: Oxford University Press, 1967.

Waltz, Kenneth N. "America's European Policy Viewed in Global Perspective." In Wolfran F. Hanrieder, ed., *The United States and Western Europe*, pp. 8–36. Cambridge, Mass.: Winthrop, 1974.

—— *Foreign Policy and Democratic Politics.* Boston: Little, Brown, 1967.

—— "International Structure, National Force, and the Balance of World Power." *Journal of International Affairs* (1967), 21:215–31.

—— *Man, the State, and War.* New York: Columbia University Press, 1954.

—— "What Will the Spread of Nuclear Weapons Do to the World?" In John Kerry King, ed., *International Political Effects of the Spread of Nuclear Weapons*, pp. 165–96. Washington, D.C.: Government Printing Office, April 1979.

Warner, Manfred. "Tactical Nuclear Weapons and the Defense of Europe." *Cyclon* (Tel Aviv) (September 1978), no. 3, pp. 24–30. Translated from *Strategic Review*, Fall 1977.

Wellnitz, B. A., ed. *LASL Panel on Tactical Nuclear Warfare, April 5–6, 1977.* Los Alamos: Los Alamos Scientific Laboratory, August 1977.

Wettig, Gerhard. "Soviet Policy on the Non-Proliferation of Nuclear Weapons," *ORBIS* (Winter 1969), 12:1058–84.

Wiesband, Edward and Damir Raguly. "Palestinian Terrorism: Violence, Verbal Strategy and Legitimacy." In Yonah Alexander, ed., *International Terrorism*, pp. 258–319. New York: Praeger, 1976.

Williams, Shelton L. *The U.S., India, and the Bomb.* Baltimore: Johns Hopkins University Press, 1969.

Willrich, Mason and Theodore Taylor. *Nuclear Theft: Risks and Safeguards.* Cambridge, Mass.: Ballinger, 1974.

Wohlstetter, Albert. "The Delicate Balance of Terror." *Foreign Affairs* (January 1959), 37:211–34.

—— "NATO and the Nth + 1 Country." In R. N. Rosecrance, ed., *The Dispersion of Nuclear Weapons*, pp. 186–221. New York: Columba University Press, 1964.

Wohlstetter, Roberta. "Terror on a Grand Scale." *Survival* (May–June 1976), 18:98–104.

Yiftah, Shimon. *Hayidan Hagarini Bamizrach Hatichon* (The Middle East in the Nuclear Era). Tel Aviv: Am Oved, 1976.

Young, Oran R. *The Politics of Force.* Princeton: Princeton University Press, 1968.

Zoppo, Ciro E. "France as a Nuclear Power." In R. N. Rosecrance, ed., *The Dispersion of Nuclear Weapons*, pp. 113–56. New York: Columbia University Press, 1964.

—— "The Nuclear Genie in the Middle East." *New Outlook* (February 1975), pp. 21–26.

Index